Marriage, Sex, and Procreation

Princeton Theological Monograph Series
K. C. Hanson, Charles M. Collier, D. Christopher Spinks,
and Robin A. Parry, Series Editors

Recent volumes in the series:

Steven C. van den Heuvel
*Bonhoeffer's Christocentric Theology and Fundamental
Debates in Environmental Ethics*

Andrew R. Hay
God's Shining Forth: A Trinitarian Theology of Divine Light

Peter Schmiechen
*Gift and Promise:
An Evangelical Theology of the Lord's Supper*

Hank Voss
*The Priesthood of All Believers and the Missio Dei:
A Canonical, Catholic, and Contextual Perspective*

Alexandra S. Radcliff
*The Claim of Humanity in Christ: Salvation and
Sanctification in the Theology of T. F. and J. B. Torrance*

Yaroslav Viazovski
*Image and Hope:
John Calvin and Karl Barth on Body, Soul, and Life Everlasting*

Anna C. Miller
*Corinthian Democracy:
Democratic Discourse in 1 Corinthians*

Thomas Christian Currie
*The Only Sacrament Left to Us: The Threefold
Word of God in the Theology and Ecclesiology of Karl Barth*

Marriage, Sex, and Procreation
Contemporary Revisions to Augustine's Theology of Marriage

STEVEN SCHAFER

☞PICKWICK *Publications* · Eugene, Oregon

MARRIAGE, SEX, AND PROCREATION
Contemporary Revisions to Augustine's Theology of Marriage

Princeton Theological Monograph Series 240

Copyright © 2019 Steven Schafer. All rights reserved. Except for brief quotations in critical publications or reviews, no part of this book may be reproduced in any manner without prior written permission from the publisher. Write: Permissions, Wipf and Stock Publishers, 199 W. 8th Ave., Suite 3, Eugene, OR 97401.

Pickwick Publications
An Imprint of Wipf and Stock Publishers
199 W. 8th Ave., Suite 3
Eugene, OR 97401

www.wipfandstock.com

PAPERBACK ISBN: 978-1-5326-7182-1
HARDCOVER ISBN: 978-1-5326-7183-8
EBOOK ISBN: 978-1-5326-7184-5

Cataloguing-in-Publication data:

Names: Schafer, Steven, author.

Title: Marriage, sex, and procreation : contemporary revisions to Augustine's theology of marriage / by Steven Schafer.

Description: Eugene, OR : Pickwick Publications, 2019 | Princeton Theological Monograph Series 240 | Includes bibliographical references.

Identifiers: ISBN 978-1-5326-7182-1 (paperback) | ISBN 978-1-5326-7183-8 (hardcover) | ISBN 978-1-5326-7184-5 (ebook)

Subjects: LCSH: Augustine of Hippo, 354–430. | Marriage—History of doctrines—Early church, ca. 30–600.

Classification: BT706 .S33 2019 (print) | BT706 .S33 (ebook)

The scripture quotations contained herein are from the New Revised Standard Version Bible: Anglican Edition, copyright © 1989, 1995 National Council of Churches of Christ in the USA. Used by permission. All rights reserved.

Manufactured in the U.S.A.   09/12/19

Contents

Acknowledgments | vii
Introduction | ix
    The State of the Contemporary Debate   ix
    Bridging the Divide   xiii
    Tradition and the Contemporary Debate   xv
    Overview of the Book   xvii

1   Sexuality in the Early Church: From Paul to Augustine | 1
    Paul on Sexual Practice in First Corinthians   2
    Paul to the Early Church Fathers   6
    Tertullian (c. 160–225)   7
    Virginity and Marriage in the Fourth and Fifth Centuries   11
    Gregory of Nyssa: Virginity versus Marriage   12
    Jovinian: By Baptism Alone   15
    Jerome: Virginity as Primary (or Only) Option   18
    The Makings of Division   21

2   The Good of Marriage | 22
    Augustine of Hippo   22
    Marriage as a Good   23
    Procreation   26
    Fidelity   45
    Sacrament   47
    Summary of the Three Goods   51
    Ascetic Hierarchy   51
    Qualifications to the Ascetic Hierarchy   58
    Contemporary Challenges to Augustine: Gender Relations   64
    Contemporary Challenges to Augustine: Desire   71
    Conclusion   75

3   Contemporary Revisions of Augustine's Theology
    of Marriage | 76
        Elizabeth Stuart: Theology of Friendship   78
        Adrian Thatcher: Theology of Progressive Relationship   96
        Eugene Rogers: Sexuality and the Christian Body   112
        Robert Song: Covenant and Calling   131

4   Mapping the Debate | 150
        Areas of Broad Agreement   151
            Fidelity and Permanence   151
            Desire as Positive Theological Category   154
            Experiential Difference   157
        Areas of Contention   161
            Sexual Difference   161
            Procreation   167
        New Claims in Christian Sexual Ethics   172
            Social Trinitarian Theology and Sex   172
            Covenant and Same-Sex Relationships   174
        Dialogue and Discernment   179

    Bibliography | 181

Acknowledgments

I AM GRATEFUL FOR the many people who offered love, support, and guidance during the completion of this project. This undertaking required my family to travel some 4,500 miles from the place that we call home. As such, I will forever treasure the many friends and adopted family members in Aberdeen, Scotland, who welcomed us with open arms. I'm also thankful for contributions that my colleagues and professors at the Divinity department have made to this project. A final word of thanks to the pastors and churches around Aberdeen who allowed me to preach . . . you continually reminded me of the audience for this work: the church.

Several folks require special mention:

>Ridgewood Baptist Church—for teaching me what it means to be a thinking, feeling, healing Christian.

>The Aghajan family—Shawn, thanks for introducing me to a whole new level of sarcasm and encouraging me to finish. Sarah and the girls, whose laughter and optimism are infectious.

>Queen's Cross Church—for being a supportive church family that allowed me to preach, play, and sing.

>The Payne Family—for knowing when we were overwhelmed and bringing us dinner.

>The Hadden Family—for embodying kind and gentle Christian service.

>Ronnie and Moira Brown—for showing us your bonnie countryside.

>The McKinlay family—for Christmas parties, puddings, and the heroic quest to find the best cake in England.

>Stanley Hauerwas—for offering the benefit of your keen intellect and wit to another Texan.

>Brian Brock—for patience, guidance, and encouragement.

Jan Miller—for making this guy's educational dream come true.

Patsy Schafer—for thoughtful and surprising conversations.

My brother, Nathan—who knows when I need to laugh and how to make it happen.

Eddie and Rochelle Schafer—Mom and Dad, I am so thankful you allowed your oldest son and daughter-in-law to disappear across the pond for four years. Your support has meant more than you know.

And most importantly, Linsey—my partner, editor-in-chief, cheerleader, and best friend. None of this would be possible without you.

Introduction

The State of the Contemporary Debate

By now, the debate taking place within the churches on the inclusion of same-sex-attracted individuals and their relationships is more than familiar; we know the trajectory of the conversation as well as the terms in which it is taking place.

Consider the recent discussion within the Church of Scotland. The question, arising from within the denomination and imposed from without by public courts, is whether the church should recognize the ordination of ministers and deacons in same-sex civil partnerships. Over the duration of the debate, the question was extended to include ministers in same-sex marriages. Two positions dominated the discussion. Revisionists argued in favor of the inclusion of "stable, committed, faithful, same-sex partnerships."[1] Based on this definition, same-sex civil partnerships share some of the relational expectations of heterosexual couples, namely, fidelity and lifelong commitment.[2] The revisionists claimed that the church should recognize the ordination of ministers in same-sex civil partnerships because of the similarities that their relationships shared with marriage. The revisionists proposed four arguments to support their position. First, they appealed to the doctrine of the Trinity. They argued that the Triune God is the basis for relationality, mutuality, and the sharing of love. Humans, created in the image of God, reflect these qualities by sharing mutual love with others. Second, the revisionists argued that humans express love through sexuality. Within their account, sexuality was described as a fluid continuum which does not neatly fit traditional binary descriptions of heterosexual or homosexual. Yet, confusingly, sexuality was also described as a category that is

---

1. McPake, "Theological Commission," 49.

2. John, *Permanent, Faithful, Stable,* originally published in 1993, provides a helpful introduction to the revisionist argument that same-sex couples can fulfill the faithfulness and permanence of marriage. As such, John argues that these relationships should be called marriage.

"relatively firmly established," and not one that is "chosen."[3] The revisionists relied more heavily on the determined, static description of sexuality to assert that the direction of one's sexual desires is "not something that [one] has chosen to do and feel."[4] The pairing of this claim with the proposition that humans are created to love, resulted in the revisionists equating sexuality and sexual desire with love. From this perspective, requiring lesbian and gay individuals to remain celibate represents a barrier to their expression of love, and, by extension, their ability to reflect the Triune God in whose image they are created. Third, the revisionists appealed to Jesus. According to their reading, the Gospels portray Jesus as the one who broke down barriers to inclusion and sought to bring the marginalized into the fold. Based on this description, the revisionists argued that if the church is to follow Jesus' example, she should include same-sex-attracted individuals, i.e., the marginalized sexual others. Finally, the revisionists chose to read Scripture through the hermeneutic lens of God's "ever-widening inclusion and acceptance."[5] The welcome of Gentiles into the covenant hinted at in the Old Testament and made more fully manifest in the New Testament, as well as Jesus' inclusion of women are cited as evidence of this reading of Scripture. Based on these moves, the revisionists asserted that the debate over the recognition of the legitimacy of same-sex relationships is primarily about love's expression and welcome of the outcast.

By contrast, the traditionalists argued in favor of maintaining the church's position of recognizing the relational vocations of marriage and celibacy as the only licit options for Christians. Because the church allows sexual activity to occur only within the context of a marriage between a man and a woman, individuals of same-sex orientation must assume a life of celibacy. The traditionalists built their case by relying primarily on the creation stories and the books of the law. First, they asserted that same-sex acts are sinful because they violate the created order and represent a threat to marriage as a created good. Second, the traditionalists contended that monogamous marriage is the only sexual practice considered licit by the Old Testament. This move allowed the traditionalists to argue that same-sex acts are sinful in a way parallel to other sexual sins described in the Old Testament law, i.e., heterosexual promiscuity and pedophilia. These claims were then applied to the contemporary setting. Relying heavily on the modern historical critical method, the traditionalists assumed a "fundamental

---

3. McPake, "Theological Commission," 45.
4. McPake, "Theological Commission," 44–45.
5. McPake, "Theological Commission," 54.

unity of scripture."⁶ As such, they asserted that the Old Testament law has relevance for all peoples, not just for the Hebrews. To support this view, the traditionalists pointed to the Jerusalem Council (Acts 15), where the church welcomed the Gentiles into the fold providing that they observe the Jewish sexual purity laws.⁷ From these arguments, the traditionalists concluded that recognizing the ordination of ministers and deacons in same-sex relationships amounts to rejecting the plain meaning of the biblical text. Thus, for traditionalists, the debate over the affirmation of same-sex relationships is concerned primarily with the authority of Scripture.

What is striking is not what is included in these two positions, but what is missing in the discussion. For example, the methodological choice to equate sexual desire with love, combined with the description of humans who image God through expressing love, leaves the revisionists no room to discuss the existence of disordered love/desire. One can presume that the revisionists would not affirm any and all displays of desire. However, it is unclear what would ground such a line of argument. Pressing further, the revisionist position lacks a detailed account of procreation and sexual difference, two key theological categories gleaned from the doctrine of creation. Regarding procreation, the revisionists asserted that marriage and sex serve purposes other than procreation. Based on the construction of the argument, the existence of alternative goods nullifies the necessity of procreation to marriage.⁸ In similar fashion, the necessity of sexual difference to marriage was summarily dismissed by the revisionists as a product of societal norms on gender and family. These moves result in the revisionists' theology of marriage and relationships being severed from the abundant theological resources found in the doctrine of creation.

The traditionalists position also has its shortcomings. First, their account relied primarily on a doctrine of creation, without reference to the rest of salvation history. But theologically speaking, creation is not an independent category; it is connected to the fall, redemption, and eschatology in the grand narrative of God's action in the world. The traditionalist decision to privilege creation to the exclusion of other doctrines leaves them unable to explore, for example, how the coming of Christ alters the church's understanding of sex and marriage. As the position is currently portrayed, the traditionalists are unable to explain why, contrary to the Jewish people, Christians do not have to marry and have children. Second, the traditionalist

---

6. McPake, "Theological Commission," 68.

7. Here, the traditionalists overstate their case. The Gentile believers are instructed to abstain from fornication, not the whole of the Jewish sexual purity laws (Acts 15:29).

8. Torrance, "Theological Forum," 9–10.

position's preference for a harmonization of the disparate texts of Scripture is also problematic. This move results in equal weight being assigned to the creation stories, Levitical commands, and the teachings of Jesus and Paul as they relate to contemporary Christian practice. The traditionalists are also required to engage in exercises of theological gymnastics to explain away difficult texts which seem to run contrary to the assertion that the Old Testament only affirms monogamous marriage.[9] A quick glance at the women included in the genealogy of Jesus in Matthew 1 illustrates this point. Jesus' lineage includes Tamar, Rahab, Ruth, and the wife of Uriah, none of whom fit the traditionalist's conviction that the Old Testament only affirms monogamous marriage. As one author points out, the traditionalist position "[does] not actually leave room for the scandals God delights in using to lead up to the incarnation."[10] Finally, the traditionalist position refers repeatedly to "sexuality," but offers no account of how sexuality maps onto other descriptors associated with human identity. It is unclear how the traditionalists would describe the interplay between sexuality, desire, gender, and sexual difference. This lack of detail results in an insufficient response to a complicated discussion.

The debate within the Church of Scotland, reminiscent of other conversations taking place in denominations throughout the West, presented two mutually exclusive options. From the traditionalist's perspective, it is a choice between submitting to or rejecting the authority of Scripture. From the perspective of the revisionists, the choice is between welcoming a more just, loving future for the outcast or retreating to the traditional, archaic position of the past. Both positions oversimplify the discussion through an uneven handling of the biblical witness paired with an insufficiently integrated theological account of humans and their relationships. The consequence of this mode of argumentation is that the two sides provide incomplete answers to key doctrinal questions surrounding marriage and sexuality. Rather than resolving the debate, the conversation between the two sides reflects the impasse that is taking place in denominations across the West. It is clear that the debate cannot be resolved while couched in these terms.

---

9. For example, the traditionalists find nothing sexual in the encounter between Ruth and Boaz on the threshing floor (Ruth 4). The story of Judah and Tamar (Gen 38), where Tamar plays the part of the harlot to attain justice, is not included in the litany of Scriptures explored by the traditionalists. See McPake, "Theological Comission," 74–80.

10. Rogers, *Sexuality and the Christian Body*, 244.

Bridging the Divide

There has been no shortage of attempts to resolve the dispute. One method has been to focus on a key theological category as it relates to a theology of sex and marriage. Responding to recent challenges to the church's theology of marriage, Christopher Roberts constructs a robust defense of traditional marriage grounded in sexual difference. Tracing arguments from the church fathers to John Paul II, Roberts asserts that God's creation of humans as male and female is significant, not merely incidental. It is as male and female beings that humans are created, elected, and redeemed. Because humans experience the breadth of salvation history as male or female, sexual difference cannot be bypassed in a discussion of sex and marriage. Roberts argues that sexually differentiated marriage and celibacy are the places where humans respond to God as men and women. Only by embracing sexual difference through embodying one of these two vocations can humans be obedient to God. When this argument is applied to the debate on same-sex relationships, Roberts concludes that celibacy is the only licit option available to same-sex-attracted individuals.[11] Thus, Roberts shows that sexual difference has consistently been a key feature of the church's theology of marriage. However, what this account achieves in depth, it sacrifices in breadth. A robust theology of marriage does not rely on an articulation of sexual difference alone. Determining how the church might understand same-sex relationships in light of its traditional theology of marriage requires an investigation of other relational categories as well: procreation, bodily desire, etc.

Another method of addressing the challenge that same-sex relationships present to the church's theology of marriage focuses on biblical interpretation. For example, one can appeal to detailed biblical exegesis to make one's case.[12] Another option is to demonstrate the ways in which the traditionalists and revisionists read Scripture as it relates to sex and marriage.[13] The goal of the latter option is to bridge the gap between the two sides by creating meaningful dialogue. In theory, allowing each side to demonstrate their use of Scripture should negate the traditionalist's claim that revisionists reject the authority of Scripture. Unfortunately, the traditionalist's readings of Scripture are characterized

---

11. Roberts, *Creation & Covenant*.

12. For traditionalist examples, see Gagnon, *Bible and Homosexual Practice*; Webb, *Slaves, Women & Homosexuals*. For a revisionist example, see Rogers, *Jesus, the Bible, and Homosexuality*. A helpful introduction to revisionist exegesis is found in Wink, *Homosexuality and the Christian Faith*.

13. Via and Gagnon, *Homosexuality and the Bible*.

by uneven literalism. And the revisionist's readings omit troublesome texts while emphasizing the distance between the contemporary reader and Scripture, leaving us wondering if the Bible has anything normative to say about contemporary sexual ethics.[14] As such, these approaches have been unsuccessful in bringing together the two sides of the debate.

While a Christian view of human sexuality is "necessarily based on the testimony of scripture," revisionists argue that the biblical witness takes for granted the sociological phenomena that influenced both the definition and practice of sexual ethics.[15] Two foundational works which explore these themes are Judith Butler's *Gender Trouble* and Michel Foucault's *History of Sexuality*. Butler argues that the problem of gender is at the heart of contemporary discussions of sexuality. Gender, a category which is constructed and employed through social norms, is given ontological status. It is then used to ensure the continuance of heteronormity and patriarchy. Butler seeks to dismantle the current construction of gender through genealogical criticism. In place of an ontological understanding of gender, she suggests a more malleable understanding of the concept based on performance.[16]

In his three-volume work on sexuality, Foucault asserts that a discussion of sexuality is only possible after the Enlightenment. He contends that "sexuality" is not a reality but a social construct created through dialogue by various power entities. Through this dialogue, a new set of categories is created in effort to gain control over the body. Over time, he argues, "sex" has become a causal principle and giver of meaning. Thus, our contemporary understanding of sex and the body did not appear in a vacuum but was created by dialogues between different points of power.[17]

The relationship between power and sexuality in Scripture and tradition is a central theme explored by feminist theology. For example, Rosemary Radford Ruether argues that the social setting in which the biblical text was written was steeped in patriarchy. As such, biblical sexual ethics is concerned with male sexuality and male access to female bodies.[18] Other feminists focus on how the use of language has influenced sexual ethics. Isherwood and McEwan argue that words have the power to create human reality and shape the world. They assert that traditional readings of the creation accounts have given males the power to name reality. This power

---

14. See Rogers, *Sexuality and the Christian Body*, 17–28; Brownson, *Bible, Gender, Sexuality*, 39–53.
15. Brubaker, "Christian View of Marriage," 28.
16. Butler, *Gender Trouble*.
17. Foucault, *History of Sexuality*.
18. Ruether, *Sexism and God-Talk*.

of naming, they contend, is on display in the institution of marriage. The language of marriage where the wife takes on the name of the husband suggest male ownership over his wife.[19] By contrast, Sarah Coakley has been critical of the trajectory of feminism. She argues that the feminist's move to equate power with patriarchy, followed by an attempt to replace patriarchy with matriarchy, is simplistic and misguided. She suggests that what is needed is a discussion of what kinds of power are legitimate in light of Christ.[20] As we will see in chapter 3, the question of whether power inequality is an inherent characteristic of marriage is one that must be taken seriously. What remains to be seen is whether criticizing the theological tradition's patriarchal prescriptions of power relations provides a workable solution to the current debate.

Another challenge to traditional Christian sexual ethics comes from Countryman. He argues that the contemporary debate has difficulty conceiving of sexual ethics apart from purity and property laws found in Scripture. In response, he gleans six principles from the New Testament which can be applied to contemporary discussions on sex and marriage. This includes giving ownership of sexuality to the individual and affirming liberal tolerance whereby one's sexual ethic cannot be imposed on another.[21] It should be noted that his approach assumes an understanding of the individual which would be foreign to the biblical text. Furthermore, it is unclear how such an approach helps the church say anything normative about sexual ethics.

Tradition and the Contemporary Debate

Stanley Hauerwas has summarized the state of the contemporary debate by asserting that there is no longer a normative understanding of sex, marriage, and family among Christians. The church does not know what these entities are or for what purpose they exist.[22] This assessment hints at something that has been lost or forgotten. In this case, I am referring to a robust theology of marriage. One of the main proposals of this book is that a conversation on same-sex relationships cannot take place apart from a wider discussion on sex, marriage and family as understood through the lens of the church's theological tradition. For this reason, I have chosen to dedicate the first half of this work to an analysis of the origins of the church's theology of marriage.

19. Isherwood and McEwan, *Introducing Feminist Theology*.
20. Coakley, *Powers and Submissions*.
21. Countryman, *Dirt, Greed, & Sex*.
22. Hauerwas, "Moral Value of the Family," 167–74.

Before engaging the work of contemporary revisionists in the second half of this book, it is necessary to have a firm understanding of what they are revising. This methodological choice requires me to wrestle with Augustine.

The reasons for engaging the work of Augustine are twofold. The first is practical. Augustine's theological vision and vocabulary shaped the Western church's thinking on sex and marriage more profoundly than any other non-biblical writer; he set the terms of the discussion on marriage and Christian sexual ethics. His three goods of marriage (procreation, fidelity, and sacrament) have held sway from the fifth century to the present day. As chapter 3 will demonstrate, contemporary revisionists are still arguing with Augustine either explicitly or implicitly.

The second reason for choosing Augustine as my primary interlocutor is the breadth of his account of marriage. Before articulating his view of marriage, he studied the various systems of thought available to him, listening to voices from within and without the Christian tradition. He also wrestled with his own sexual experiences, allowing Scripture to be a lens through which he interpreted those experiences. In these ways, Augustine is similar to many contemporary authors. However, as we will see in chapter 2, the range of considerations which Augustine addresses in his theology of marriage is wider than that of many contemporary accounts. Though it was formulated in the fifth century, his theology of marriage addresses a plethora of issues central to the contemporary discussion: sexual desire, bodies, gender, and power, to name a few. These are familiar points in the contemporary debate, but Augustine also infuses unfamiliar elements into the discussion. While many modern accounts of marriage offer no reason why the institution exists or for what purpose people have children, Augustine's framework gives answers to both questions. In summary, Augustine provided a systematic theological account, insuring his position on marriage and sex made sense of the entire biblical witness and the preceding doctrinal tradition. This study of Augustine will prepare us for the various ways that contemporary authors are criticizing, appropriating, and rejecting the church's theology of marriage.

My engagement with Augustine is not an attempt to discover/recover what he was really trying to say about sex and marriage, as if such a feat were possible. Furthermore, the overarching aim of this work is not to ensure that the church remains true to Augustine's theology of marriage. Throughout this enquiry, we may well discover that we affirm some of Augustine's responses to issues of sexuality and are forced to leave others behind. Such an outcome should not surprise the reader. The questions of Augustine's day, as well as the cacophony of voices wishing to weigh in on the church's fourth-century discussion of sexuality, differ from our own in some respects. This variance in setting may require a contemporary pastoral response that would be unimaginable to the great Bishop of Hippo. However, his methodology will aid us as we seek theologically sound replies to the contemporary debate. With this in mind, I intend to focus on Augustine's writings as "loci of ongoing debates and readings, as occasions for reflection and insight."[23] My choice to engage Augustine is intended to push us beyond the terms of the current debate toward the underlying doctrinal concerns so often glossed over by that debate. To that end, in the second half of this work I will place Augustine in conversation with contemporary authors who are criticizing, appropriating, and rejecting the church's theology of marriage as they wrestle with what it means for a Christian to embody sexual ethics today. Through this dialogue, I will identify areas of relative consistency between the revisionists and the theological tradition, key doctrines that are being challenged, and newer theological arguments being employed to create space for same-sex relationships. This methodology runs contrary to revisionists and traditionalists whose arguments often assume that these doctrinal questions are already settled. Reopening these questions allows us to ask new and interesting questions. For example, rather than enquiring whether same-sex-attracted individuals and their relationships should be affirmed or condemned, we can query what the church has to learn from the difference exhibited by gay and lesbian Christians and their relationships. By exploring areas of broad agreement between the revisionist authors, as well as the many competing crosscurrents that exist in their work, my aim is to provide language and theological avenues to reframe the contemporary discussion on marriage and same-sex relationships.

Overview of the Book

The foregoing suggests a two-part construction. The first half, composed of chapters 1 and 2, will provide an analysis of the origin of the church's theology of marriage. Its aim is to elucidate the wide-ranging parameters within which the church's discussion of same-sex relationships can take place. The second half, comprised of chapters 3 and 4, will examine four contemporary authors who seek to revise that theology in an attempt to make space for same-sex relationships. These sections will unfold as follows:

    The aim of chapter 1 is to provide an overview of the church's discussion of the body, sex, and marriage from Paul through the fifth century. Focusing on key theologians who made unique contributions to this conversation, this chapter seeks to describe their theological positions and the consequences of

---

23. Rees, *Romance of Innocent Sexuality,* 148.

those positions. While an exhaustive study of these figures and their views is beyond the limitations of this project, my intent is to define the range of intellectual positions available to Augustine as he crafted his theology of marriage. As we will see, by the turn of the fifth century, clear lines were drawn in the church's discourse on the body, marriage, and sex. Similar to the present day, the discussion was dominated by two extreme positions. Augustine, bishop of the North African city of Hippo, had the unenviable task of navigating a middle course between these extremes.

Chapter 2 presents a descriptive analysis of Augustine's theology of marriage. His treatise, *The Good of Marriage* (401), serves as the primary text of inquiry with other writings used to demonstrate the depth and richness of his views on marriage and sexuality. While I will explore writings that span the breadth of Augustine's career, priority will be given to his more developed work written in his middle-to-late years. Following a brief section setting the theological landscape into which Augustine was responding, the chapter will begin with Augustine's defense of marriage as a good. Next, I will provide a detailed description of his three goods of marriage: procreation, fidelity, and sacrament. As with any author whose work spans decades, there is some amount of change and growth in Augustine's theology. In these sections, I will endeavor to demonstrate areas of relative stability as well as zones of development in Augustine's thought. The last two sections of this chapter will address concerns that arise from reading ancient texts from the perspective of a modern setting. Namely, the apparent foreignness of certain Augustinian themes. Addressing the first of these themes, one that is vital to understanding his theology, requires placing marriage in the context of Augustine's sexual hierarchy. Finally, the chapter will engage two contemporary challenges to Augustine's theology of marriage: power in gender relations and sexual desire.

In chapter 3, I examine the work of four contemporary authors who seek to revise the church's traditional theology of marriage. I have chosen authors who provide distinct, significant theological contributions to the question of same-sex relationships as it relates to the church's theology of relationship. As such, this chapter will serve as an introduction to the field of contemporary Christian sexual ethics, with an eye toward teasing out the many points of doctrinal debate within the discussion on same-sex relationships. I will begin with Elizabeth Stuart, who argues that marriage is a patriarchal institution that should be rejected and replaced by friendship as the preferred model for relationships. In her criticism of marriage, Stuart rejects each of the three goods of marriage and supplies three goods of friendship to take their place. Next, I will engage the work of Adrian Thatcher who argues that, contra Stuart, marriage should be revised, not abolished.

Thus, Thatcher maintains the importance of fidelity and permanence to Christian marriage but rejects procreation as a necessary good. Third, I will examine the work of Eugene Rogers who, like Thatcher, upholds fidelity and permanence, but reassesses the importance of procreation. Rogers provides a rationale for Christian marriage which he believes is broad enough to include both heterosexual and same-sex couples. Finally, I will analyze the work of Robert Song who defends Christian marriage as a creation good, while exploring the importance of the advent of Christ for the possibility of a new relational vocation grounded in eschatology. The chapter will proceed by examining each author's theology of marriage/relationship and the implications of that theology for Augustine's three goods of marriage. Finally, I will seek to put the author in dialogue with the work of Augustine. The purpose of this exercise is not to judge each author based on his or her agreement with Augustine, but instead to discover how Augustine might both challenge certain lines of thought and illuminate new pathways that might not be available to each author on his or her own terms.

In the concluding chapter, I will undertake the constructive task for which chapters 1–2 on the origins of the church's traditional theology of marriage and chapter 3 on contemporary revisions of that theology have prepared us. Here, I will address the various questions and conflicts that have been brought to light by engaging Augustine's thought with that of the contemporary revisionists. This chapter will begin by indicating areas of relative consistency between the revisionists and the theological tradition. Next, I will examine key traditional doctrines that are being challenged by the revisionists. I will conclude by highlighting newer theological arguments being employed to revise the church's theology of marriage and create space for same-sex relationships. Identifying new theological claims that are beginning to peak out in the conversation will also reveal areas for future inquiry.

The daunting challenge before us is summarized by Oliver O'Donovan. He writes:

> What if the challenge gays present the church with is not emancipatory but hermeneutic? Suppose that at the heart of the problem there is the *magna quaestio*, the question about the gay experience, its sources and its character, that gays must answer for themselves: how this form of sensibility and feeling is shaped by its social context, how it can be clothed in an appropriate pattern of life for the service of God and discipleship of Christ? But suppose, too, that there is another question corresponding to it, which non-gay Christians need to answer: how and to what extent this form of sensibility and feeling has emerged in specific historical conditions, and

how the conditions may require, as an aspect of the pastoral accommodation that changing historical conditions require, a form of public presence and acknowledgment not hitherto known? These two questions come together as a single question: how are we to understand together the particularity of the age in which we are given to attest God's works?[24]

This book is a response to O'Donovan's invitation. Contrary to the typical traditionalist response, this project is not primarily a discussion of genital activity or a list of practices in which one engages or refrains based on one's reading of Scripture. It also does not follow the standard revisionist path which assumes a place of enlightened superiority over all that came before it. Instead, this book is a work of hermeneutics which seeks to engage the contemporary discussion on the legitimacy of same-sex relationships with the grand theological narrative handed down by the church. My hope is that this work will serve a small part in reframing the terms of the debate taking place within the church.

---

24. O'Donovan, *Conversation Waiting to Begin*, 117.

Sexuality in the Early Church: From Paul to Augustine

THIS CHAPTER OFFERS A brief survey of ancient discussions by the early church fathers on the nature of the body, sex, and marriage. Its aim is to trace the developments and refractions of that discussion from Paul through the fifth century. Focusing on key theologians who made unique contributions to this conversation, I seek to explore their theological positions and the consequences of those positions. Beginning this project with these ancient authors serves as a reminder that theology is not formed *ex nihilo*. Likewise, we do not read Scripture in a vacuum. Our theological reflection and biblical interpretation are colored by the great cloud of witnesses that came before us. The same was true for Augustine. Like us, he was influenced by his theological predecessors who provided a variety of positions which guided his thought.

This chapter begins by examining the Apostle Paul's response to a debate raging within the Corinthian Church concerning a Christian understanding of the body, sex, and marriage. As we shall see, the detailed solution he provided in 1 Corinthians 7 bequeathed a series of unresolved questions and problems to subsequent theologians. Next, I will examine Tertullian's theology of marriage by surveying three works spanning his career. Though his early work demonstrates a positive view of marriage, Tertullian's later writings challenge the inherent goodness of the institution. His wariness of sex and sexual desire would have a profound impact on Christian thinking about the body in the subsequent theological tradition. Next, I will examine the contributions of three fourth- and fifth-century theologians to the church's ongoing discussion of marriage: Gregory of Nyssa, Jovinian, and Jerome. While an exhaustive study of these theologians and their views is beyond the limitations of this project, the intention of the chapter is to define the range of intellectual positions available to Augustine as he crafted his theology of marriage in the early fifth century.

Paul on Sexual Practice in First Corinthians

Paul addressed the topic of sexual ethics in several of his letters, but perhaps his greatest contribution to the subject comes from his first letter to the Corinthians. As Rowan Williams writes, "If this letter had been lost in the post, Christian Ethics would have been very different, since there is more here on sexual relationships than in all the rest of the New Testament."[1] One major issue of contention for the church in Corinth was how Christians should understand the body. Based on evidence from Paul's letter, the church was split into two factions. One group within the church affirmed adopting an ascetic lifestyle. Those in favor of asceticism asserted that baptism and initiation into new life with Christ required a complete break from what came before. After baptism, they contended, a Christian should not replicate the activities, attitudes, and institutions of his or her previous life. When this conviction was applied to the body, it was argued that all Christians should commit themselves to lives of sexual abstinence by renouncing marriage, avoiding intercourse in marriage, and divorcing pagan spouses.[2] By contrast, the second group of Corinthian Christians emphasized the freedom that accompanied their new life in Christ. They argued that life in the Spirit freed Christians from all earthly rules concerning the body. Essential to this assertion was the conviction that Christians are primarily spiritual beings, rather than physical. Therefore, how a Christian uses the body is of little importance. This understanding of Christian freedom led to a variety of irregular expressions of sexuality within the Corinthian church.[3]

The Apostle Paul had the difficult task of navigating these extreme understandings of the body and sexual expression as he attempted to help the Corinthians become a cohesive community of faith.[4] In response to the Corinthian Christians who espoused an ascetic mandate for all believers, Paul encourages the practices of celibacy for single individuals and continence for those who are married, but argues that these lifestyles should not be required for the church as a whole. Let's briefly dissect this

---

1. Williams, "Forbidden Fruit," 27.
2. Brown, *Body and Society*, 54.
3. Coleman, *Christian Attitudes to Marriage*, 106.
4. Brock and Wannenwetsch have made convincing arguments that Paul's primary concern in 1 Corinthians 7 is calling Christians to chastity over *porneia*, rather than elevating celibacy over marriage (*Malady of the Christian Body*, 136–55). However, theologians of the second through fifth centuries read this chapter as an exhortation to celibacy with a concession given to marriage. As the purpose of this chapter is to prepare us for the range of intellectual positions available to Augustine, I have chosen to interpret the passage in line with the Church Fathers we will examine later in this chapter.

two-part argument. On the one hand, Paul wants all Christians to adopt a celibate or continent lifestyle. Paul responds to the claim made by the ascetic Christians that "it is well for a man not to touch a woman" (1 Cor 7:1)[5] by declaring his desire "that all were as I myself am" (1 Cor 7:7), i.e., continent.[6] Paul sees marriage as a distraction from one's participation in the body of Christ.[7] He also notes that marriage brings with it anxieties of "how to please [one's spouse]" (1 Cor 7:33). These anxieties divide one's attention between the things of God and earthly interests. In response to the distractions that accompany married life, Paul wants his readers to be "free" to serve God with undivided attention (1 Cor 7:32-34). On the other hand, Paul understands continence to be a gift from God and argued that this gift is not bestowed upon all Christians. He writes, "But each has a particular gift from God, one having one kind and another a different kind" (1 Cor 7:7). Since not every Christian receives this gift, the church cannot expect all Christians to live continent lives.

While affirming continence as the ideal for Christians, Paul also made room for marriage and marital intercourse. Marriage is a necessary institution, in part, because it allows a place for the appropriate expression of sexual desire. Based on his hamartiology, Paul does not seem to believe that sexual urges can be entirely socialized or ordered.[8] Because of this conviction Paul allows for marriage in order to protect Christians from the sins of lust and fornication. As he is so eloquently translated, "For it is better to marry than to burn" (1 Cor 7:9 KJV).[9] As Otten points out, this statement "was not exactly a ringing endorsement of marriage, thus

---

5. While this verse has traditionally been interpreted as a statement of Paul's view on sex and marriage, other interpretations bring this reading into question. Charles Talbert reads 1 Corinthians 1:1 as a Corinthian—not Pauline—claim (*Reading Corinthians*, 37). And Witherington argues that this statement might have been a slogan used by those in favor of asceticism, rather than revelation of Pauline conviction (*Women in the Earliest Churches*, 40). A comprehensive look at the consensus of modern biblical studies that Paul is quoting a slogan of the ascetic Corinthian Christians is found in Garland, *1 Corinthians*, 247–51.

6. This reading hinges on the belief that Paul was either unmarried or not sexually active as of the writing of 1 Corinthians.

7. Butting, "Pauline Variations," 84.

8. Brown, *Body and Society*, 55–56. See also Brock and Wannenwetsch, *Malady of the Christian Body*, 138.

9. While all other scriptural quotations come from the NRSV, in this case the KJV translation captures the force with which several theologians in the early church argued against marriage as a viable option for Christians.

setting in motion a whole series of problems regarding the interpretation of marriage in the Christian tradition."[10]

Paul's second argument against the church's wholesale adoption of continence was rooted in his concern for mission. Paul believed that continence would be a barrier for new converts. With procreative marriage being an integral part of the Jewish and Roman worldviews, Paul feared that continence could become a rigid wall that distinguished Christians from the outside world. Forced continence threatened to destroy the structure of the Roman household, which Paul used to disseminate his teachings throughout the city.[11] Perhaps this is why the egalitarian vision which bookends First Corinthians, of a community created through the critique and collapse of worldly dominion (1 Cor 1:26–29) and completed by the work of Christ (1 Cor 15:24), does not go as far as the modern reader would like in addressing the hierarchical structures governing male/female relationships in the first-century Roman world.[12] A more detailed examination of this issue is reserved for later in the chapter. To state the matter more positively, for Paul, bearing witness to the work of Christ is the one thing a Christian can do that has eternal significance. This calling can be accomplished regardless of one's place in the world and does not require the elimination of the existing structures of power and authority.[13]

In response to those in the Corinthian Church who espoused a hyper-spiritualized understanding of Christian freedom from earthly rules, Paul rejects the body/soul dualism inherent in their beliefs. At first glance, it appears that Paul would affirm the separation of body and soul espoused by some Corinthian Christians. For example, he asserts that the body is "sown in dishonor" (2 Cor 15:43); it is an "earthen vessel" vulnerable to illness and frustration (2 Cor 4:10–11). However, while Paul made distinctions between body and soul and between flesh and spirit, he did not divorce the concepts from each other. Following Jewish tradition, Paul "did not separate existence from embodiment."[14] Body/soul and flesh/spirit were tropes he used to discuss the orientation of the entire person in relation to God. For Paul, the body is naturally weak because it is susceptible to the "power of the flesh," which leads to human sin. Here, flesh is not synonymous with the body. Throughout Paul's writings, the flesh came to represent the body's

---

10. Otten, "Augustine on Marriage," 400.
11. Brown, *Body and Society*, 54.
12. Butting, "Pauline Variations," 85.
13. For example, see 1 Cor 11:2–16; Witherington, *Conflict & Community*, 178–79.
14. Coleman, *Christian Attitudes to Marriage*, 106.

weakness to temptation and rebellion against God.[15] At the same time, he viewed the flesh as an enemy that had been conquered through the cross and the resurrection. When an individual participates in Christ's death and resurrection through baptism, the individual transitions from a life of bondage to the flesh to a life of freedom in the Spirit.

Paul asserts that bodies hold theological significance. He makes two arguments to support this claim. First, Paul highlights the essential connection between body and spirit on display in the act of prostitution (1 Cor 6:15–19). The one who has sex with a prostitute "becomes one body with her" (v. 16). In the same breath, Paul writes, "But anyone united to the Lord becomes one spirit with him" (v. 17). These statements reflect, for Paul, an essential connection between the categories of body and spirit. Brock and Wannenwetsch argue that in Pauline theology, "The body is not a separable aspect of/from the person. Rather the ensouled body is the person."[16] This logic continues as Paul contends that the body is the "temple of the Holy Spirit" (v. 19). For Paul, the body is not a prison from which one escapes, but a location in which the sanctifying work of the Spirit takes place.[17] Second, Paul points to the conviction that Christians will one day experience bodily resurrection (1 Cor 15).[18] While the body is a place where humans experience the effects of sin, it is also the site of redemption and resurrection. In the resurrection, bodies are perfected, not discarded. Bodies are the location for the human experience of salvation history. Thus rejecting the body in favor of the spirit is not a viable option for Christians. If Christians are to live life before God in the body, then obedience to God requires an ordering of the body and bodily desire.

Hence, Paul's discussion of the body in his letter to the Corinthians served a larger ecclesiastical purpose. Paul connected the individual Christian body to the body of the Christ. "Just as the body is one and has many members, and all the members of the body, though many, are one body, so it is with Christ" (1 Cor 12:12). Paul's appeal to a unified body of believers carries with it three implications. First, since all Christians are a part of one body, individual actions, including seemingly private, sexual actions, affect the rest of the body of Christ.[19] Second, whether one has been granted the gift of marriage or celibacy, all Christian are called to glorify God with their bodies. Finally, it is assumed that the actions of the body of Christ

---

15. Brown, *Body and Society*, 48.
16. Brock and Wannenwetsch, *Malady of the Christian Body*, 127.
17. Butting, "Pauline Variations," 84.
18. Coleman, *Christian Attitudes to Marriage*, 106.
19. Coleman, *Christian Attitudes to Marriage*, 107.

(the church) will be seen by those outside the church. For Paul, the church's conduct in relation to sex and the body is connected to its witness to the world. Thus, the primary question of inquiry is not what sexual activities are allowed or prohibited, but what the sexual lives of Christians communicate about God, Christ, and the church.

While Paul provided direction to Christians concerning appropriate methods of sexual communication (1 Cor 7), his mode of argumentation raised four questions that continued to occupy the minds of theologians for several centuries after Paul. First, if celibacy and continence are preferable to marriage, is marriage part of God's original plan for humankind, or does it represent a detour to accomplishing God's purposes? To put the question another way, is marriage prelapsarian or postlapsarian? Second, is marriage a good in itself, or is it a relative good only when compared to an evil like lust or fornication (1 Cor 7:9)? Third, does continence or celibacy represent a form of moral perfection? The final question was extrapolated from the logic of Paul's argument. If Christians are encouraged to adopt a celibate or continent lifestyle, surely virginity must be the best option. As a consequence, later theologians asked, if virginity is elevated above marriage, do married people have a place in the church? We now turn our attention to the various ways in which the early Fathers of the church sought to navigate these questions.

Paul to the Early Church Fathers

In the two centuries after Paul, the early church did not regard marriage and sexuality as major points of contention. It does not appear that the early church created a distinctly Christian marriage ceremony, but instead followed Roman civil customs.[20] Moreover, sexuality did not dominate writings of the early church Fathers. These writers were content to support New Testament household codes and encourage their congregations to avoid sexual immorality.[21] The early church fathers did not champion chastity and continence, but instead focused on ordered sexuality.[22] However, it was not long before a shift occurred in the church's attitude toward marriage and sexuality. This change occurred, in part, due to fluctuating political realities in the second century. Increased persecution during this period led some Christians to see marriage as superfluous. As more Christians suffered martyrdom, earthly concerns of sex, marriage, and procreation were viewed as

---

20. Coleman, *Christian Attitudes to Marriage*, 107.
21. Coleman, *Christian Attitudes to Marriage*, 123.
22. Brown, *Body and Society*, 58.

"less important" than preparing for life in heaven.[23] Whereas we might say that one's stance on issues of sexuality is the contemporary litmus test of one's faith, willingness to face martyrdom was the key distinguishing characteristic of a Christian in the second and third centuries.

Tertullian (c. 160–225)

While much of the Christian church experienced persecution at the hands of the Roman Empire, the same cannot be said for Christians in Carthage at the turn of the third century. In response to this less hostile setting, Christian apologist Tertullian found a new marker of Christian distinctiveness: chastity.[24] A brief examination of three of Tertullian's writings on marriage will highlight the distinctive ideas that he brought to the church's discussion of the body, sex, and marriage.

To His Wife (c. 200–206)

In one of his early works, entitled *To His Wife*, Tertullian writes on the subject of remarriage. Here, Tertullian reveals a positive disposition toward marriage, calling it an "institution blessed by God for the reproduction of the human race. It was planned by Him for the purpose of the propagation of humankind. Hence, it was permitted; but only once may it be contracted."[25] This statement reveals several distinctive features of Tertullian's theology of marriage. First, marriage is a good because it is part of the divine plan, though Tertullian does not mention if he believes that marriage is prelapsarian or postlapsarian. Second, there is an inherent connection between marriage and procreation; procreation is the telos of marriage. Finally, marriage is designed by God to be monogamous. As we will see, Tertullian's definition of monogamy is somewhat more robust than the modern use of the term referring to having one spouse at a time.

After acknowledging the many reasons why someone might yearn to remarry (sexual desire, social stability, loneliness, ambition, desire for children, etc.), Tertullian encourages his spouse to remain single after his death. He cites three arguments in favor of rejecting remarriage. First, he appeals to the divine will. Tertullian believes that all things submit to the will of God. God controls both life and death; no one dies without God willing it. Based on this conviction, Tertullian writes, "Therefore, when God wills that

23. Coleman, *Christian Attitudes to Marriage*, 126–27.
24. Brown, *Body and Society*, 77.
25. Tertullian, *To His Wife* 1.2.

a woman lose her husband in death, He also wills that she should be done with marriage itself. Why attempt to restore what God has put asunder?"[26] According to Tertullian, the death of one's spouse is a divine sign that one's marrying days are over. Based on this logic, remarriage represents a rejection of God's will for one's life. Second, Tertullian warns of the limitations that accompany a second marriage. He notes that both church law and Scripture's decrees place strict boundaries on individuals who marry a second time. In Tertullian's context, both the deaconate and dedicated widowhood were reserved for individuals who had only been married once. Finally, Tertullian appeals to the widow's place in the church's sexual hierarchy. In an unusual move for this era, Tertullian places widowhood above virginity. He writes, "Chastity (of widowhood) is most praiseworthy when it is sensible of the right it has sacrificed and knows what it has experienced. The condition of the virgin may be regarded as one of greater felicity, but that of the widow is one of greater difficulty."[27] Widowhood is elevated in Tertullian's theology based on the distinct challenge this way of life presents. The widow has experiential knowledge of what she is giving up. Hence, Tertullian calls virginity a grace, while widowhood is a virtue because it is accomplished by one's "own efforts" and "personal endeavor."[28]

Tertullian closes the letter to his wife by noting the "heroic" difficulty of persevering in continence after the death of a spouse.[29] Because of this challenge, Tertullian pardons individuals who cannot sustain the monogamous widow's life. While discouraging the practice, he acknowledges that remarriage is not sinful so long as the new spouse is a Christian. Christian remarriage has a place in Tertullian's theology precisely because Christ unifies the couple through marriage. They are "two who are one in hope, one in desire, one in the way of life they follow, one in the religion they practice. They are as brother and sister, both the servant of the same Master. Nothing divides them, either in flesh or in spirit."[30] Marriage and, despite his best efforts, remarriage serve positive roles in the lives of the couple.

In this early example of Tertullian's theology, monogamous marriage is seen as a gift from God for the purpose of procreation. Christian marriage also exists for the good of the couple, as both partners are unified in their service to God. Remarriage is discouraged but permitted. And the life of the widow is elevated above that of the virgin based on the widow's

26. Tertullian, *To His Wife* 1.7.
27. Tertullian, *To His Wife* 1.8.
28. Tertullian, *To His Wife* 1.8.
29. Tertullian, *To His Wife* 2.1.
30. Tertullian, *To His Wife* 2.8.

experiential knowledge of what she is sacrificing for Christ. Compared to other theologians of the third and fourth centuries, Tertullian's letter is a glowing affirmation of Christian marriage. Yet, in only a few short years, his perspective takes a sharp turn.

Exhortation to Chastity (c. 205–12)

By roughly 205, the tone of Tertullian's rhetoric on marriage and sexuality begins to change. *Exhortation to Chastity* reveals a major shift in his theology of marriage. This change coincides with Tertullian's introduction to Montanist teachings. This sect emphasized continual new outpourings of the Spirit which supersede previous revelations from God. Accompanying this supersessionist bent was a renewed focus on moral rigorism.[31] In *Exhortation to Chastity*, Tertullian's previous affirmation of the inherent goodness of marriage is brought into question in three ways. First, Tertullian appeals to Paul's concession for marriage in 1 Corinthians 7:9. Commenting on this verse, Tertullian argues that marriage is considered a good only "when it is compared with the greatest of all evils (punishment)."[32] However, he argues, goods should only be spoken of in absolute terms, not in comparison to an evil. Based on this logic, Tertullian contends that if the negative point of comparison (i.e., punishment) is removed, then the good of marriage is nullified. Second, Tertullian challenges the telos of marriage: procreation. He argues that before the coming of Christ, marriage and its command to be fruitful and multiply was a prophetic sign pointing to the coming of the church. Now that the church is a present reality, the procreative command has been superseded. He writes, "The precept of continence . . . and the restriction placed on intercourse, which is the seeding of the race, have abolished the ancient command to increase and multiply."[33] For Tertullian, procreation no longer has any value, thus abolishing it as a telos of marriage. Third, Tertullian challenges the goodness of marriage by altering his use of the sexual hierarchy. While marriage is discussed in positive terms in *To His Wife*, here Tertullian argues that marriage represents a fall "from the level of immaculate virginity" into the trough of "incontinence."[34] To illustrate this move, he compares looking lustfully at a woman who is not one's spouse with the sexual desire that one has for one's spouse. The

---

31. González, *Early Church*, 76. See Olson, *Story of Christian Theology*, 31–33, 91–93.
32. Tertullian, *Exhortation to Chastity*, 47.
33. Tertullian, *Exhortation to Chastity*, 52.
34. Tertullian, *Exhortation to Chastity*, 57.

argument is constructed so that marital desire is equated with adulterous desire, leading Tertullian to conclude that marriage is essentially fornication. Tertullian gleefully admits that his doctrinal position is "destructive of all marriage, even monogamy," however, he believes that this is justified because sex, "the shameful act which constitutes [the essence of marriage], is the same as fornication."[35] In Tertullian's sexual hierarchy, virginity, not widowhood, is now placed on one end of the spectrum with fornication on the other. However, when marriage is equated with fornication, the effect is to contrast the good of virginity with the evil of marriage.

Toward the end of this work, Tertullian reveals the primary logic driving his new theology of marriage. He asserts that the "use of sex even in marriage repels the Holy Spirit."[36] For Tertullian, the senses of the body are connected to one's experience of the divine. Therefore, the body must be trained or regulated so that one might more ably experience the movement of the Spirit. As Peter Brown notes, Tertullian's statement is "the first consequential statement . . . of the belief that abstinence from sex was the most effective technique with which to achieve clarity of soul."[37] This belief would have a lasting impact on the Western Christian world.

Monogamy (c. 217)

By the completion of *Monogamy*, Tertullian, fully immersed in Montanist teachings, was convinced that the moral code set forth in the Scriptures needed to be updated for his contemporary setting. This revision is accomplished through a new word spoken by the Holy Spirit.[38] Much of this work repeats themes from *Exhortation to Chastity*, with one key addition. In a discussion of remarriage, Tertullian argues that the marriage bond is not broken by death. Even when a spouse dies, he argues, the living partner "owes a debt of undivided affection" to the deceased spouse.[39] Here, Tertullian's condemnation of remarriage takes on an eschatological dimension. While he acknowledges Jesus' statement to the Saducees denying the existence of marriage in heaven (Matt 22:30), he asserts that this statement does not deny that we shall be "bound to spouses who have gone before us in death."[40] Rather than death severing the marriage bond, Tertullian envisions marital

---

35. Tertullian, *Exhortation to Chastity*, 57.
36. Tertullian, *Exhortation to Chastity*, 59.
37. Brown, *Body and Society*, 78.
38. Brown, *Body and Society*, 76.
39. Tertullian, *Monogamy*, 91.
40. Tertullian, *Monogamy*, 92.

partners being more closely bound together in the eschaton. He argues for a continuity of the marriage bond after death because in heaven "we shall be conscious of our own identity as well as the identity of those we love."[41] If a widow is allowed to remarry after the death of her husband, the husband's heavenly life would be disrupted. Instead of seeking remarriage, Tertullian asserts that widows and widowers should pray for their spouses and honor them through living a continent life. Thus, the marriage bond is not loosened even by death.

Tertullian's life and work illustrate the live debate taking place in the early church on marriage and sexual ethics. As we have seen, he articulates contrasting viewpoints on the nature of the institution and its place in the church. To this conversation, Tertullian bequeathed three significant ideas. First, though he was not the first Christian theologian to identify procreation as the telos of marriage, he was the earliest to claim that both marriage and the result of the couple's sexual relationship (i.e., procreation) are good. His inability to maintain this position would complicate the church's ongoing dispute. Second, he introduced the concept of a sexual hierarchy based on renunciation. Under this rubric, one's place in the church is determined, in part, by one's level of sexual activity. The more sex a Christian has, the lower they rank amongst God's people. This idea is closely connected to Tertullian's third contribution, namely, his claim that sexual activity is a barrier to encountering the divine, a barrier that can only be overcome through a commitment to abstinence. This wariness of sex and sexual desire continued to color the church's discourse on human sexuality for centuries.

Virginity and Marriage in the Fourth and Fifth Centuries

While the first inklings of an ascetic hierarchy in Christian thought can be traced to the writings of Paul, virginity, chastity and continence were not widely practiced among Christians until the fourth century. This shift toward ascetic sexual practices coincided with a rise in Christianity's stature in the Roman Empire, accompanied by a decline in persecution and martyrdom. Throughout the second and third centuries, the socio-cultural identifying markers that distinguished Christians from non-Christians were easy to identify. Christians were those who were willing to suffer and die for their commitment to Christ. However, after the conversion of Constantine and the elevation of Christianity from a minority sect to the religion of the Roman Empire, the dividing line between Christians and pagans became

41. Tertullian, *Monogamy*, 92.

more muddled. As a result, Christians began to draw a new set of distinctions, not between Christians and pagans, but between Christians and other Christians. Where the previous mark of faithfulness was a willingness to face persecution and martyrdom, the new measure of one's obedience to God was determined by one's sexual activity, or lack thereof. Virginity replaced martyrdom as the sign of Christian uniqueness.[42] This change left the nagging question of what to do with marriage and married Christians. Two dominant positions provided answers to the quandary. Respected leaders of the early church, such as Gregory of Nyssa and Jerome, declared virginity to be the ideal mode of life for Christians. As a result, they viewed married Christians, at best, as second-class citizens within the church. This assessment was challenged by Jovinian, who argued that the practice of virginity should not be elevated over marriage. Thus, a clear boundary line was drawn between ascetic and married Christians, and this division threatened to rend the unity of the church.

In order to provide a general overview of the church's fourth- and fifth-century discussion on the body, sex, and marriage, I will briefly examine the writings of three authors from this period: Gregory of Nyssa, Jovinian, and Jerome. These authors present distinct positions in the early church's ongoing debate about the relationship between Christian faith and the body. As contemporaries of Augustine, their arguments represent a key segment of the intellectual positions available to the Bishop of Hippo.

Gregory of Nyssa: Virginity versus Marriage

Gregory of Nyssa (c. 335–95) was one of the fourth-century church's champions of virginity. He was not against marriage, per se. After all, he was probably a married bishop.[43] However, he longed for the perfection he perceived to exist in virginity.[44] In making the case for virginity in his aptly titled work, *On Virginity*, Gregory spends a great deal of time discussing the dangers and heartaches associated with marriage. He notes, for example, that husbands experience the possibility of losing a wife or child during birth, and that wives are threatened by the grief which accompanies the loss of a husband. Gregory acknowledges that while each person experiences death, the deep friendship developed within marriage makes the couple

---

42. Otten, "Augustine on Marriage," 394.

43. Scholarship is divided on whether or not Gregory of Nyssa was married. However, Otten indicates that Gregory was married to a woman named Theosebeia. See Otten, "Augustine on Marriage," 390; Brown, *Body and Society*, 296.

44. Brown, *Body and Society*, 299.

"twice as vulnerable" to the heartache of mortality.[45] In light of these hardships, Gregory argues it is better to forego marriage and choose a life of virginity, which is immune to such worldly troubles. Hence, the primary way that Gregory endorses virginity is by accentuating the problems associated with marriage. Here, Gregory follows Tertullian's method of elevating virginity by contrasting it with marriage.[46] For him, virginity and marriage are as different "as heaven is from earth."[47]

Gregory's affirmation of virginity is connected to his understanding of the fall. He begins his bifurcate argument by asserting that sin fundamentally changed the physical composition of humans. According to Gregory, the first humans were created asexual. The logic supporting this claim is the conviction that sexual difference exists for the purpose of procreation. Procreation is needed to ensure the continuance of the human race in a context where humans suffer death. However, death did not exist prior to the fall. As such, there would have been no need for procreation and, by extension, sexual difference. This train of thought leads Gregory to the conclusion that sexual differentiation was a "safety device" installed in humankind by God which became active at the fall.[48] Following this reasoning to its logical end, he concludes that procreative marriage was made necessary by human sin. Gregory asserts that when Adam and Eve were cast out of paradise they "became colonists of this place . . . where marriage was contrived as a consolation for death."[49] For Gregory, marriage and procreation were, at best, afterthoughts in creation. At worst, they represent a deviation from God's original plan. Since both marriage and procreation are attached to death, Gregory encourages Christians to choose the life of virginity.[50] In anticipation of those who might use sexuality as a scapegoat for the origin of sin or equate it with divine retribution, Gregory provides two caveats. First, he asserts that sexual differentiation did not cause the fall but was the result of the fall. Humans cannot blame sin on their sexual composition and are therefore still responsible for the consequences of sin.[51] Second, Gregory is quick to note that sexuality is not an emblem of divine punishment for human sin. Instead, sexuality is "a privileged sign of God's abiding care," similar to the garments of skin which God gave to help humans endure life

---

45. Gregory of Nyssa, *On Virginity* 3.12.
46. Otten, "Augustine on Marriage," 391.
47. Gregory of Nyssa, *On Virginity* 2.13.
48. Brown, *Body and Society*, 296.
49. Gregory of Nyssa, *On Virginity* 12.46.
50. Gregory of Nyssa, *On Virginity* 13.46–47.
51. Gregory of Nyssa, *On Virginity* 12.41–42.

after the fall. Based on these interpretations of creation and the fall, Gregory views both sexual difference and procreative marriage as gifts of grace.[52] In spite of these caveats, both categories remain postlapsarian detours to fulfilling God's purposes in the world.

The second part of Gregory's argument on the relationship between sin and the human body is his assertion that the fall fundamentally altered the way in which humans perceive time. He argues that before the advent of sin, humans experienced time in a pure way; they lived without fear of time. After the fall, time was tainted by dread of the future because of the approaching reality of one's death. Based on this interpretation, Gregory argues that marriage, sex, and children represent attempts to avoid the incessant march of time.[53] According to Brown, Gregory understands marriage to be a sign of society's fear of death, while sex and procreation are the "last outward stopping [places] of Adam and Eve in their sad exile from Paradise."[54] Gregory argues that the solution to this dilemma is to reject marriage and procreation entirely, thereby refusing to acquiesce to death's demand for captives in the form of children.[55] In this framework, virginity represents a rejection of time's ceaseless journey toward death and a return to the pure time that Adam and Eve experienced before the fall. Thus, Gregory's affirmation of virginity is a criticism of the pride expressed by humanity's desire to avoid death through marriage and procreation.

In his treatise, Gregory made two significant contributions to the church's ongoing debate on the nature of marriage and sexuality. First, he clearly articulated the position that sexual difference and procreative marriage are divergences from God's original plan for humankind. While Gregory attempted to maintain a pastoral tone by describing these categories as gifts from God, his mode of argumentation made it difficult for him to ascribe any inherent goodness to sexual difference and procreation. Second, through his discussion of sin, time, and the self, Gregory conceived of virginity as a return to the purity of a pre-lapsarian era. This stance left later theologians to wonder whether virginity represented a form of moral perfection. If so, then any deviation from perfection, including procreative marriage, might be sinful.

---

52. Gregory of Nyssa, *On Virginity* 7.31. See also Otten, "Augustine on Marriage," 398.

53. Gregory of Nyssa, *On Virginity* 3.12; 14.48–49.

54. Brown, *Body and Society*, 298.

55. Gregory of Nyssa 3.16.

Jovinian: By Baptism Alone

Gregory of Nyssa's elevation of virginity over marriage did not go unchallenged. Jovinian (died c. 405) was one of the chief opponents of the ascetic movement sweeping through the church during the fourth century.[56] Before being condemned as a heretic in 393, Jovinian was an influential monk in Rome who experienced the support of many Roman clergymen. Like most individuals convicted of heresy during this time period, none of Jovinian's writings survive. However, his ideas can be partially reconstructed with a degree of confidence from the writings of his contemporary critics, namely Ambrose and Jerome.[57]

Jovinian felt compelled to respond to the damage he perceived being done to marriage and married Christians by the ascetic movement and its hierarchy of sexual behavior. Rather than elevating some members of the church over others, Jovinian sought to level the field by challenging the ascetic trajectory of the church. We will briefly examine three of his arguments.[58] First, he asserts that virgins and celibates receive no added merit for their actions. It should be noted that Jovinian did not criticize celibacy itself; after all, he was a celibate monk. His concern was the tendency for Christians to draw distinctions within the church based solely on the elevation of ascetic sexual practices over marriage. He points to the fourth-century practice of veiling virgins as evidence of this tendency. Jovinian argues that through this ritual consecration of young women, the personal and private choice to dedicate oneself to God through virginity became a public spectacle used to assert the virgin's superiority over married women.[59] This practice, he contends, leads to increased pride in individuals who ranked higher on the presumed ascetical hierarchy, resulting in further division within the body of Christ. According to Jovinian, it is not appropriate to draw distinctions among Christians based on their choice to be married or celibate. The more fundamental distinction is that which differentiates those inside the church from those outside the church: baptism. Once an individual enters the faith through baptism, whether that person chooses

---

56. Hunter, "Virgin," 283.

57. Hunter, "Reconstructing Jovinian," 393.

58. Jovinian is credited with a fourth proposition against asceticism, which does not pertain to this discussion. He argued that Satan cannot overcome the baptized Christian. Here, Jovinian balances individual and communal concerns. He focuses on the church's communal power over evil, while acknowledging that individual Christians continue to sin after baptism. While Christians continue to sin, they do not lose the benefits of salvation, namely, baptism. Hunter, "Reconstructing Jovinian," 17–19.

59. Hunter, "Reconstructing Jovinian," 10–14.

to be a celibate, a virgin, a widow, or a married person is of limited consequence.[60] Through this argument, Jovinian rejects the implementation of an ecclesial hierarchy based on sexual practice.

To support his move, Jovinian cites biblical texts which affirm the place of married people within the people of God. He also highlights the important role that sex and reproduction play in salvation history. Abraham and Sarah's sexual relationship, which led to the birth of Christ, is Jovinian's prime example. Based on these illustrations, he argues that the Hebrew Scriptures do not elevate celibacy over marriage. According to David Hunter, Jovinian believed that the "necessity of sex in salvation history was a permanent reminder to celibate Christians that they [do] not merit any special status before God."[61] Next, Jovinan argues that sex, marriage, and procreation continue to serve a purpose once the Incarnation was complete. While celibacy became an option once the Messiah had been born, Jovinian claims that the New Testament preserves procreative marriage as a licit option for the people of God. He cites the celebration of the birth of John to Zachariah and Elizabeth as evidence of this claim (Luke 1:5–25, 57–66). He also points to Paul's instruction to bishops and elders, requiring them to be husbands of one wife (1 Tim 3:2).[62] If virginity were the preferred mode of life for Christians, presumably leaders of the church would be required to set an example by adopting this ascetic practice. Instead, they are called to monogamous marriage. Thus, Jovinian argues that both the Hebrew Scripture and the New Testament demonstrate continuity on their affirmation of marriage. Based on this evidence, Jovinian argues, there is no scriptural basis to elevate virginity over marriage. Baptism, not virginity, is the primary marker which distinguishes people from one another.

In his second challenge to asceticism, Jovinian criticizes the dangerous theological assumptions supporting the elevation of virginity over marriage. To illustrate this point, he discusses the practice of fasting. Like his arguments on virginity, Jovinian does not reject fasting as a legitimate Christian practice. There are times when fasting is wholly appropriate. But there are other moments that call for a feast. Jovinian finds evidence to support both of these claims in the life of Jesus. He acknowledges that Jesus and the disciples fasted, but notes that they also ate and drank in such a manner that they were accused of gluttony. How is it possible to affirm both fasting and excessive eating as acceptable Christian practices? For Jovinian, this answer hinges on the attitude with which one eats and fasts. He argues that

---

60. Hunter, "Reconstructing Jovinian," 13–14.
61. Hunter, "Reconstructing Jovinian," 15.
62. Hunter, "Reconstructing Jovinian," 16.

pride undoes the good accomplished by fasting in the same way that eating without gratitude turns a celebratory feast into gluttony. This leads Jovinian to contend that there is no difference between humbly abstaining from food and eating with an attitude of thanksgiving. In this discussion of eating and fasting, Jovinian is concerned with excessive asceticism or "the elevation of ascetic over non-ascetic practices," which he believes demonstrates a warped view of creation.[63] Extreme asceticism, he argues, runs dangerously close to dualism, a view that posits creation as evil or tainted, as something to be avoided. By contrast, Jovinian sees creation as a good gift from God. The proper human response to this good gift, he argues, is thanksgiving. Jovinian takes the logic of food as a good gift from God and applies it to sex and marriage. He concludes that idealizing virginity and continence as the preferred or only means of living the Christian life runs dangerously close to rejecting the goodness of sex and marriage as gifts from God.

Finally, Jovinian challenges the ascetic hierarchy through a discussion of eternal rewards. He argues that all Christians, married and celibate, will receive the same reward in heaven. The logic of this statement turns on Jovinian's understanding of baptism. According to Jovinian, a Christian's salvation, preservation, and eternal reward come through baptism, not through ascetic accomplishment. Furthermore, any reward bestowed on a Christian is a gift from God, and therefore cannot be earned through human activity.[64] If one's salvation and reward are based solely on the agency of God, Jovinian concluded, then there is no reason to elevate virginity or continence over marriage. All baptized Christians share in the holiness of the church and in the rewards promised to its members.

Though the church ultimately disagreed with his position, Jovinian made two contributions to the church's ongoing dialogue on sex and marriage. First, he was one of the few theologians in the fourth and fifth centuries to consistently affirm that bodies and their various sexual functions were created before the fall. Describing bodies and sex as prelapsarian enabled Jovinian and later theologians to affirm the inherent worth of these categories, rather than dismissing them as effects of the fall. Second, Jovinian broadened the discussion by placing the creation categories of sex and marriage alongside baptism and salvation. Such a move enabled Jovinian to emphasize the significance of salvation while relegating sexual practice to a place of lesser import. This argument was an underappreciated gift to a church being torn apart by disagreements over the hot theological topic of the day.

63. Hunter, "Reconstructing Jovinian," 20.
64. Hunter, "Reconstructing Jovinian," 21–22.

Jerome: Virginity as Primary (or Only) Option

One of the strongest proponents of virginity during this period was Jerome (331–420) an ascetic teacher who spent the majority of his career in Bethlehem. Jerome differed from the majority of church leaders in the fourth century in two ways. First, while many male church leaders abhorred companionship with members of the opposite gender, Jerome had a number of female students and was an advocate for the education of virtuous Christian women. Second, Jerome made a place for celibate women, not just virgins.[65] This decision appears to be a practical move as most of his students were continent widows. Such an arrangement reflected the social setting of the church in the fourth century. During this period, the typical continent woman was a widow, not a woman who had chosen virginity from the time of her youth. Widows tended to be from wealthy families. As such, they were controllers of property and were financially independent. These influential women often attained leadership positions within the church, where they engaged in "paraclerical" roles such as offering advice, praying for the laity, etc.[66] The presence of female leadership in the church, not doubt, influenced Jerome's understanding of sexuality, in general, and male/female relations in particular.

Jerome's generous attitude toward women is grounded in his understanding of the body. Similar to Gregory or Nyssa, Jerome argues that humans were created asexual. He writes, "Let us read the beginning of Genesis, and we shall find Adam, that is man, called both male and female."[67] Yet, Jerome takes the argument one step further than his predecessor. He asserts that humans were spiritual beings prior to the fall. Not only sexual characteristics, but also physical bodies were bestowed on humans as a result of sin. Since neither sexual differentiation nor bodies existed, Jerome contends, marriage and its procreative telos would not have been possible in a prelapsarian world. He reasons that if sin had not entered the world, Adam and Eve would have lived in perpetual virginity. "But after they sinned, and were cast out of Paradise," he writes, "they were immediately married."[68] Here, bodies, sexual differentiation and marriage are the direct result of the fall. For Jerome, this assertion had two implications for how Christian men

---

65. Hunter "Virgin," 291–92. At this time, the church made a distinction between the two categories. Celibacy was a label that could apply to an individual prior to marriage or after the death of a spouse. Virginity, by contrast, was a term reserved only for individuals who made a lifelong commitment to refrain from marriage and sex.

66. Brown, *Body and Society*, 150–52.

67. Jerome, *Against Jovinianus* 1.29.

68. Jerome, *Against Jovinianus* 1.16; cf. 1.29.

and women interact. On the one hand, because men and women are now sexual beings, they are a source for mutual temptation. Therefore, specific rules are required to govern interaction between the sexes. On the other hand, since Christians are primarily spiritual beings, they have the ability to live unaffected by bodily desire. Christians can transcend bodily desire in this life through the transforming power of Christ.[69] Thus, it is possible for Christian men and women to form partnerships based not upon sexual desire but on desire for Christ displayed through virginity.

In spite of Jerome's affirmation of the interaction of Christian men and women, he continued the tradition of differentiating between Christians based on a hierarchy of sexual practice. Virgins were elevated above widows, who were above continent married people, who were privileged above the ordinary, married Christian who engaged in sexual intercourse. Jerome's elevation of virginity relies on his reading of 1 Corinthians 7. Following Tertullian's interpretation, Jerome argued that Paul makes a concession for marriage. A concession is, by definition, less than the good. Therefore, the concession of marriage is not the good that Paul desires for Christians. Based on this logic, he contends, it follows that marriage can only be considered good when compared to the evil of punishment for lust.[70] Therefore, Jerome concludes that marriage is not a good in itself; it is merely a lesser evil. It is difficult to see how such a position leaves room for either marriage or married people within the church. It is important to follow the logic of the argument. If all evil, regardless of degree, is sinful and marriage is evil, then those who marry engage in sin. As a result, virginity becomes the only licit option available to Christians.

In making his case for virginity as the ideal mode of life for the Christian, Jerome points to examples of virginity in Scripture. First, he appeals to the Virgin Mary's role in the Incarnation. Jerome poses the rhetorical question, "If virginity be not preferred to marriage, why did the Holy Spirit not choose a married woman, or a widow?"[71] In response, Jerome instructs both men and women to follow the example of Mary, the perpetual virgin mother of Jesus.[72] Second, he argues that the apostles had either been virgins or had been continent in marriage.[73] The underlying assumption is that sex is a barrier to interaction with the divine. Jerome contends that

---

69. Brown, *Body and Society*, 373. See Jerome, *Against Jovinianus* 1.16, where salvation, or the "putting off of the old man," is equated with overcoming sexual desire through Christ.

70. Jerome, *Against Jovinianus* 1.7–9.

71. Jerome, *Against Jovinianus* 1.32.

72. Jerome, *Perpetual Virginity of Mary*, 11–43.

73. Jerome, *Against Jovinius* 1.26.

"any believer, cannot pray unless he [abstains] from sexual intercourse."[74] While the stain of sex applies to all Christians, Jerome believes it is most pronounced in the lives of priests who have the holy obligation to pray for their people. This logic leads Jerome to conclude that pastors, teachers, and other church leaders should follow the apostles' example by committing themselves to celibacy in marriage or, preferably, virginity. In his passionate defense of virginity, Jerome went so far as to say that married clergy, even if they are celibate, are merely individuals that the church is forced to employ when true virgin priests are not available.[75] In summary, for Jerome, sexual intercourse reduces an individual's status in the church, whether that person is clergy or laity.

Jerome's valorization of virginity had important consequences for his theology of marriage. For example, he found himself unable to articulate potential positive effects of Christian marriage for the couple. Instead, his description of the institution of marriage was thoroughly negative. He writes, "Having a wife is a heavy burden if one cannot dismiss her except on the ground of fornication. For what if she were a drunkard, hot-tempered, badly behaved, lustful, a glutton, inconstant, quarrelsome, or abusive. . . . Like it or not, one must put up with her, for one has subjected one's self to servitude while one was still free."[76] Here, marriage is conceived as bondage, while virginity is seen as a form of freedom. As one would imagine, this pessimistic account of marriage made remarriage unthinkable for Jerome. He asserts that first marriages are regrettable, because they signify the giving of the self to the flesh.[77] And second marriages are one step from the brothel.[78] Here, the connection between marriage and sin in Jerome's theology is clearly displayed, as marriage is equated with offering oneself over to lust.

While Jerome's position faced a series of challenges in the fourth century, he influenced the church's discussion of sex and bodies in two ways.[79] First, his description of bodies, sexual difference, and procreative marriage as postlapsarian entities left Jerome and subsequent theologians with little room to discuss their inherent goodness. If there is any goodness to be found in bodies and sex, they cannot be construed as the result of sin. Second, though not the first to articulate an "ascetic hierarchy, ranked according to degrees

---

74. Jerome, *Against Jovinianus* 1.34.

75. Jerome, *Against Jovinianus* 1.34.

76. Jerome, *Commentary on Matthew*, 223–24.

77. More than other authors of this period, Jerome equated Paul's use of the "flesh" with sexual desire. See Brown, *Body and Society*, 376–77; Jerome, *Letter 22/5*, 23–27.

78. Jerome, *Against Jovinianus* 1.13, 15.

79. See Brown, *Body and Society*, 378; Hunter, "Virgin," 295.

of sexual renunciation," Jerome's influence resulted in this schema becoming the church's primary model for understanding the sexual life of the Christian.[80] Third, by placing virginity at the top of the hierarchy and contrasting it with married life, Jerome, along with several of his contemporaries, won the argument in the fourth century. But in the process, they nearly destroyed marriage as a viable option for Christians.

The Makings of Division

By the turn of the fifth century, clear lines were drawn in the church's discourse on the body, marriage, and sex. The discussion was dominated by two extreme positions. One position exalted virginity at the expense of marriage; the other left little room for virginity, celibacy, or other forms of ascetic life. Augustine (354–430), bishop of the North African city of Hippo, had the unenviable task of navigating a middle course between these extremes. Willemein Otten summarizes the challenging task set before Augustine: "When called upon to defend virginity, how can [Augustine] do so while avoiding the simple solution that celibacy makes one sinless? In placing virginity above marriage, how can he avoid indicting marriage as an institution infected by human corruption? . . . [Choosing either option amounts to] sowing further discord in the Church."[81] The church's discussion of sexuality in the fifth century was characterized by tension. It is with these tensions in mind that we turn to Augustine's theology of marriage.

---

80. Hunter, "Virgin," 294.
81. Brown, *Body and Society*, 396.

2

The Good of Marriage

Augustine of Hippo

AUGUSTINE IS A TOWERING figure in the history of the Western church. His theological vision and themes have shaped subsequent Western Church tradition perhaps more than any other writer since Paul. "For good or for ill, he is in the West the Second Founder of the Faith," as Mathewes observes.[1] His historical stature tempts modern readers to conflate the historical Augustine with an image passed down over the centuries of Saint Augustine the Latin Father. In truth, Augustine was a complex figure. He wore a variety of occupational and ministerial "hats," including bishop, pastor, theologian, shepherd, crisis arbiter, etc. Furthermore, he wrote to a variety of audiences with incredible rhetorical skill, and his theological views exhibit movement and change over time.[2] The effect of this eclectic mixture on the contemporary reader of Augustine is twofold. First, because of his rhetorical ability, it can be difficult to pigeonhole Augustine into a particular position. Second, because of the vast quantity and the dynamic nature of his writings, Augustine is quoted to support a wide variety of views. Perhaps it is in these two characteristics that the modern reader can find the humanity in the writings of St. Augustine. "Like us, he struggled for clarity, changed his mind, and operated within a fairly limited range of intellectual options whose parameters he did not set."[3]

It was in response to a variety of complex theological and ecclesial circumstances that Augustine penned *The Good of Marriage*. Jovinian argued that baptism is the only distinction that matters between people, and therefore there is no added merit for those who practice virginity. His views threatened to negate the validity of ascetic lifestyles and had wide ranging theological and social implications for the church. During this period, the church was also engaged in fierce debate with rival groups, such as the

---

1. Mathewes, "Original Sin," 40.
2. Nikkel, "Goodness of Creaturely Existence," 185.
3. Mathewes, "Original Sin," 40.

Manichees, over the nature of the body, and, by extension, the legitimacy of marriage and procreation for the Christian life. The Manichees believed that creation is a battleground where the forces of light and darkness vie for supremacy. In this system, divine spiritual light has been imprisoned in physicality by darkness. Therefore, activities of the flesh, like marriage and reproduction, are "a plot used by the Darkness to keep the Divine Light trapped in the flesh."[4] Because of their dualistic conception of the world, the Manicheans understood both marriage and procreation to be intrinsically evil. Finally, Jerome and Gregory of Nyssa contrasted virginity with marriage, elevating the former while denouncing the latter, thereby threatening to destroy marriage as a viable option for Christians. Not unlike the contemporary setting, the fifth-century church was splintered over disagreements about the body and sexuality, and their relationship to the faithful witness of the Christian.

This chapter presents a descriptive analysis of Augustine's response to this divisive setting. His treatise *The Good of Marriage* (401) will serve as the primary text of inquiry with other writings incorporated to demonstrate the depth and richness of his views on marriage and sexuality. While I will attempt to present texts which span Augustine's career, priority will be given to his more developed work found in his middle-to-late years. I will begin with Augustine's defense of marriage as a good, followed by a detailed description of his three goods of marriage: procreation, fidelity, and sacrament. These sections will demonstrate areas of relative stability as well as areas of development in Augustine's thought, an effort that will distinguish peripheral concerns from key concepts in Augustine's understanding of sex and marriage. I will proceed by placing marriage in the context of Augustine's sexual hierarchy, allowing Augustine to discuss how marriage should be understood in relation to virginity and continence. Finally, I will engage two contemporary challenges to Augustine's theology of marriage. The first is a discussion of power in gender relations. The second challenge addresses Augustine's impact on the church's understanding of sexual desire.

Marriage as a Good

Augustine responded to the various fourth- and fifth-century critics of matrimony by affirming the goodness of marriage. Augustine begins his first direct treatise on marriage by defending the institution on historical grounds. Unlike several of his early works where Augustine employs an allegorical interpretation of the creation account, in *The Good of Marriage*,

---

4. Jungling, "Passionate Order," 319

he uses a more concrete, historical interpretation.[5] Here, the creation story marks the beginning of human history. The first man was created from the dust of the ground, and the first woman was created from the man's rib. For Augustine, the creation of woman from man signifies that from the beginning, man and woman were bound together by the "bond of blood relationship."[6] It is significant that Augustine describes the bonded relationship between the first couple as a marriage. Some of the early church fathers rejected this notion outright, allowing them to assert that marriage is a postlapsarian institution that represents a deviation from the divine plan.[7] In response to this view, Augustine argues that marriage is a gift from God instituted before Adam and Eve sinned.[8] Arguing that the first couple was married shortly after the time of their creation allows Augustine to assert that marriage is a prelapsarian good, instituted by God from the beginning of human history. As such, the first marriage represents the ideal human relationship; it is the source of all successive relationships and should be revered by subsequent humans.

Second, in order to demonstrate that marriage is a good, Augustine points to the social dimension of marriage. Augustine argues that humans are created by God to be relational beings. In the garden, God made the man and declared, "It is not good that the man should be alone" (Gen 2:18). In response, God provided a partner for the man. Based on these events, Augustine concludes that humans were made to live in community. He asserts that God designed human nature in such a way that it "is something social and possesses the capacity for friendship as a great and natural good."[9] Augustine takes this general statement about human nature and applies it to the marriage relationship. He contends that the marriage bond is characterized by friendship and "the natural companionship between the two sexes."[10] In Eden, husband and wife experienced the fullness of their union. There, Augustine argues, "between husband and wife there was a faithful partnership of genuine love, an alertness of mind and body in true

---

5. While Augustine would be comfortable describing the interpretation of Genesis found here as "literal," in contemporary circles, the word "literal" has connotations associated with fundamentalism's biblicism that do not apply to Augustine. Therefore, I have refrained from using the word "literal" and instead chosen to describe Augustine's interpretation in *The Good of Marriage* as "concrete" to contrast with his allegorical interpretation of Scripture found in several of his other works.

6. Augustine, *Good of Marriage*, 9.

7. See Tertullian, *Monogamy*, 5; Gregory of Nyssa, *On Virginity* 12.43–46.

8. Augustine, *Continence*, 192.

9. Augustine, *Good of Marriage*, 9.

10. Augustine, *Good of Marriage*, 12.

concord."[11] Sin, however, fundamentally altered the way partners relate. According to Augustine, the sexes are now sources of mutual temptation, and the marriage bond is a chain to which one is tied.[12]

While sin may have changed the way humans relate, Augustine remains convinced that sin has not totally destroyed the bond of friendship that exists between man and woman.[13] In spite of sin's impact on human relationality, marriage continues to be the foundational communal relationship between man and woman and the basis of other social relations. In *The Good of Marriage*, Augustine describes the bond of marriage between the first man and woman as "the first natural tie of human society."[14] He expands on this idea in his much later work, *City of God* (426), "And in this case [God] created one single individual, but not so that man would be left alone, bereft of human society. Rather, God's purpose was that the unity of human society and the bond of human intimacy would be all the more strongly commended to human beings if they were linked to one another not only by likeness of nature but also by the sense of kinship."[15] Here, Augustine connects notions of familial blood relations and procreation to the unity of humankind. The link of common ancestry, grounded in the first marriage and perpetuated by the "bond of human intimacy," serves as the basis for all human social relationships.

Third, Augustine appeals to the New Testament to support his defense of the good of marriage. For example, he points to Scripture's prohibition of the remarriage of a divorced person while their spouse is still living (Rom 7 and 1 Cor 7).[16] The implication of these Scriptures is that the biblical witness presents marriage as a lifelong good. To further support his argument, Augustine also points to the teachings of Jesus.[17] While Moses allowed a man to divorce a woman if "he finds something objectionable about her" (Deut 24:1), Jesus limited the grounds for divorce to adultery (Matt 5:31–32). If

11. Augustine, *City of God* 14.26.
12. Augustine, *Confessions* 6.20.
13. Otten, "Augustine on Marriage," 399.
14. Augustine, *Good of Marriage*, 9.
15. Augustine, *City of God* 12.22.
16. Augustine, *Good of Marriage*, 12. "Thus a married woman is bound by the law to her husband as long as he lives; but if her husband dies, she is discharged from the law concerning the husband. Accordingly, she will be called an adulteress if she lives with another man while her husband is alive. But if her husband dies, she is free from that law, and if she marries another man, she is not an adulteress" (Rom 7:2–3). Paul also affirms this view in 1 Corinthians: "A wife is bound as long as her husband lives. But if the husband dies, she is free to marry anyone she wishes, only in the Lord" (7:39).
17. Augustine, *Good of Marriage*, 12.

marriage were not a good, then presumably the New Testament would allow for easier termination of the relationship. However, by narrowing the legitimate reasons for divorce from any fickle dissatisfaction among married partners to a violation of fidelity, Augustine argues that Jesus defended the goodness of marriage. Augustine also points to the episode in John's Gospel where Jesus attended a wedding in Cana and performed his first miracle (John 2). Jesus' presence at a wedding and his statements which limit the grounds for divorce indicate that marriage is a good. Finally, Augustine affirms marriage by highlighting statements by the Apostle Paul on the sexual relationship between the married couple. Augustine states that Paul distinguished between non-procreative sex and marriage. On the one hand, Paul made a concession for married couples to engage in sex to avoid the sins of lust and fornication (1 Cor 7:5–6). On the other hand, he clearly stated that "if you marry, you do not sin" (1 Cor 7:28). Thus, while Paul made an allowance for non-procreative sex, he offered no such pardon for marriage.[18] Furthermore, Augustine argues, concessions are only made in instances where the goodness of a thing is in question. Since Paul provided no pardon for marriage, then a pardon is not necessary. If a pardon is not necessary, then it can be inferred that marriage is a good. Based on this set of arguments, Augustine affirms marriage as a viable option for Christians.

Augustine summarizes his position by identifying three goods of marriage: "The good, therefore, of marriage among all nations and all men is in the cause of generation and in the fidelity of chastity; in the case of the people of God, however, the good is also in the sanctity of the sacrament. . . . These are all goods on account of which marriage is a good: offspring, fidelity, sacrament."[19] It is to these three goods of marriage that I now turn my attention.

Procreation

As we will see in chapter 3, Augustine's first good of marriage is one of the primary theological barriers to the church's affirmation of same-sex relationships. Each of the revisionists that we will examine is required to provide a response to the challenge presented by procreation. As such, it is necessary to gain a robust understanding of procreation and its theological relationship to Christian marriage. To that end, more space will be dedicated to teasing out Augustine's understanding of procreation as it relates to marriage than the remaining two goods of fidelity and sacrament. However,

18. Augustine, *Good of Marriage*, 24.
19. Augustine, *Good of Marriage*, 47–48.

before directly addressing his description of procreation, it is necessary to take a step back. Procreation is tied to bodies, which are linked to the physical creation. To understand Augustine's account of *proles*, it is necessary to begin with his theology of creation.

Augustine's mature cosmology is the culmination of a lifetime of interacting with a variety of sources including Manichaeism, Plotinus' Neoplatonism, and Nicene Christianity. Manichaean cosmology combined a form of dualism and materialism. In the Manichaean creation myth, good and evil are eternal entities in perpetual conflict. According to Manichaean story, evil attacked the realm of divine goodness. Because God is good, God did not respond to the provocations of evil with force, but chose to surrender. In doing so, God placed a part of God's self in the world. This piece of the divine mingled with evil, defined as physical matter, in an effort to restrain evil. Thus, the world is a mixture of good and evil in constant, chaotic struggle.[20] This same dualistic struggle, they argued, is evident in human nature. The Manichees asserted that the human soul is of divine origin. However, the first humans (Adam and Eve) were the product of two animals who devoured other creatures. Under the influence of evil, these animals then mated, producing human offspring. The result of this genesis, the Manichees asserted, is that subsequent humans are comprised of two natures: good and evil. Because of their bifurcate nature, humans cannot bring about their salvation. Salvation requires the unilateral action of God, who awakens the human to her true, divine nature, thereby making her a new creation.[21] In response to God's saving action, humans are called to shun the physical world and fleshly activities in pursuit of the spiritual. Augustine was a convert to the Manichaean system for roughly a decade before rejecting several of the underlying premises of the position. As we shall see, Manichaean thought continued to influence Augustine's reading of Scripture as it relates to sex and marriage.

Augustine's introduction to the work of Plotinus provided an alternative to materialism of Manichaean cosmology. Plotinus' system shared several traits with Manichaeism, and these similarities aided the development of Augustine's thought as he transitioned from a Manichaean system to a Neoplatonic cosmology.[22] Plotinus affirmed a dualistic conception of the cosmos. In Plotinus' system, the good creator, who is immaterial, immutable, and eternal, is located at the top of the hierarchy of being. Matter, also eternal and unchanging, is located at the bottom. Since God is good, matter

---

20. BeDuhn, *Augustine's Manichaean Dilemma*, 75–80.
21. BeDuhn, *Augustine's Manichaean Dilemma*, 81–92.
22. BeDuhn, *Augustine's Manichaean Dilemma*, 173–90.

is equated with evil. In this system, Plotinus argued, humans have fallen from a state of spiritual perfection into the physical world. Like the rest of creation, humans desire to return to a "state of perfectly ordered spiritual contentment in the being of God."[23]

Augustine's cosmology retains positions characteristic of Manichaean, Neoplatonic, and Nicene Christian views.[24] Augustine rejects the Manichees' materialistic view of a physical divine being who battles against the forces of evil, while retaining their understanding of the world as a creative act of a good God. Also, while affirming some of the dualistic features of Plotinus' system, particularly the elevation of the spiritual over the physical, Augustine dismisses the notion that the physical is inherently evil. Following Aristotle, Augustine argues that matter is a substance, but it is not evil. He affirms that the physical creation was created good. Augustine locates the source of creation in the will of God.[25] In this framework, creation is not the result of any need located within the Godhead. God existed eternally before the moment of creation in complete self-sufficiency. Instead, Augustine describes creation as an overflow of God's goodness and generosity.[26] Everything that exists originates from and has its source in this benevolent God. Augustine writes, "From [God] comes all mode, all form, and all order; from him comes measure, number, and weight; from him comes all that exists in nature, whatever its kind and whatever its rank in value. From him comes the seeds of forms, the forms of seeds, and the motion of both seeds and forms. He gave also to flesh its origin, its beauty, its health, its fruitfulness in propagation, the disposition of its limbs, and their apt harmonious arrangement. He also gave memory, sensation, and appetite to the irrational soul; and to the rational soul, in addition, he gave mind, intelligence, and will."[27] Thus, in his mature view, Augustine asserts that the physical universe is good because it is created by a good God who has declared it to be good.

After creation, God's interaction with the world shifted from that of creator to one who manages and sustains creation.[28] According to Augustine, God chose for created things to behave in a specific, ordered way. To accomplish this, every created thing was given a nature by God.[29] For example, fire naturally seeks to rise to the heavens and rocks possess a

---

23. Jungling, "Passionate Order," 317.
24. BeDuhn, *Augustine's Manichaean Dilemma*, 187–88.
25. Augustine, *On Genesis* 1.4.
26. Augustine, *Literal Meaning of Genesis* 1.11; *City of God* 12.17.
27. Augustine, *City of God* 5.11.
28. Augustine, *Literal Meaning of Genesis* 6.18.
29. Augustine, *City of God* 7.29.

God-given desire to go down to the ground.[30] When a created thing behaves according to its created nature, according to its kind, it seeks to be no more and no less than what God designed it to be. All created things "as long as they continue to be, have their own proper measures, numbers and destinies. So all things, properly considered are worthy of acclaim."[31] According to Augustine, the goodness or worth of a thing is directly connected to its behaving according to its nature. When this occurs, a created thing reaches its properly ordered place where it experiences rest.[32] There is no longer any movement or struggle, nor is there any sense of need or necessity because the created thing experiences perfection in God.

Augustine applies this overarching description of cosmological order to humans. He argues that humans "are something good, deriving our being from him who made all things very good, ourselves included."[33] Like the rest of creation, God created humans and gave them a nature comprised of two parts: body and soul. God has ordained that the soul should rule over the body.[34] However, he argues, the superior quality of the soul does not invalidate the goodness of the physical body. He writes, "The bodies themselves, which we wear far more intimately and closely than any garment, are by no means to be scorned. They are no mere adornment or external aid but belong to human nature itself."[35] Augustine is convinced that because God is the source of all natures and God is good, that God can only create good natures. Since human nature is comprised of both body and soul, both body and soul were created by God and declared good from the beginning.

In Augustine's day, belief in the inherent worth of the body was not a given. This was due primarily to disagreements about the composition of human nature. Are humans primarily body, soul, or a combination thereof? This question was further complicated by a discussion of the effects of sin on human nature. There were a variety of ways of negotiating the relationship between sin and the body during the fourth and fifth centuries. The

---

30. Augustine, *Literal Meaning of Genesis* 2.6.

31. Augustine, *Literal Meaning of Genesis* 3.25.

32. The concept of an ordered creation seeking its proper place is found throughout Augustine's works with various emphasis. Things reach their proper place individually, but also when they find their place within the greater created order (*Literal Meaning of Genesis* 3.37). The connection between proper place and rest is linked to Sabbath, where God rested on the seventh day (*Literal Meaning of Genesis* 4.16). Because God is the source of all that is, creation can only find its proper place in God (*Literal Meaning of Genesis* 4.34).

33. Augustine, *Literal Meaning of Genesis* 4.27.

34. Augustine, *City of God* 9.9.

35. Augustine, *City of God* 1.13.

Manichees believed that the physical and the spiritual were two natures in perpetual conflict with one another. They viewed humans as primarily spiritual beings that "fell" into physical bodies. Thus, bodies were seen as punishment for sin. Augustine strongly disagreed with this view. In his first major treatise on the book of Genesis, he quipped that the Manichees "find their own bodies displeasing . . . to the extent of denying that God is the maker of bodies."[36] As we have seen, Gregory of Nyssa also disagreed with the notion that bodies are punishment for sin. He compared bodies, particularly the sexed body, to the garments of skin which God provided to the first couple after the fall (Gen 3:21). Thus, bodies were a sign of God's gracious provision and protection. While he held a more positive view of bodies than that espoused by the Manichees, Gregory's belief in the postlapsarian nature of bodies gave him little room to discuss their inherent worth.[37] Jerome argued that humans are spiritual beings that were given bodies after the fall. Humans must endure bodies during this life, he asserted, but the soul will escape the body and humans will live a spiritual existence in the next life.[38] For Jerome, the body and its desires are highly suspect.[39]

The advent of sin problematized the relationship between body and soul in Augustine's theology as well. In Eden, Augustine argues, the first humans experienced a unity of body and soul/will, a perfect harmony of master and servant. After the fall, the will no longer governs the body.[40] Instead, the body is ruled by desire. According to Augustine, sin and its punishment also have devastating consequences on the composition of the body. After the fall, the body is subject to decay and death. The postlapsarian human is born into a "body that is doomed to die. There is never a time when death is not at work in him."[41] Thus, sin affects the entire human, both body and soul. Yet, Augustine is quick to assert that though the body has been marred by sin, the body is not the cause of sin. He writes, "It is not the body in itself, but rather the body as it became due to sin and sin's punishment, that weights down the soul."[42] Augustine also rejected the idea that physical bodies are either a result of the fall or punishment for sin. Augustine views bodies, along with the rest of the physical creation as gifts

36. Augustine, *Genesis Manichees* 2.38.
37. Gregory of Nyssa, *On Virginity* 12.43–46.
38. For the majority of his career, Jerome believed in the individual's ability to transcend bodily desire in this life. After being charged with heresy, Jerome rejected this view. See Brown, *Body and Society*, 379–83.
39. Brown, *Body and Society*, 376.
40. Augustine, *City of God* 13.12–15.
41. Augustine, *City of God* 13.10.
42. Augustine, *City of God* 12.16.

which God intended from the beginning. Even though our bodies die in the postlapsarian world, they are still good. In a rhetorical question aimed at the Platonists' desire to escape the body in favor of a spiritual existence, Augustine writes, "If our creation is a divine gift, even if we are created mortal, how can it be a punishment to return to these bodies—to return, that is, to benefits divinely bestowed on us?"[43] Hence, the problem for Augustine is not the physical or the body, per se, but the corruption of the body, which is a result of the division created by sin between the body and the will within the self. Based on these convictions, Augustine argues that humans do not achieve their proper place in God's created order by escaping the body, but through achieving unity of the various parts of the person: body and soul.[44] Augustine writes, "To attain happiness, therefore, there is no need to flee from all bodies but only from bodies that are corruptible, burdensome, oppressive, and death-bound—not, that is from bodies such as God's goodness created for the first human beings but rather from bodies such as sin's punishment compelled them to be."[45] Thus, while bodies have been corrupted by sin, they are good in their created nature.

Augustine's assertion of the inherent goodness of the body is not only grounded in his protology, he also supports his argument with his eschatology. In *On the Trinity*, Augustine indicates that the body has eschatological importance. He envisions a time when the body shall be renewed after "the spirit of man has been piously subjected to God . . . [then] it shall have a body that is happily subject to it, and this happiness shall remain forever."[46] According to Augustine, the Christian's eschatological hope is not an escape from the body, but a renewal of the unity of body and soul. However, this renewed body does not represent a return to bodies as they existed before the fall. Augustine argues that Adam's body was mortal, and he was required to eat and drink in order to preserve and sustain it. By contrast, Augustine has in mind a transformation of the body in the eschaton.[47] Augustine envisions this transformed, eschatological body as a spiritual body that will exist without any need or necessity.[48] Need and necessity will be eliminated because the human has found its proper place in God, the ultimate source

---

43. Augustine, *City of God* 12.27.

44. Augustine, *City of God* 14.3. According to Augustine, sin distorted the unity of body and soul to the degree that humans are enslaved to sin and can no longer choose the good. The restoration of the unified self begins with God's grace, but the process of restoration will only be completed in the *eschaton* (*City of God* 13.22–23).

45. Augustine, *City of God* 13.17.

46. Augustine, *Trinity*, 15.25.

47. Augustine, *City of God* 13.20–23.

48. Augustine, *Continence*, 204; *City of God* 13.22.

of all goodness. While today some humans seek the good in the body and a few even seek the good from the soul, in the eschaton, Augustine asserts, humans will seek it "from both, from the whole man."[49] Thus, the telos of the divine plan for humankind is the restored unity of body and soul oriented toward the good. In *City of God*, Augustine leaves no doubt that God has ordained that humans will live this life and the next in the body. As humans have experienced sin in the body, they will also experience redemption and resurrection in the body. For Augustine, the body is the vehicle for the human experience of salvation history.[50]

Augustine provides further logic for the good of the body by appealing to the body of Jesus. In the Incarnation, Christ took on a physical, human body. Augustine then makes a bold statement about the continuity of the human body with Christ's incarnational body, saying the human body "is the kind of body that the first Adam had. . . . It is also the kind of body that we ourselves have now. . . . And it is also the kind of body that Christ originally condescended to assume for our sake."[51] For Augustine, Christ's taking on of a human body is validation of the body's inherent worth. Augustine also points to the resurrected body of Christ. The body of Christ was killed on the cross, but that same body was transformed in the resurrection. The gospel writers indicate that the risen Christ was not a floating spirit, but a kind of physical body that could share in a meal (John 21) and be touched (John 20). Augustine asserts it was "Christ's (risen) body, with which he ascended into heaven." Therefore, both the Incarnation and the Resurrection validate the worth of the body.

Finally, Augustine defends the goodness of the body by asserting that Christians are members of Christ's body. In 1 Corinthians 6:15, Paul writes, "Do you not know that your bodies are members of Christ?" While it can be argued that this passage refers to spiritual bodies, Augustine relates this verse to physical bodies. Commenting on this verse, he writes, "And unquestionably this refers to the faithful of both sexes."[52] In Augustine's theology, it is not possible to differentiate between the sexes except with reference to their physical bodies. Thus, Augustine interprets this verse as saying that we are members of Christ's body in our physical bodies.

In summary, bodies are good because they were created as part of human nature from the beginning of the divine plan. Humans experience the totality of salvation history (creation, fall, redemption, and eschaton) in

---

49. Augustine, *City of God* 8.8.
50. Augustine, *City of God* 8.8, 16–23.
51. Augustine, *City of God* 8.23.
52. Augustine, *Excellence of Widowhood*, 117.

the body. Both the Incarnation and the Resurrection occurred in a physical body. Finally, Christians participate in the church, the body of Christ, through their bodies. These arguments in support of the goodness of the body are the foundation upon which Augustine builds a case for his first good of marriage: procreation.

Augustine's understanding of procreation and its relation to intercourse and marriage developed throughout his career. Gaining an in-depth appreciation of this relationship in his theology requires a brief survey of Augustine's treatment of *proles* from his early to his later writings. In one of his early works, *On Genesis: Against the Manichees* (388–389), Augustine argues that procreation and intercourse would not have occurred prior to the fall. Here, in a move reminiscent of Gregory of Nyssa, procreation is linked to death and sin. If humans had not sinned, they would not die, and therefore procreation would not have been necessary. This leads Augustine to conclude that in the garden, "those two human beings would not have had human children unless they had sinned."[53] This reading of the creation story leads Augustine to interpret the command to "be fruitful and multiply" (Gen 1:28) allegorically. Though he condemns interpretations that equate procreation as a punishment for sin, he views procreation as a result of the fall.[54] Writing a decade later, Augustine's position becomes a bit more muddled. Here, in *Confessions* (397), Augustine asserts that procreation is the purpose of marriage. He expands this argument in two ways. First, Augustine argues that marriage channels lustful desires toward their proper, procreative end.[55] Second, he notes a qualitative difference between his ongoing sexual relationship with an unnamed woman and a marriage "contracted for the purpose of founding a family."[56] In both cases, the link between marriage and procreation is clear, but Augustine does not indicate whether procreation is prelapsarian or postlapsarian. Similar to *Confessions*, in *The Good of Marriage* (401), Augustine directly connects procreation with the divine command to "be fruitful and multiply."[57] Yet, this treatise does reveal a shift in Augustine's thinking. Here, because this command was given before the fall, Augustine is convinced that prelapsarian procreation was part of God's plan from the beginning. However, whether prelapsarian procreation would have been the result of physical sexual intercourse between the first couple or whether generation could have occurred by some

53. Augustine, *Genesis Manichees (Revisions)*, 37.
54. Augustine, *Genesis Manichees* 2.29.
55. Augustine, *Confessions* 2.3; 6.22.
56. Augustine, *Confessions* 4.1.
57. Augustine, *Good of Marriage*, 10.

other means is not yet settled in Augustine's mind. Augustine dedicates the majority of chapter 2 of this work to a detailed discussion of the various ways that Adam and Eve might have brought forth children. At this point in his career, Augustine is content to leave the question unanswered.

In his later writings, the place of procreation in human history is more settled. Whereas in his early works, Augustine interprets the creation story allegorically, in *Literal Meaning of Genesis* (416), Augustine affirms both a historical/concrete and allegorical reading of the creation story. He asserts that the various elements of the story "stood for something other than what they were, but all the same they were themselves bodily realities."[58] Based on this interpretation, creation is a real event in history, and that event points to a spiritual truth. By the time he completed this work, Augustine argued that procreation was part of the divine plan from the beginning, and therefore could not be considered sinful. He makes two arguments to support this proposal. First, he asserts that God made creatures in such a way that "none of them was created just to exist once and for all by itself, whether to continue forever, or to pass away with none to succeed it."[59] It is in the natures of creatures to multiply. These natures were created by God and granted to creatures from the beginning of time. Therefore, procreation is not an afterthought or a consequence of sin. Augustine applies this premise to humankind. He argues that human bodies, like other physical creatures, were created mortal.[60] Since human bodies are mortal, some mechanism is required for human existence to continue. Procreation is that mechanism. In this work, Augustine asserts that procreation would have occurred before the fall, and he is mostly convinced that procreation would have been the result of physical intercourse.[61] Second, Augustine appeals to the divine blessing to "be fruitful and multiply." He notes that in the Genesis text, this blessing is first pronounced to non-human creatures, but is later repeated to humans. Augustine writes, "It was, however, necessary to repeat [the blessing] for man, in case anybody should say that there is any sin in the business of procreating children, as there is in the lust involved in fornication or in

---

58. Augustine, *Literal Meaning of Genesis* 8.8. See also Augustine, *Literal Meaning of Genesis* 8.9–11, 13; 9.12, 20–22; 11.38–39, 50–55.

59. Augustine, *Literal Meaning of Genesis* 3.19.

60. For Augustine, this is true whether or not sin had occurred. Even if sin had not occurred, humans would enjoy life in the body and then be translated into a spiritual existence, rather than experience earthly, bodily life eternally.

61. Augustine, *Literal Meaning of Genesis* 3.33. Augustine still leaves the possibility that procreation could have occurred by other means, though he believes this to be an unlikely option.

the immoderate use, or rather, misuse, of marriage."[62] Against his opponents who equate procreation with lust and therefore with sin, Augustine distinguishes between lustful and licit sex in marriage, with licit sex being that which is connected to procreative ends. This move, paired with his conviction that procreation is prelapsarian, allows Augustine to argue that procreation is a good of marriage.

In *City of God* (426), Augustine continues to hold the tension between both a historical and an allegorical reading of the creation accounts. In this work, Augustine argues that the real, historical events of creation symbolize the divine/human relationship. For example, he asserts that the daily cycle of light, evening, and darkness described in Genesis 1 represent the human creature's turning toward and away from God. Light is when the human is directed toward God, evening is turning from God, and night is when the creature is abandoned by God who is the source of light.[63] Later in *City of God*, Augustine applies his historical-allegorical reading of creation to procreation and the command to be fruitful. He writes, "For our part, however, we have no doubt that to be fruitful and multiply and fill the earth, in accord with God's blessing, is a gift of marriage and that God instituted marriage from the beginning, prior to man's sin, by creating male and female, each sex being plainly evident in the flesh."[64] Here, the command to be fruitful and multiply is directed to actual, human marriages that exist for procreative ends. However, Augustine also asserts, "There is nothing inappropriate, of course, about giving all of this a spiritual sense."[65] While privileging a historical, physical interpretation of the command to be fruitful and multiply, the mature Augustine makes room for an allegorical reading of this text. In Augustine's view, both interpretations are needed to properly honor the creation story. This tension has profound implications for contemporary issues of marriage and procreation. This is an important development to which I will return in chapter 4.

By the completion of *City of God*, Augustine has firmly decided that both procreation and marital intercourse were part of God's plan from the beginning:

> For God created man righteous; he is the author of natures, not vices. But man, willingly depraved and justly condemned, gave birth to depraved and condemned offspring. For we were all in that one man, since we all were that one man who fell into sin through the woman who was made for him prior to sin. The

---

62. Augustine, *Literal Meaning of Genesis* 3.21.
63. Augustine, *City of God* 11.7.
64. Augustine, *City of God* 14.22.
65. Augustine, *City of God* 14.22.

> specific forms in which we were individually to live as particular individuals had not yet been created and distributed to us, *but the seminal nature from which we would all be propagated was already present.*[66]

Here, Augustine summarizes several themes from his previous works. According to Augustine's cosmology, God created things with a nature, and that nature is good because it was created by God. Sin represents a deviation from the good nature that God created. A part of human nature is the ability to procreate through sexual intercourse. By identifying procreative intercourse as part of human nature, Augustine affirms that both procreation and intercourse are prelapsarian. Since procreation is not an afterthought or a result of sin, but instead is part of God's plan for creation, then procreation was instituted by God and can be considered good. Augustine summarizes, "The nuptial blessing, bidding the married couple to be fruitful and multiply and fill the earth . . . was given before they sinned precisely so that people would realize that the procreation of children belongs to the glory of marriage, not to the punishment of sin."[67] Thus, procreation is a good which was ordained by God from the beginning, and this good is inseparably linked to marriage in Augustine's theology.

With this overview in mind, let us turn our attention back to the primary text of inquiry: *The Good of Marriage*. Here, the connection between procreation and marriage is already on full display. Augustine argues that in order for a relationship to be called a marriage, the couple must be open to the possibility of children. In support of this claim, Augustine appeals to the Apostle Paul, who encouraged young widows to marry for the purpose of bearing children (1 Tim 5:14).[68] Commenting on this verse, Augustine asserts that it was not enough for Paul to encourage widows to marry. They are instructed to marry for a purpose, namely, procreation. In the *Good of Marriage*, Augustine also defends the good of procreation by appealing to his protology. Drawing on Plotinus' cosmology, Augustine understands creation to be a hierarchy located between two poles: heaven and earth. Heaven and the angels represent perfection, and therefore are located at the top of the hierarchy of created things. Formless matter is located at the bottom of the hierarchy. Augustine argues that God is bringing order and form to the

---

66. Augustine, *City of God* 13.14 (my emphasis).
67. Augustine, *City of God* 14.21.
68. Augustine, *Good of Marriage*, 48. "So I would have younger widows marry, bear children, and manage their households, so as to give the adversary no occasion to revile us" (1 Tim 5:14).

shapeless matter in the act of creation.[69] Thus, it is God's desire for formlessness to be formed. Augustine uses this concept of formlessness being formed as a defense of procreation as a good of marriage. Some of his opponents had argued that intercourse, even for procreative purposes, is sinful. If, as Augustine contends, marriage exists for the purpose of procreation, then the argument that procreative intercourse is sinful represents a direct challenge to marriage as a good. To counter his opponents' argument, Augustine asserts that their belief in the sinfulness of procreative intercourse is grounded in an incorrect understanding of the Hebrew Scriptures. They believe that sex is sinful, Augustine contends, because "the Law orders a man to be purified even after marital intercourse."[70] While he acknowledges that Scripture calls for purification after sexual intercourse, this requirement does not indicate that sex is sinful. To support this claim, Augustine asserts that the act of procreative intercourse is an example of formlessness being formed. As such, it follows God's pattern for creation. Here, Augustine employs an allegorical use of creation language to make his point. He suggests that both male seed and female menstruation represent "a certain material shapelessness."[71] God intends for this shapelessness to take form in the conception of a child. Thus, Augustine argues, the purification laws of the Old Testament point to a spiritual truth. The Hebrew Scriptures, which require a purification for the "formless flow" of intercourse and menstruation in order that they might be formed, points to "the mind [which] must be formed."[72] Therefore, marital intercourse is not sinful, but it must be ordered or formed by engaging in sex for procreative purposes. Thus, both marriage and procreation are goods, but in Augustine's theology of marriage, they are goods when paired together.

This description of the relationship between marriage and procreation allows Augustine to distinguish between procreative and non-procreative sexual intercourse within marriage. Non-procreative sexual intercourse is "that [which] comes about through incontinence, not for the sake of procreation and at the time with no thought of procreation."[73] For Augustine, non-procreative sex is tied directly to lust, because it "goes beyond the necessity [of procreation and] no longer obeys reason but passion."[74] By

69. Augustine, *Confessions* 12.3–8.
70. Augustine, *Good of Marriage*, 38.
71. Augustine, *Good of Marriage*, 38–39.
72. Augustine, *Good of Marriage*, 38.
73. Augustine, *Good of Marriage*, 24
74. Augustine, *Good of Marriage*, 24. For a more thorough analysis of these terms, see the section on ordered sexuality later in this chapter.

contrast, procreative sex is intercourse in which the couple engages solely for the purpose of generation, not as a response to lustful desires of the flesh. According to Augustine, procreative sex alone "is without fault and it alone belongs to marriage."[75] Thus, Augustine argues that licit marital intercourse is sex in which the couple engages solely for the purpose of procreation. In order to keep marital intercourse connected to its proper, procreative telos, Augustine denounces any attempt to prevent the bringing forth of children through sexual intercourse. According to Augustine, a faithful couple must not "refuse to have children nor act in any evil way so that they will not be born . . . if both or either one of these conditions is lacking, I do not see how we can call this a marriage."[76] For Augustine, the act of preventing children nullifies procreation as a good of marriage, and therefore nullifies the nature of marriage itself.

In *Adulterous Marriages* (419–20), Augustine reveals a portion of his logic for keeping marriage attached to procreation. Here, he acknowledges that some Christians are in the habit of engaging in non-procreative intercourse, or worse, deliberately attempting to remove the possibility of procreation from the sex act. To reinforce his argument in favor of keeping marriage attached to its procreative telos, he appeals to the Genesis 38 account of Onan spilling his seed on the ground rather than engaging in Leverite marriage.[77] Summarizing his interpretation of this event, Augustine writes, "Onan, son of Judah did this, and God killed him for it."[78] For Augustine, there is a direct correlation between the spilling of semen and the judgment of God which resulted in Onan's death. Judgment was necessary because the spilling of seed was an example of divorcing sex from its procreative ends. Unfortunately, Augustine's reading of Scripture and the corresponding logic derived from that interpretation misses the point of the passage. Leverite marriage was concerned with care for widows and providing an heir who would continue the family line. Onan's act was sinful because it disregarded care for a widow, not because he spilled his seed. However, this criticism would not disrupt Augustine's robust defense of the claim that openness to procreation is a necessary component of marriage.

Though he affirms an essential connection between marriage and procreation, Augustine does provide two caveats to this position. First, while a willingness and intent to procreate is necessary for a relationship

---

75. Augustine, *Good of Marriage*, 24.

76. Augustine, *Good of Marriage*, 15.

77. Leverite marriage was commanded in Deuteronomy 25:5–6, but was part of social custom during the time of Onan.

78. Augustine, *Adulterous* 1.12.

to be considered a marriage, Augustine does have space in his theology of marriage for couples that are unable to procreate. He argues that not every marriage is required to bring forth children. Therefore, a sterile couple is still considered to be married, so long as they do not seek to prevent children. Second, Augustine claims that the good of marriage extends beyond a couple's childbearing years. Here, he appeals to the companionship between the married couple. This companionship flourishes even in old age when, Augustine presumes, the elderly couple no longer engages in sexual intercourse.[79] Thus, while procreation is an essential component of marriage and the two should never be intentionally separated from each other, the good of marriage extends beyond procreation.[80] If this were not the case, it would be impossible to discuss the marriage of elderly partners or the marriage of partners who are unable to procreate.

When surveying his vast corpus, it is difficult to determine the weight that Augustine assigns to procreation related to the other goods of marriage. In some chapters of *The Good of Marriage*, it appears that procreation is the primary (perhaps only?) good that Augustine associates with marriage. In chapter 17, he writes, "Marriage itself among all races is for the one purpose of procreating children, whatever will be their station and character afterwards; marriage was instituted for this purpose, so that children might be born properly and decently."[81] This view is echoed in *Confessions*, where "marriage[s] are contracted for the purpose of founding a family."[82] Augustine continues this line of thought in *City of God* (426), where he argues that God "instituted the union of male and female to serve the propagation of offspring."[83] The marriage of the sexually differentiated couple exists so that they might procreate. Perhaps the strongest example is found in *Adulterous Marriages* where Augustine writes, "Propagation of children, therefore, is in fact the primary, natural, and legitimate purpose of marriage."[84] Here, procreation is the singular reason for marriage, and Augustine appears to negate the possibility of additional, auxiliary ends. Yet, in another chapter of *The Good of Marriage*, Augustine says that marriage and sex contribute to the friendship of the couple.[85] Whether or not Augustine believed that procreation was the only purpose of marriage,

79. Augustine, *Good of Marriage*, 12.
80. Augustine, *Holy Virginity*, 68.
81. Augustine, *Good of Marriage*, 33.
82. Augustine, *Confessions* 4.2.
83. Augustine, *City of God* 8.30.
84. Augustine, *Adulterous Marriages* 2.12.
85. Augustine, *Good of Marriage*, 22.

it is clear that he saw procreation as a vital good that cannot be separated from marriage or marital intercourse.

It seems that Augustine realized the demanding nature of his instruction to restrict marital sex for the purpose of procreation. He understood that most Christians would struggle to adhere to this teaching. To bridge the gap between teaching and practice, Augustine developed the concept of "venial fault."[86] Augustine conceded that there would be times in marriage when a partner would be overcome by lustful desire. In order to avoid the greater sin of adultery, the tempted partner could engage in a lesser or "venial sin" by requesting that their spouse engage in non-procreative sexual intercourse. In this situation, the partner who requests non-procreative intercourse commits a "venial sin." According to Augustine, the very act of requesting intercourse is seen as a display of weakness. However, the partner who engages in intercourse for the good of the weaker partner does not sin. Granting sex to a weaker partner is a sign of spiritual maturity. Augustine argues that the partner who does not "demand the carnal debt but renders it" attains a "higher grade of sanctity."[87] Thus, paying the conjugal debt to aid a partner in their weakness is seen as a demonstration of holiness. Summarizing this point, Augustine writes, "It is no sin to render the conjugal debt, but to exact it beyond the need for generation is a venial sin."[88] He bases this conclusion on the Apostle Paul who "conceded as a favor" non-procreative sex in marriage.[89] Contrary to Jerome, who equated non-procreative sex with adultery, Augustine argues that the partner who pays the "conjugal debt" to their spouse is neither an adulterer nor a fornicator because, for Augustine, a proper marriage is one where spouses intercede for the weaknesses of their partner.

For the spouse who requests non-procreative intercourse, it is the institution of marriage which differentiates the venial sinner from an adulterer or fornicator who commits a mortal sin. Referring to the weak spouses who request non-procreative intercourse, Augustine writes, "In the marriage of these [individuals] there is this good, that they are married."[90] According to Augustine, overindulging in sex within marriage is better than even a single event of sex outside marriage. He writes "even though there is an excess in the things that have been granted to be used, this is much more tolerable than a

---

86. Hunter, "Making of Marriage," 79.
87. Augustine, *Good of Marriage*, 29.
88. Augustine, *Good of Marriage*, 17.
89. Augustine, *Good of Marriage*, 16.
90. Augustine, *Good of Marriage*, 16.

single or rare deviation in those things which have not been granted."[91] This is true, Augustine argues, because certain activities "belong to marriage."[92] Even when sex outside marriage is pursued for the proper end of intercourse (i.e., procreation), this act of intercourse is not considered licit. It is the institution of marriage which legitimizes intercourse, whether procreative or non-procreative. Thus, while non-procreative sex is sinful, marriage acts as a cover or pardon for the stain of lustful sex. Yet, while marriage covers the stain of non-procreative intercourse, Augustine makes clear that marriage is not a license for excessive expressions of lustful sex. He asserts that non-reproductive sex "is not permitted because of marriage, but because of the marriage it is pardoned."[93] If both partners are overcome with concupiscence and desire non-procreative sex, "they do something that manifestly does not belong to marriage."[94] This discussion of licit and illicit intercourse demonstrates the importance of procreation to Augustine's theology of marriage. It is the procreative telos of marriage which allows for the distinction between licit and illicit sex in marriage.

It should be noted that the link between marriage and procreation has remained steady for the majority of the church's history. As we have discussed, part of the reason for this consistency is theological. Another is experiential. For example, in Augustine's day, it was easily recognizable that intercourse led to the generation of children. However, with the advent of inexpensive, reliable, readily available birth control in the twentieth century, the link between sex and procreation is not as obvious. As a result, it is no longer clear that marriage and marital sex exist for the purpose of procreation. This highlights a key issue to which we will return in chapter 3, namely, if sex is severed entirely from procreation in a theology of marriage, then a new foundation for sexual ethics within marriage would need to be constructed.

While Augustine understands procreation to be a necessary good of marriage, he qualifies this position by calling all Christians, both married and single, to lives of chastity and continence. He writes, "Would that all men had this wish [to be continent].... Much more quickly would the City of God be filled and the end of time be hastened."[95] This exhortation to continence represents a shift from the Old Testament command to be fruitful

---

91. Augustine, *Good of Marriage*, 25.
92. Augustine, *Good of Marriage*, 30.
93. Augustine, *Good of Marriage*, 16. Augustine connects excessive, lustful intercourse with Paul's discussion of excessive sexuality among the Gentiles in Romans 1 (*Good of Marriage*, 24–25).
94. Augustine, *Good of Marriage*, 24.
95. Augustine, *Good of Marriage*, 23.

and multiply. The question is, how does Augustine understand this new instruction to be consistent with God's command in Genesis? To support the call to marital chastity, Augustine appeals to the "mysterious difference in times" between the Old Testament and the New Testament.[96] During the days of the patriarchs, he reasons, the Incarnation had not occurred; the promise of Christ's coming had yet to be fulfilled. In order to realize the divine promise that God would create a people from whom the messiah would come, marriage was required for the patriarchs who "possessed their wives for the work of procreation."[97] Therefore, Augustine argues, abstaining from procreative intercourse was not an option in the Old Testament. After the coming of Christ, procreation was no longer a necessity. To put it another way, *proles* no longer held the same value in salvation history. Augustine finds evidence to support this claim in Ecclesiastes. Before Christ "there [was] a time for embracing," whereas after Christ, the "time for refraining from all embrace" (Eccl 3:5) has arrived.[98] Augustine also sees that difference in times demonstrated by comparing the Old Testament example of Ruth with the New Testament prophetess Anna (Luke 2:36–38). Whereas Ruth did not have children and sought a husband for that purpose, Anna "knew that it was now the time when Christ would be better served, not by the duty of bearing children but by dedicated continence, not by making her body fertile in marriage but by making her conduct chaste in widowhood."[99] Not only does Augustine point to the Incarnation as support for marital continence, he also argues that this mode of life became a viable option for Christians because of the teaching of Jesus. In a conversation between Jesus and his disciples about difficulties associated with marriage and divorce, "[The] disciples said to [Jesus], 'If such is the case of a man with his wife, it is better not to marry.' But [Jesus] said to them, 'Not everyone can accept this teaching. . . . Let anyone accept this who can'" (Matt 19:10–12). With the words, "Let anyone accept this who can," Augustine argues that marital continence became the preferred mode of Christian life both inside and outside marriage. Hence, "from that time up till now and henceforward to the end, he who possesses continence puts it into practice."[100]

Yet, Augustine does not want the reader to assume that continence is a new development. He seeks to demonstrate a level of continuity between the Old and New Testament on this topic. To accomplish this, Augustine draws a

---

96. Augustine, *Good of Marriage*, 31.
97. Augustine, *Good of Marriage*, 29.
98. Augustine, *Adulterous Marriages* 2.12.
99. Augustine, *Excellence of Widowhood*, 118–19.
100. Augustine, *Good of Marriage*, 43.

distinction between the marriages of the patriarchs and the marriages of his contemporaries. First, he argues that while his contemporaries often marry to curb lustful desires, the patriarchs married "because of the obligation of procreation, not overcome by passion, but motivated by piety."[101] For the patriarchs, sexual intercourse was "not [the result of] lust but duty to be joined with women by the law of marriage."[102] If the patriarchs had been given the option of marital continence, he contends, they would joyfully have refrained from intercourse with their spouses. Second, Augustine argues that even the desire for children had a different motivation in the Old Testament. He asserts that his contemporaries' desire for children is the result of instinct for survival or other "carnal" desires.[103] By contrast, Augustine describes the patriarchs' desire for children as "spiritual, because it was in accordance with the mystery of the time . . . the work of piety itself was to propagate children even carnally."[104] Though they engaged in sexual intercourse with their spouses, the patriarchs' only motivation was to fulfill God's command to procreate. Their obedience pointed to an inward quality of spiritual continence. Third, Augustine argues that this ascetical approach to marital intercourse was shared by both the patriarchs and the matriarchs. He writes, "So it was that even holy women burned, not with sexual desire for sexual union, but with zeal for their duty to have children, and there is no reason to doubt that they would not have wanted the sexual act, if children could have been born some other way."[105] Therefore, continence has always existed, and "only the difference in the times made the works of the fathers (and mothers) diverse" from the actions of continent married people today.[106]

Throughout his discussion of procreation and continence, Augustine is attempting to hold together a delicate tension. On the one hand, he calls all Christians, both married and single, to the higher good of continence. On the other hand, Augustine argues that the higher good of continence does not nullify procreation as a good (albeit lesser good) of marriage,

---

101. Augustine, *Good of Marriage*, 29. After the Incarnation, procreation is no longer a priority. If the primary telos of marriage is removed, marriage is no longer a necessity. Indeed, Augustine asserts that after Christ, marriage exists for tempering and ordering lustful desires rather than being primarily for procreation. Augustine writes, "Unless the weakness of the flesh is an obstacle, even a first marriage should be rejected" (*Excellence of Widowhood*, 119).

102. Augustine, *Good of Marriage*, 32.

103. On carnal desire as motivation for children, see Augustine, *Good of Marriage*, 34. On instinct, see Augustine, *Good of Marriage*, 37.

104. Augustine, *Good of Marriage*, 34.

105. Augustine, *Excellence of Widowhood*, 118.

106. Augustine, *Good of Marriage*, 33.

thereby making room for both continence and procreative marriage. By asserting that all marriages must be open to the possibility of procreation, thus making procreation a necessary good of marriage, Augustine ensures that marriage is attached to its rightful end.

Before concluding this section on the first good of marriage, we must briefly examine the eschatological character of procreation in Augustine's thought. While he understands procreation to be a telos of marriage, procreation is not an end unto itself. According to Augustine, procreation exists for the purpose of populating the City of God.[107] Placing marriage, procreation, and the family in service to the church makes procreation a time-sensitive activity. Indeed, when the pre-ordained number of saints have been born to fill the heavenly city, Augustine envisions a day when "a final limit would be put to the whole business of birth."[108] This eschatological view means that marriage, intercourse, and procreation exist primarily for God and the church. Augustine highlights this connection in two ways. First, he downplays temporal, earthly claims made upon marriage and procreation by privileging the church over biological family ties. The transmission of inheritance or keeping the family name alive are not the primary purposes of marriage and procreation for Christians. This is true because Jesus taught Christians "to value our spiritual family more highly than relationship by birth."[109] Second, Augustine extends this argument by discussing the link between parenting and the church. Augustine readily acknowledges that there is more to procreation than the physical act of making a child. A more holistic definition of procreation means "children should be welcomed with love, brought up with kindness, [and] given a religious education."[110] Augustine believes that in order for children to populate the heavenly city, they must be raised in the faith. Therefore, he places greater priority on the raising of children, rather than their begetting.[111] Thus, marriage exists for procreation, and procreation for the raising of children for the City of God.[112]

---

107. Augustine, *Excellence of Widowhood*, 134; *City of God*, 14.10.
108. Augustine, *Literal Meaning of Genesis*, 3.33.
109. Augustine, *Holy Virginity*, 69.
110. Augustine, *Literal Meaning of Genesis* 9.12.
111. Augustine, *Excellence of Widowhood*, 124.
112. Augustine, *Holy Virginity*, 74.

Fidelity

Augustine identifies fidelity as the second of his three goods of marriage. In support of this claim, Augustine appeals to empirical evidence in society. He argues that humans acknowledge the good of fidelity in small matters. If fidelity is acknowledged in "material and base things," then it should be honored even more in marriage.[113] For Augustine, fidelity is more than faithfulness or commitment. He defines fidelity as a "power" or "authority" over the body of one's spouse. Augustine's understanding of fidelity is derived from Paul's statement in 1 Corinthians 7:4, "For the wife does not have authority over her own body, but the husband does; likewise the husband does not have authority over his own body, but the wife does." According to Augustine, fidelity, or power over a spouse's body, is not reserved merely for the male spouse to exercise over the female spouse. Fidelity is demanded equally by both the husband and the wife. Any violation of the marital good of fidelity amounts to adultery, regardless of whether infidelity is "by the instigation of one's own lust or by consent to the lust of another . . . intercourse with another [is] contrary to the marriage compact."[114]

Augustine's discussion of fidelity is not limited to outward actions which give the appearance of fidelity. He is also concerned with the intention behind an individual's actions. Throughout *The Good of Marriage*, Augustine rarely pronounces straightforward judgment on an individual's actions. Instead, he acknowledges that human action always includes a level of ambiguity. In the case of marital unfaithfulness, Augustine does not merely condemn the sinful actions of an adulterer. Instead, he enters the murky waters of the motivations behind his or her actions. This nuanced position allows Augustine to argue that the various adulterers he describes are considered more or less sinful/faithful based on their motivations.[115] For Augustine, right action, in this case, fidelity, must be accompanied by right motivation.

While a great deal of Augustine's discussion of fidelity in *The Good of Marriage* is concerned with physical sexual encounters, he expands the concept of faithfulness in his other works. In his *Commentary on the Lord's Sermon on the Mount*, Augustine addresses Jesus' statements on adultery.[116] Here, Augustine describes two different kinds of marital fidelity. When a

113. Augustine, *Good of Marriage*, 13.

114. Augustine, *Good of Marriage*, 13.

115. Augustine, *Good of Marriage*, 14, 40, 45.

116. "You have heard that it was said, 'You shall not commit adultery.' But I say to you that everyone who looks at a woman with lust has already committed adultery with her in his heart" (Matt 5:27–28).

married person refrains from engaging in bodily intercourse with another outside the bonds of marriage, he displays fidelity to his partner. However, when a married person refrains from adultery of the heart, he demonstrates even greater fidelity to his partner. For Augustine, the starting point for moral inquiry is not an outward act, but the will. He argues that sin occurs within the self by following a three-step pattern of "suggestion, pleasure, and consent."[117] Suggestion occurs when memory or bodily senses stimulate the will toward sinful desire.[118] Augustine describes suggestion as a kind of persuasion. Yet suggestion to sinfulness, in itself, is not sin. Augustine argues that this is true because "persuasion is not compulsion."[119] Humans constantly battle against sinful suggestion but are in no way compelled to sin. The next stage in the progression toward sin occurs when the will takes pleasure or enjoyment in the suggestion. However, even at this stage, sin has not occurred. Augustine points to the example of desiring food while in the midst of fasting. It is possible to crave and experience pleasure at the thought of food without giving consent to the craving. At this stage both suggestion and pleasure can be repressed by reason. However, if an individual reaches the third stage where the will consents to the sinful suggestion and pleasure, "then a sin is fully committed in the heart, and it is known to God, even though it be not made known to men through the medium of any act."[120] Thus, for Augustine, marital fidelity is concerned with bodily sexual encounters. Having intercourse with someone other than one's spouse violates the marital good of fidelity. But within his understanding of sin and the self, fidelity involves more than avoiding the physical act of adulteraty. Fidelity, like all forms of obedience, begins with the will. If a married person experiences the suggestion and pleasure of adultery and gives consent of the will to that sinful impulse, he has broken fidelity with his spouse, whether or not he engages in the physical act of adultery. According to Augustine, both sin and obedience occur within the self before action is ever taken.[121] Thus, fidelity involves both outward and inward faithfulness to one's partner.

In his theology of marriage, fidelity, when isolated from the other goods, is an insufficient basis for marriage. Augustine writes, "The question is also usually asked whether this case ought to be called a marriage: when a man and a woman (he not being the husband nor she the wife of another) . . . have intercourse not for the purpose of procreating children but only for the sake

---

117. Augustine, *Commentary*, 53.
118. Elsewhere, Augustine uses the term "concupiscence" to discuss "suggestion."
119. Augustine, *Commentary*, 54.
120. Augustine, *Commentary*, 53.
121. See also Augustine, *Holy Virginity*, 72; *Continence*, 192–93; *City of God* 1.28.

of intercourse itself, with this pledge between them, that he will not perform this act with another woman, nor she with another man. Yet perhaps not without reason this can be called wedlock, if this has been agreed upon between them even until the death of one of them."[122] In response to this hypothetical situation, Augustine argues that if the relationship is lacking the intent to be both procreative and faithful, the relationship cannot be called a marriage. He concludes, "The crown of marriage, then, is the chastity of procreation and the faithfulness in rendering the carnal debt."[123]

Sacrament

While the first two goods apply to all marriages, sacrament applies only to Christian marriages. While Augustine uses the word in a variety of ways in his writings, in his theology of marriage the term "sacrament" is connected to the permanence of the bond of matrimony. Appealing to both Romans 7:3 and 1 Corinthians 7:39, Augustine argues that to divorce and remarry while your spouse is still living amounts to adultery.[124] Augustine comments on these verses, "If [a woman] did not have this bond with her husband while he was alive, she could marry someone else without being accused of adultery. Hence, if she is bound as long as her husband is alive, she cannot be said to be freed from this bond in any way except by the death of her husband."[125] He continues, "A woman does not begin to be the wife of any second husband, unless she has ceased to be the wife of the first. She ceases to be the wife of the first, however, if her husband dies."[126] Therefore, marriage is a lifelong bond severed only by the death of a spouse. To illustrate his point, Augustine compares the permanence of marriage to the perpetuity of ordination.[127] In the same way that the sacrament of ordination can be removed from a clergy person only through death, "the marriage bond is not loosed except by the death of a spouse."[128] In another work, Augus-

---

122. Augustine, *Good of Marriage*, 15.

123. Augustine, *Good of Marriage*, 25.

124. "Accordingly, she will be called an adulteress if she lives with another man while her husband is still alive" (Rom 7:3); "A wife is bound as long as her husband lives. But if the husband dies, she is free to marry anyone she wishes, only in the Lord" (1 Cor 7:39).

125. Augustine, *Adulterous Marriages* 2.3.

126. Augustine, *Adulterous Marriages* 2.4.

127. Interestingly, nowhere in *The Good of Marriage* does Augustine appeal to the metaphor of Christ's relationship with his bride—the church (Eph 5:22–30)—as evidence to support the sacramental bond between husband and wife.

128. Augustine, *Good of Marriage*, 48.

tine compares the permanence of marriage to the sacrament of baptism. He writes, "When someone guilty of some crime is excommunicated, the sacrament of rebirth [baptism] remains present in that person, and that person does not lose that sacrament even if he or she is never reconciled with God. In the same way, when a wife is divorced for committing adultery, the bond of the marriage union remains in her, and she does not lose that bond even if she is never reconciled with her husband. She will lose it, however if her husband dies."[129] For Augustine, it is as if marriage, like baptism, permanently alters the composition of a human being. Once one has entered the institution, it is a part of that individual and cannot be removed in this life. With this point, Augustine draws an important distinction between baptism and marriage. Whereas the permanence of baptism rests on God, who does not die, the marriage bond relies on humans who are mortal. Therefore, the permanence of baptism is never broken while the sacrament of the marriage ends with the death of a spouse.

While Augustine mentions the sacrament of marriage throughout *The Good of Marriage*, his most comprehensive description of this term and its relationship to divorce and remarriage is found in *Adulterous Marriages* (419–20).[130] In this work, Augustine examines the teachings of Jesus on divorce, and notes inconsistencies with the gospel accounts. For example, in the book of Matthew, Jesus allows for divorce only in the case of adultery (Matt 5:32). In a later Matthean text, Jesus appears to allow for both divorce and remarriage in the case of adultery (Matt 19:9). In these texts, adultery is the only justification for divorce and (possibly) remarriage.[131] However, neither Mark nor Luke allows for remarriage after divorcing an adulterer.[132] In order to navigate this tension, Augustine concludes that Matthew should be read in light of Mark and Luke, both of whom provide no justification for remarriage after divorce.[133] Thus, Augustine concludes that while adultery may justify

---

129. Augustine, *Adulterous Marriages* 2.5. This is the first instance that I've seen where Augustine compares the sacrament of marriage to the sacrament of baptism.

130. Hunter, introduction to *Adulterous Marriages*, 139. This work represents the only Christian work in the first five centuries dedicated entirely to the topic of divorce and remarriage. Here, Augustine responds to Pollentius, whose views are reconstructed from Augustine's writings. Apparently, Pollentius taught that Jesus allowed for divorce and remarriage when one's partner was an adulterer. He also allowed for divorce, but not remarriage, for other reasons as well. His position represented a major break in the church's teaching on divorce and remarriage.

131. Augustine, *Adulterous Marriages* 1.1, 8–9.

132. "Anyone who divorces his wife and marries someone else, commits adultery by her, and if a wife divorces her husband and marries someone else, she commits adultery" (Mark 10:11–12). Nearly identical wording in Luke 16:18.

133. Augustine, *Adulterous Marriages* 1.12. Augustine cannot fathom disagreement

divorce, it does not allow for remarriage. To state it another way, Augustine concludes that the permanence of the marriage bond does not depend on the good of fidelity. While adultery provides the only grounds for divorce, a violation of fidelity does not dissolve the marriage bond. Augustine's concern for maintaining the permanence of marriage is not only grounded in his desire to be faithful to Scripture, but also in a practical pastoral concern. For example, he fears that allowing remarriage in the case of adultery would result in encouraging adultery as a means of dissolving marriage.[134] If one grows tired of his spouse, he could provoke his spouse to commit adultery, thus freeing himself from the marriage bond. In this case, adultery becomes a "get-out-of-marriage-free card." Augustine wants to avoid this scenario altogether. This pastoral concern leads him to conclude that even when a married couple divorces, they are not allowed to remarry. The formerly married parties "are wedded persons even though separated."[135] Marriage, Augustine argues, is a "nuptial pact which [once it] has been entered upon . . . is not nullified by separation."[136] According to Augustine, uniting with another after divorce, even when divorcing because of the unfaithfulness of a spouse, violates the permanence of marriage.

In an attempt to further protect the permanence of marriage, Augustine rules out several possible justifications for divorce. First, he argues that a nonconsensual desire for continence by one partner is not grounds for divorce. The reason for this conviction rests on the fidelity of marriage as described in 1 Corinthians: "The wife does not have authority over her own body, but her husband does; and likewise the husband does not have authority over his own body, but his wife does" (1 Cor 7:5). Once married, both partners must consent to continence. While continence is a good which Augustine considers to be greater than the good of procreative marriage, divorcing a spouse who either cannot or will not commit to continence would have unintended consequences for the weaker spouse. In this case, divorce would result in the greater good of continence for one spouse, but it would probably propagate

---

between the gospels and must harmonize the differing accounts. The logic of his privileging of Mark and Luke is twofold. First, it is possible that Matthew only recorded part of what Jesus said, while Mark and Luke recorded the whole. Second, Augustine notes the existence of textual variants in his copy of Matthew which make the text ambiguous. There are two major questions regarding this method of interpretation. First, are there textual variants in Mark or Luke? If there are, then Augustine's reasoning for privileging Mark and Luke falls. Second, are the grounds for privileging Mark and Luke sufficiently strong, or could he just as easily have privileged Matthew?

134. Augustine, *Adulterous Marriages* 2.5.
135. Augustine, *Good of Marriage*, 19.
136. Augustine, *Good of Marriage*, 18.

the sin of adultery in the other spouse who cannot live the continent life.[137] Creating the possibility (probability?) of sinfulness in one's spouse nullifies the good of continence by violating the good of fidelity. In this instance, care for the weakness of one's spouse trumps the desire for continence, thereby eliminating continence as a justification for divorce.

Second, Augustine argues that an inability to procreate is an insufficient cause for divorce. To put it another way, the sacrament or permanence of marriage does not rely on the good of procreation. Augustine is concerned that allowing for divorce because of sterility of one partner would lead to an increase in divorce. He writes, "That motive of having children would drive husbands not only to divorce adulteresses, but even to divorce women of great chastity, if they happen to be sterile."[138] Augustine acknowledges that while marriage exists for the purpose of procreation and therefore all marriages must be open to bringing forth children, some marriages will not lead to generation. In this case, separation and remarriage would increase the odds that the barren couple would be able to procreate, thereby obeying God's command to "be fruitful and multiply" (Genesis 1:28). However, based on the teachings of Jesus on divorce, Augustine concludes that this practice is not allowed by Scripture. While the bond between married people "is tied for purpose of procreation, it is not loosed for the purpose of procreation."[139] This is true, in part, because procreation is less of a priority after the Incarnation, but also because of Augustine's conviction that the sacramental bond of fellowship between married couples is a good that operates independently of the good of procreation.[140]

While Augustine tries to keep the good of sacrament working alongside the other goods, it seems that this final telos is the only one that remains in effect regardless of whether the other two goods are fulfilled. Sacrament does not rely on either of the other two goods. Even if fidelity is violated and the marriage is infertile, the sacramental bond remains a good of marriage. Augustine argues that it is permissible to refrain from getting married, but after joining together, it is not permissible to break the marriage bond.[141] He writes, "Once, however, marriage is entered upon in the City [that is, Church] of our God, where also from the first union of the two human beings marriage

---

137. Augustine, *Adulterous Marriages* 1.4–7.
138. Augustine, *Adulterous Marriages* 2.11.
139. Augustine, *Good of Marriage*, 18.
140. Augustine, *Good of Marriage*, 31.
141. Augustine, *Good of Marriage*, 29.

bears a kind of sacred bond, it can be dissolved in no other way except by the death of one of the parties. The marriage bond remains."[142]

Summary of the Three Goods

While Augustine consistently affirms three goods or ends of marriage, his ordering of these goods varies occasionally in his works. In two locations, he lists the marital goods as fidelity, procreation, and sacrament.[143] In two other instances in a later work, Augustine further alters the order of the goods, by referring to fidelity, sacrament, and procreation.[144] Answers vary as to why Augustine modified the order of the goods. Perhaps he changed his formulation of the goods to address a specific doctrinal challenge.[145] Perhaps the modifications indicate that the valuation of the importance of each of the goods was not set in Augustine's mind. What is clear is that from his first formulation of the goods in 401 CE to the end of his career, Augustine consistently affirmed three teloi of marriage. All three are necessary to Augustine's theology of Christian marriage. He writes, "Certainly marriages have their value. It is not because they produce children, but because they produce children honorably, because they do so lawfully, because they do so chastely, because they do so in a social role, and because they educate those children without favoritism, soundly and perseveringly, and because they maintain marital fidelity, and because they do not abuse the sacrament of matrimony."[146]

Ascetic Hierarchy

One of the key features of Augustine's theology of marriage is what Peter Brown calls "an ascetic hierarchy, ranked according to degrees of sexual renunciation."[147] Though he hints at the structure of this hierarchy in *The Good of Marriage*, perhaps the clearest description is found in *Holy Virginity*. Here, Augustine writes, "We, on the other hand, relying on the reliable and salutary doctrine of the holy Scriptures, not only say that marriage is not a sin, but also rank it as inferior both to virginity and to celibate widowhood."[148]

142. Augustine, *Good of Marriage*, 31.
143. See Augustine, *Literal Meaning of Genesis* 9.7; *Against Julian* 3.16.30; 5.12.46.
144. Augustine, *Against Julian* 2.7.20; 3.25.57.
145. Haflidson, "Outward, Inward, Upward," 51–68.
146. Augustine, *Holy Virginity*, 74.
147. Brown, *Body and Society*, 404.
148. Augustine, *Holy Virginity*, 80.

Based on this definition, we can deduce that consecrated virginity is located at the pinnacle of Augustine's hierarchy, followed by widowhood. The next place on the hierarchy is occupied by continent married persons. For while continence is always considered a good, it is a greater good when practiced by a virgin. Augustine writes, "In no way can it be doubted that the chastity of continence is better than the chastity of marriage."[149] The position occupied by continent married people is followed by married individuals who engage in sexual intercourse only for the purpose of procreation. For Augustine, the presence of sex in marriage reduces the position of partners to a status below marital continence.[150] Married individuals who engage in non-procreative sex in order to appease lustful desires occupy the lowest level of the hierarchy of licit sexual behavior.

While an ascetic hierarchy based on one's sexual practice did not begin with Augustine, his use of the concept is unique for his time. Jerome, one of Augustine's contemporaries, used the hierarchy to denounce marriage. By comparing marriage to fornication, thereby contrasting virginity with marriage, Jerome argued that virginity is the only option for the obedient Christian, while marriage is nothing short of sin.[151] On the other side of the argument, Jovinian rejected the sexual hierarchy entirely stating that there is no difference between married Christians and virginal Christians. Baptism, he argued, is the only significant distinction between persons. Therefore, there should be no distinctions between Christians based on sexual practice. Augustine believed that the views espoused by both Jerome and Jovinian represented improper or partial uses of Scripture. Augustine used the sexual hierarchy as a means for finding a middle way between these two positions. In response to Jerome's attempt to elevate virginity by comparing marriage with fornication, Augustine argues that Jerome presents an incorrect analogy. He writes, "All will be good in comparison with that which is worse." This form of comparison relativizes both marriage and fornication, effectively transforming marriage into an evil while making fornication a good.[152] Augustine asserts that because marriage is a good, it must be compared to other goods. In this case, virginity is the proper analogue to marriage. By comparing marriage with virginity, Augustine is able to maintain that virginity is a greater good, without nullifying the good of marriage. In response to Jovinian, who rejected the sexual hierarchy altogether,

149. Augustine, *Good of Marriage*, 44.
150. Jungling, "Passionate Order," 321.
151. Brown, *Body and Society*, 377.
152. Augustine, *Good of Marriage*, 20. Augustine makes a similar argument about comparing marriage to divorce. The proper analogy is essential to the argument. See also *Adulterous Marriages* 1.23.

Augustine argues that virginity allows Christians to follow Christ in a way that is inaccessible to married Christians. Though all Christians are called to follow Christ, virgins can follow Christ in his virginity. Augustine writes, "The special joy of Christ's virgins is not the same as that of non-virgins, even if they too are Christ's. . . . Rightly you follow him by virginity in body and heart, wherever he goes."[153] While all Christians can imitate Jesus' obedience in spirit, virgins follow Christ not only in spirit, but also in body, exhibiting obedience as a more unified self. Therefore, while married and unmarried Christians experience the joys of eternal life, virginity is a greater good and will receive greater reward in the City of God. Yet, lest he devolve into Jerome's position, Augustine is quick to note that affirming a greater reward for virginity does not imply punishment for marriage.[154] If marriage is a sin, then virginity would not receive a greater reward. Christians would simply be encouraged to refrain from the sin of marriage and live as faithful virgins. Yet the Apostle Paul is clear, "If you marry, you do not sin" (1 Cor 7:28). Thus, marriage is a good, but virginity is a greater good.

Why does Augustine consider virginity to be better than marriage? For one so intent on defending the good of marriage, it seems counterintuitive to recommend the avoidance of the same institution. Investigating this tension requires an examination of the logic behind Augustine's sexual hierarchy. In support of his conviction that virginity is superior to marriage, Augustine supplies three arguments. First, he argues that, in many ways, marriage brings "present distress" which should be avoided.[155] Jealously among spouses, the difficulties of raising children, and the heartache that accompanies the death of a spouse are but a few of the burdens associated with marriage. Elsewhere, he says that marriage is accompanied by "tribulation of the flesh, without which marriage cannot exist."[156] Intercourse, he argues, is example of this tribulation. For Augustine, intercourse is that which "interferes with prayer" and which "marriage does not force but endures.[157] If married people experience distress from marriage and from intercourse

---

153. Augustine, *Holy Virginity*, 85.

154. Against Tertullian and Jerome, who interpreted Paul's desire for Christians to remain unmarried as a condemnation of marriage.

155. Augustine, *Holy Virginity*, 74–75. Here, Augustine follows Gregory of Nyssa in appealing to the heartache associated with marriage. See in Gregory of Nyssa, *On Virginity*, 12–15.

156. Augustine, *Good of Marriage*, 28.

157. Augustine, *Good of Marriage*, 30. Here we see hints of Tertullian's argument regarding sex and the experience of the divine. In this passage, Augustine may be saying that sex, like a host of other activities, requires valuable time that could otherwise be devoted to prayer. In any case, Augustine stops short of calling sex a barrier to one's experience of the divine.

in particular, Augustine believes that virgins will be "free" by avoiding sex and marriage altogether[158] By his choice of terms, it appears that Augustine viewed marriage as a form of bondage, with virginity being freedom from the affliction of marriage. Augustine's conception of marriage as bondage connects to his understanding of the fall. On his reading of the Genesis text, Eve was deceived by the serpent, but Adam willfully chose to engage in sin. Concerning this event, Augustine writes, "They were alone with each other, two human beings, a married couple; and we must believe that it was not because he thought she was speaking the truth that he was seduced into transgressing God's law but because he yielded to the tie that bound them together."[159] Here, Augustine identifies the relationship between the first couple, the marriage bond, as an influence on Adam's decision to sin. As a result, sin has corrupted the marriage relationship and turned it into a source of distress and temptation. According to Augustine, since marriage contributed to placing the first couple in bondage to sin, and sin has so disfigured the marriage bond resulting in marriage being a burden, it is better to forego that hardship altogether.

Second, Augustine supports his claim that virginity is superior to marriage with a discussion of affections. According to Augustine, marriage divides the affections, while virginity allows for singular focus on God. For example, he argues that the unmarried woman "thinks only of this, how she might please the Lord," while the married person "does so less because she is thinking also of the things of the world, how she might please her husband."[160] In a subsequent work, *On Holy Virginity*, Augustine provides another example to illustrate the logic behind the unity of affections. He argues that a married woman seeks to please one man. This singular focus of affection indicates that the relationship is a good. By contrast, an unmarried woman desires to please many men in her pursuit of a husband. Because her affections are divided, this is considered a lesser good. Augustine points his reader toward a third example: the consecrated virgin who wants only to please God. This singular focus of affection toward God, illustrated by the life of the consecrated virgin, is the highest good.[161]

Third, to illustrate his sexual hierarchy, Augustine describes two different types of goods: goods which exist "for their own sake" and goods "which are necessary for something else."[162] While both are types of goods,

---

158. Augustine, *Good of Marriage*, 29.
159. Augustine, *City of God* 14.11.
160. Augustine, *Good of Marriage*, 26.
161. Augustine, *Holy Virginity*, 73.
162. Augustine, *Good of Marriage*, 21–22.

those which exist for their own sake are considered greater goods. According to Augustine, goods for their own sake include "wisdom, health, and friendship," among others.[163] Necessary goods include food, which exists for the greater good of nourishment, as well as marriage and intercourse, which exist for the greater goods of procreation and "friendly association."[164] Augustine argues that it is not wrong for an individual to use the goods necessary for something else, but it is better to use them in such a way that the individual does not need those goods. In applying this logic to marriage, Augustine writes, "For this reason it is a good to marry, since it is a good to beget children . . . but it is better not to marry, since it is better for human society itself not to have *need* of marriage."[165] Here, the issue for Augustine is not whether one uses the goods of marriage and intercourse, but the necessity which is often associated with their use. Humans are allowed to use certain goods, so long as humans are "not bound by these goods and are able to use them when there [is] no need."[166] Augustine argues that it is impossible for a person to "use them properly unless he is able also not to use them."[167] This is true because, in Augustine's cosmology, having need points to a disordered life which has not found its rightful place in God. Augustine applies this discussion of goods to marriage and virginity. Some individuals, he argues, need marriage in order to pacify lustful desires. Others are able to live the virginal life and therefore do not need marriage. These latter individuals are higher on the hierarchy because they are free from necessity. Augustine argues that those who are able to practice virginity "step down" into marriage, while those who are unable to control their lustful urges "step up" into marriage.[168]

As previously mentioned, while Augustine defends marriage as a good, he also encourages all Christians, both married and single, to practice continence. Broadly speaking, Augustine describes continence as the "putting to death" of sinful impulses.[169] Referencing Colossians 3:5, Augustine writes, "What, therefore, does he [the apostle] want them to put to death, as the work of continence, other than those impulses that are still alive and in their own way intruding, without any consent from our mind and without

---

163. Augustine, *Good of Marriage*, 22.
164. Augustine, *Good of Marriage*, 22.
165. Augustine, *Good of Marriage*, 22 (my emphasis).
166. Augustine, *Good of Marriage*, 41.
167. Augustine, *Good of Marriage*, 41.
168. Augustine, *Good of Marriage*, 33.
169. Augustine, *Continence*, 213.

being put into effect by our bodies?"[170] This passage reflects Augustine's understanding of the relationship between the body, the will, and sin. For Augustine, humans were created body and soul. It is possible to distinguish between body and soul, however, both parts are required to describe a whole human. The soul is the higher or more noble part of a person because it contains the intellect or the will. It is the will that governs the body. Augustine applies this understanding to Adam and Eve's sin, "Thus, the evil act—that is, the transgression of eating the forbidden food—was committed by people who were already evil, and it would not have been committed if they had not already been evil."[171] Sin begins, not with outward action, but with evil desires in the mind or the will.[172] The term that he designates for these evil desires is concupiscence. Unlike Jerome's assertion that humans can overcome concupiscence, Augustine is convinced that after the fall, not even the most righteous person can fully eradicate evil desires. The final victory over concupiscence will only come in the eschaton. In this life, humans are in a continual struggle between consenting to evil desires and refraining from giving consent. Yet, Augustine argues that God has provided a way for humans to win the daily struggle against concupiscence. He writes, "The evil of carnal desire is not conquered except by the good of continence."[173] Thus, Augustine's hamartiology allows him to affirm a general description of continence as a turning away from evil desires.

While Augustine affirms general definitions of concupiscence and continence, the terms take on a more specific meaning when Augustine applies them to his theology of marriage. Consider his discussion of the differences between prelapsarian and postlapsarian sexual intercourse. In his later work, Augustine argues that intercourse existed in Eden as part of God's good, created order. In the garden, the first humans experienced the ideal sexual relationship. Because of his understanding of the relationship between the will and the body, Augustine envisions prelapsarian sex as a purely rational operation. He is convinced that there would have been little or no excitement or pleasure in prelapsarian sex. Man's seed would have come forth "by the quiet and normal obedience of his members to his will's command."[174] It should be noted that Scripture does not indicate whether the first humans engaged in intercourse before the fall, or if they experienced pleasure or

---

170. Augustine, *Continence*, 212. "Put to death, therefore, whatever in you is earthly: fornication, impurity, passion, evil desire, and greed (which is idolatry)" (Col 3:5).

171. Augustine, *City of God* 14.13.

172. Augustine, *City of God* 1.18. Elsewhere, Augustine describes sin as a disease of the soul (*City of God* 9.17).

173. Augustine, *Continence*, 195.

174. Augustine, *Marriage and Concupiscence* 7.773.

excitement during sexual intercourse. However, Augustine's argument about the nature of prelapsarian sex is grounded in his anthropology and hamartiology, working backwards from clear features of the fall account. Based on Augustine's convictions about the will's governance of the body, he concludes that prelapsarian sex was "undisturbed by lustful passion, and that the motion of the organs of generation, like that of any other member of the body, was not instigated by the ardor of lust, but directed by the choice of the will."[175] By contrast, in postlapsarian marriage, intercourse and human sexuality has been so distorted by sin that they bear little, if any resemblance to that which was created by God and declared to be good.[176] Desire for sex is now disordered, and this disordered desire "taints marriage, body, and the sexual embrace."[177] Whereas before sin, humans would not have engaged in intercourse as a result of lustful urges, after sin, procreation is accomplished by the power of the genitals, rather than by the obedience of the genitals to the will. Thus, Augustine describes the difference between postlapsarian and prelapsarian intercourse as a problem of the will no longer controlling the body, but the body being controlled by concupiscence.

Continence, understood as a general turning away from evil desire, also becomes more clearly defined when Augustine appropriates the term for his theology of marriage. For example, Augustine argues that marriages in the Old Testament existed primarily for the purpose of begetting children to bring forth the birth of the Messiah. After the coming of Christ, procreation no longer holds the same value. While contemporary marriage is still connected to procreative ends, Augustine argues, it exists primarily to curb concupiscence. In the context of marriage and sexuality, this term refers to lustful desires of the flesh. Since procreation, and therefore, marriage, no longer hold the same value in salvation history, Christians are encouraged to avoid the difficulties associated with marriage by practicing the higher life of virginity. Virginity is the practice of continence which foregoes the bonds of marriage. However, Augustine notes, virginity is a gift that has not been given to all. In order to keep individuals from burning with lustful desires, Scripture permits those who are unable to control their lustful urges to marry. Thus, marriage exists for weaker Christians who cannot "hold to a higher order of life" but are in "a kind of bondage to desire."[178] Augustine argues that marriage is a good, in part, because it chastens one's desire. This happens in two ways. First, the expression of sexual desire is limited to one's

---

175. Augustine, *Original Sin* 40.749.
176. Jungling, "Passionate Order," 323.
177. Kelly, "Sexuality and Concupiscence," 93.
178. Augustine, *City of God* 1.9.

spouse in marriage. Second, sexual desire is confined to procreation or paying the conjugal debt. Augustine expresses this idea clearly, "Continence in marriage usually allows some freedom to these carnal desires, but it reins them in and keeps them under control. Not even in marriage are they let go with unlimited freedom."[179] In summary, Augustine argues that continence can be practiced by both married and unmarried individuals. Within marriage, continence is the chastening of one's sexual desires through limiting or avoiding intercourse. Outside the bonds of marriage, continence is displayed by the practice of virginity.

Qualifications to the Ascetic Hierarchy

While Augustine holds virginity and continence in high regard, he does not consider these goods to be the chief Christian virtues. He asserts that obedience is the "the mother of all virtues."[180] This is true, he argues, because "there can be obedience to precepts without virginity, but there cannot be this obedience without chastity."[181] Here, Augustine makes a distinction between obedience and both continence and virginity on the basis of what Scripture commands versus what Scripture recommends. Relying on his reading of Paul, Augustine argues that Scripture has a series of commands which must be followed if one is to be considered obedient. For example, Paul commands that divorced individuals refrain from remarriage (1 Cor 7:10–11). However, in other areas, Scripture allows more freedom. In 1 Corinthians 7:6, the Apostle Paul recommends virginity and makes a "concession" for marriage. While Scripture commands obedience with regard to the remarriage of divorced people, Augustine argues, virginity is recommended but never commanded. Based on this distinction between command and recommendation, Augustine writes, "On this account, then, there can be obedience without virginity, because virginity is of counsel, not of precept."[182] Augustine wants to hold on to a tension where he acknowledges virginity as a greater good, while preserving the lesser good of marriage as a viable option for obedient Christians. He contends that "marriage and virginity are, it is true, two goods, the second of them is the greater. . . . However, it is better to have everything that is good in a lesser degree than to have a greater good with a great evil."[183] On the one hand, it is possible to practice virginity and

---

179. Augustine, *Continence*, 212. See also Augustine, *Excellence of Widowhood*, 116.
180. Augustine, *Good of Marriage*, 46. See also Augustine, *City of God* 14.12.
181. Augustine, *Good of Marriage*, 46.
182. Augustine, *Good of Marriage*, 46.
183. Augustine, *Good of Marriage*, 45.

still be disobedient in a variety of other ways. In response to this tendency, Augustine makes clear that practicing virginity does not give one license to be disobedient in other areas of life. On the other hand, it is possible to be married and be faithful to God. To illustrate this claim, Augustine points to Abraham, who, though he was not a virgin, was obedient to the point of sacrificing the child of promise (Gen 22:1–19). Thus, Augustine concludes, "Greater, indeed, is the good of obedience than the good of continence."[184]

Augustine further clarifies his understanding of asceticism by arguing that the practice of virginity and continence must be connected to the teachings of the church.[185] In a discussion of the good intentions of one pursuing a continent life, Augustine writes, "It is especially necessary, therefore, that the good of [this] intention be enhanced and fortified by sound doctrine."[186] For Augustine, virginity and continence are worth nothing apart from the church; he considers the practice virginity outside the church to be heretical.[187] Providing a culinary illustration, Augustine writes, "But, as the meals of the just are better than the fasting of the sacrilegious, so the marriage of the faithful is placed above the virginity of the unbeliever."[188] It is clear that for Augustine, even the chief virtue of obedience is not primarily an individual striving for moral perfection. Proper obedience is that which is dedicated to God.[189] One can only discuss the good of the sexual hierarchy within the boundaries of the church. To put it another way, for Augustine, sexual hierarchy is affirmed under the umbrella of the unity of the church. Marriage, virginity, widowhood are goods of relative value, but they are very good in relation to the whole of the body of Christ. Virginal Christians are Christians before they are virgins. To emphasize this point, Augustine writes, "So great is the excellence of Christian marriage, therefore, that they are even members of the body of Christ. Nevertheless, while the excellence of chastity in widowhood is greater, it does not follow that in this state of life a Catholic widow is something greater than a member of Christ, but among the members of Christ she occupies a place superior to that of the married woman."[190] Here, Augustine gives primacy to the body of Christ over ascetic distinctions. He clearly asserts that individuals are members of the body

---

184. Augustine, *Good of Marriage*, 45.
185. Augustine, *Continence*, 211.
186. Augustine, *Excellence of Widowhood*, 123.
187. Hunter, "Virgin," 299–300.
188. Augustine, *Good of Marriage*, 20.
189. Augustine, *Holy Virginity*, 73.
190. Augustine, *Excellence of Widowhood*, 114.

of Christ before any elevation or distinction between married, virginal, or widowed Christians can be made.

Not only does a proper ascetic life require the teaching of the church, it must also be accompanied by participation in the work of the church. For Augustine, continence (refraining from evil) is not sufficient grounding for the Christian life. Avoidance of evil must be paired with doing good. Augustine likens this view to a discussion of law and grace. Continence, like the law, is a negation or negative command. The negative command tells one what not to do, however, Augustine argues that this is insufficient. His concern is pastoral in nature. Augustine worries that merely denying sexual desires will result in desire rearing its head in a different and more destructive way, further enslaving the Christian. He compares this phenomenon to the loss of one of the physical senses. If one loses sight, the body compensates by focusing the body's energy into the remaining senses. Applying this analogy to sexual renunciation, Augustine writes, "In the same way, when sensuality is denied the pleasure of sexual union, it turns with greater energy to the pursuit of money, and so changing the direction of its attack from one to the other it becomes even more passionate toward the new objective."[191] Thus, humans do not live by renunciation alone. The negative command is insufficient because it provides no positive command of what a Christian is to do. Augustine argues that renunciation must be accompanied by a pursuit of justice. Justice, like grace, provides a positive account of how a faithful Christian should live.[192] Thus, according to Augustine, renouncing sex must be accompanied by service to God. As Willemian Otten puts it, "For Augustine, the ultimate importance of one's lifestyle depends on the contribution it makes to the City of God."[193]

It should be noted that, for Augustine, virginity and continence in no way represent a form of works-based righteousness. His teaching on chastity should not be separated from his belief that the Christian lives by the grace of God. For Augustine, salvation is not determined by one's failure or success at following a moral code. He argues, "What makes the body holy is not that its members are intact or that they have not been defiled by touch."[194] Rather, it is the soul's relationship to God. For Augustine, human nature has been entirely distorted by sin, which leaves humans unable to make any positive contribution to their salvation. Human striving, then, does not restore human nature. Based on this conviction, Augustine implores his

---

191. Augustine, *Holy Virginity*, 132.
192. Augustine, *Continence*, 202.
193. Otten, "Augustine on Marriage," 401.
194. Augustine, *City of God* 1.18.

audience, "Therefore, O human creature, do not live according to yourself; by doing that you became lost."[195] Restoration of human nature, described by Augustine as the reunification of body and soul, is accomplished only by God's grace. Therefore, continence and virginity should be chosen in response to God's grace, not in an effort to earn divine favor. Augustine's commitment to grace allows him to argue that it is possible for seemingly upright, holy, chaste individuals to be excluded from salvation, while gluttons and sex addicts can be saved by grace through faith.[196]

To support the argument that outward, ascetic action does not determine one's standing before God, Augustine points to the scriptural examples of Jesus and John the Baptizer. On the one hand, Augustine notes that Jesus ate food and drank wine, and he was accused of gluttony. Yet, Christians do not doubt his continence. On the other hand, John the Baptizer refrained from most food and beverage. Augustine asserts that both Jesus and John used food and wine rightly, though they used them differently. Both Jesus' use of earthly goods and John's abstinence were done in service to God. Both displayed continence because of the way they used or refrained from goods in specific circumstances. Therefore, the good of continence does not rely solely on outward action. For Augustine, continence is a "disposition of the soul, [that is] to be shown . . . in practice in accord with the opportunity of the time and circumstances."[197] The state of the soul is connected to outward actions, but time and circumstances also influence proper outward display of inward belief. Therefore, Augustine encourages Christians to practice "continence, indeed, not of the body but of the soul," in response to God's gift of grace.[198]

While ascetic commitment should be a display of gratitude to the salvation of God, Augustine notes that virginity and continence can also lead to a sense of entitlement. In response to some of his contemporaries who might have some level of hubris associated with their practice of sexual renunciation, Augustine accentuates the dangers of pride associated with mere outward obedience.[199] He provides four reasons why ascetic practice

---

195. Augustine, *Continence*, 198–99.

196. Kelly, "Sexuality and Concupiscence," 86–87.

197. Augustine, *Good of Marriage*, 42.

198. Augustine, *Good of Marriage*, 40.

199. Otten, "Augustine on Marriage," 401. The relationship between sin and pride is one of the distinct features of Augustine's theology. He identified pride as a sickness of the soul, which causes the individual to love the self as opposed to God. For Augustine, pride is the source of human sin. By locating the origin of sin in pride, as opposed to the physical human body, Augustine could argue that the body is good and therefore not the source of evil.

is not a source of pride. First, virginity and continence are gifts from God. Therefore, the ability to maintain a virginal life relies on God's work, not on human striving.[200] Since God is the source of the gift and the means of its fulfillment, those who practice the ascetic life should respond to God in gratitude. Augustine writes, "For there is no true virtue except the virtue that is directed toward the end where man's good is actually found, the good than which there is no better."[201] Second, virginity and continence are only viable options after the coming of Christ. Before the Incarnation, "the Law . . . called him accursed who did not rear children in Israel. . . . Afterwards, the fullness of time came . . . from that time up till now and henceforward to the end, he who possesses this continence puts it into practice."[202] If the coming of Christ initiates the time when continence can be practiced, then living a continent life should bring glory to Christ, not to humans. Third, Augustine contends that pride over one's ascetic lifestyle is the result of comparing oneself to others based solely on the good of continence. He argues that "it is not right to compare men with men in some one good. For, it can happen that one does not have something that the other has, but he has something that is to be valued more highly."[203] Continence and virginity are two goods among many greater and lesser goods displayed by individuals in the church. While virginity may rank higher than chastity in marriage, both fall short of the greater good of martyrdom.[204] For Augustine, martyrdom is the ultimate example of an individual's allegiance to Christ. Yet unlike virginity and continence, whose fruits are easily recognizable, martyrdom is a good that remains hidden inside the Christian until the moment of death. It may be that a married, sexually active Christian is ready to lay down her life for Christ and a virgin is not. Augustine's point in this discussion is to emphasize the limits of human knowledge, especially in matters of the soul. Thus, comparing Christians and their various gifts becomes a pointless exercise in self-idolization. Rather than comparing Christians to other Christians, Augustine asserts that Christ, who reigns over all, should be a Christian's point of comparison. By that

---

200. Augustine, *Holy Virginity*, 97–98. Augustine repeats the claim that chastity and virginity are gifts of grace in *City of God* 1.28.

201. Augustine, *City of God* 5.12.

202. Augustine, *Good of Marriage*, 42–43.

203. Augustine, *Good of Marriage*, 45.

204. Augustine, *Holy Virginity*, 99–100. In *City of God*, Augustine describes martyrdom as another form of baptism. Confessing Christ in the face of martyrdom has salvific power, even if the confession is made by an unbaptized (*City of God* 13.7). See also Augustine, *Excellence of Widowhood*, 98–99.

standard, there is no reason for a continent lifestyle to result in pride.[205] Fourth, Augustine draws a distinction between the good of a thing and its use. He argues that it is possible to use the good of continence in an evil way. In another work, Augustine writes, "A man makes a good use of a good thing when he dedicates his continence to God. He makes a bad use of a good thing, when he dedicates his continence to an idol. He makes bad use of an evil thing, when he loosely gratifies his concupiscence by adultery. He makes a good use of an evil thing, when he restrains his concupiscence by matrimony."[206] When individuals take pride in the higher status afforded to the continent within the church or in their ability to avoid sin through the practice of continence, Augustine contends that the good of continence is replaced by the evil of idolatry. Ultimately, celebrating self-righteousness or personal works causes one to be the "enemy of Christ's grace."[207] Therefore, Augustine requires that those who practice the higher calling of virginity also embody a higher standard of humility. This is true because "obedience can belong only to the humble."[208]

This complex use of an ascetic hierarchy allows Augustine to maintain a delicate balance by arguing that while virginity is a greater good, choosing virginity does not condemn the lesser good of marriage. He writes "These are all goods on account of which marriage is a good: offspring, fidelity, sacrament. Yet to seek Christ above and in place of marriage and its goods is "better and indeed holier."[209] At the same time, the qualifications discussed above highlight similarities between Augustine's position and that of Jovinian. For example, both theologians argue that, when it comes to drawing distinctions between individuals, salvation is primary, and asceticism is secondary. Second, both are concerned with the potential pitfalls associated with dividing Christians into different groups. Third, both challenge the notion that outward action equates to holiness. Finally, Augustine's elevation of obedience as the chief Christian virtue undercuts attempts to elevate continence and virginity. If all Christians are called to obedience and Augustine approves a variety of ways for a follower of Jesus to be obedient, then there is no reason to privilege one mode of obedience over another. This is a move that Jovinian would have welcomed.

205. Augustine, *Holy Virginity*, 87–88, 92.
206. Augustine, *Against Pelagius* 57.182.
207. Augustine, *Excellence of Widowhood*, 127.
208. Augustine, *City of God* 14.13.
209. Augustine, *Good of Marriage*, 48.

Contemporary Challenges to Augustine: Gender Relations

The last two sections of this chapter will address concerns that arise from reading ancient texts from the perspective of a modern setting, namely, the apparent foreignness of certain Augustinian themes. Perhaps nowhere is the distance between the modern reader and Augustine more evident than when examining the impacts of Augustine's teaching on the relationship between the sexes in marriage.

Augustine asserts that a properly ordered marriage is one in which the husband rules and the wife obeys. He makes two moves to support this claim. He begins his defense of gender hierarchy by appealing to the rule of singularity. He writes, "For, by a law of nature things that are ruled love singularity."[210] According to Augustine, the world is comprised of dualities where one entity rules and the other submits. When this concept is applied to the human relations, he asserts that it is natural for the male to rule and the female to submit. Here, he appeals to what contemporary theologians call natural law, where human experience of what occurs in the natural world informs the shape of human social practice.[211] Augustine continues, "Things that are ruled, indeed, are subjected not only each one to an individual master, but also, if natural or social conditions allow, many of them are not unfittingly subjected to one master."[212] To illustrate his conviction that men are created to rule and women to serve, Augustine points to the practice of polygamous marriage. At first glance, it would seem that polygamy runs counter to the divine plan for marriage found in the creation accounts. However, Augustine argues that the Old Testament practice of polygamy is "not against the nature of marriage."[213] This is true, he contends, because God has ordered the world in such a way that men can produce children with many women at once, but women can only bring forth one child at a time. Thus, Augustine asserts that during the days of the patriarchs, husbands were allowed to have many wives, but wives

---

210. Augustine, *Good of Marriage*, 34.

211. It should be noted that in his later works, Augustine is less convinced that postlapsarian humans have the capacity to recognize the real or the natural due to the effects of sin on human reason. Augustine argues that appeals to natural law are problematic because of (1) variety in nature, (2) the limited nature of human perspective, and (3) the freedom and power of God (*Literal Meaning of Genesis* 3.12; 6.25–27). Augustine also argues that reason is lost in sin (*Continence*, 198). Sin has rendered the bodily senses "unreliable and deceptive" (*City of God* 8.7).

212. Augustine, *Good of Marriage*, 34.

213. Augustine, *Good of Marriage*, 34

were allowed only one husband. Based on this evidence, he concludes that the divine order, observed in nature and in society, dictates that husbands rule over their wives. Second, Augustine provides a theological rationale for his support of gender hierarchy by appealing to the order of the human/divine relationship. Building on his assertions about polygamy, Augustine argues that many women can be subjected to one man in marriage "just as many souls are properly subjected to the one God."[214] Next, he gives this claim a christological turn in order to make application to the contemporary setting. Just as Old Testament polygamy points to all races being "subject to one man—Christ," contemporary marriages, consisting of one man and one woman, are the fulfillment of the prophetic sign found in the Old Testament.[215] When viewed through a christological lens, polygamy foreshadows monogamy. Yet in both cases, the rule of singularity dictates male rule and female submission.

At this point the questions must be raised: is Augustine the subjugator of women?[216] On the one hand, Augustine's account of gender relations clashes with twenty-first-century notions of equality. For example, women's voices and perspectives do not play a prominent role in Augustine's account of marriage. In chapters 11 and 12 of *The Good of Marriage*, Augustine discusses the difficulties associated with the institution, namely the tendency for marriage to divide the affections. As he describes his understanding of the experience of a wife, Augustine seems quick to generalize that experience by applying it to the lives of all married women. Lamenting the divided affections of married women, Augustine writes, "Not without reason, is it doubted whether [Paul] said this of all married women or of such women of this type who are so numerous that almost all women can be considered the same."[217] Also, it appears that Augustine, either consciously or unconsciously, understands male bodies and male perspectives to be normative.[218] For example, in his commentaries on Genesis, Augustine assumes a male experience of arousal as normative. He provides no account of female sexual arousal. Consider another example. In his discussion of the sexual relationship between married people, Augustine argues that spouses may engage in intercourse for procreative purposes or for paying the conjugal debt to their spouse. However, "when the husband wishes to use the member of his wife" in another manner, "the wife is more shameful *if she permits this* to take

---

214. Augustine, *Good of Marriage*, 35.
215. Augustine, *Good of Marriage*, 36.
216. See Primavesi, *From Apocalypse to Genesis*, 205–15, 227–31.
217. Augustine, *Good of Marriage*, 27.
218. Burrus et al., *Seducing Augustine*, 4.

place with herself rather than with another woman."[219] Augustine is quick to denounce a wife for allowing herself to be used in an unworthy manner, but does not question whether the wife would have a choice in the matter. When Christian wives are instructed to be submissive to husbands who rule over them, it is unlikely that a wife would be afforded the opportunity to decline a husband's "unnatural" sexual request. Augustine's hasty judgment reveals the phallocentrism of his worldview.[220]

Reading Augustine on contemporary questions of gender relations is further complicated by his sexed anthropology, a concept that remains relatively stable throughout his career. Key to Augustine's anthropology is the assertion that humans are comprised of body and soul. The soul, which contains the intellect and the will, is higher than the body. Therefore, the soul should govern the body. In *Genesis Against the Manichees* (388–89), Augustine provides further descriptors of this division of the human. Reason, described as "manly," must rule over the "animal" body.[221] The inference is that man is equated with reason and woman is identified with the animal part of the human which must be controlled. Later in the same work, Augustine applies the gender hierarchy, where males are to rule over females, to the individual. He argues that every person has a male and female part. He writes, "In this way what can be seen more clearly in two human beings, that is, in male and female, may be considered a single person; that the interior mind, like the manly reason, should have as its subject the soul's appetite or desire."[222] Here, woman is equated with desire, a lower category in Augustine's anthropology. Augustine finds further evidence to support his case in the creation of woman from man's rib. He argues that this event signifies the "joining together" of the rational with that which "yields compliance to reason."[223] When feminine desire and animal body submits to manly reason, the result is an ordered human, a kind of "wedded couple in the self."[224] For Augustine, the goal is for the body to submit to soul, and for the desires of the flesh to "comply with [reason] and thus [cease] to be of the flesh."[225] However, if fleshly desire is equated with femininity, is Augustine encouraging a "masculinization" of all Christians?

---

219. Augustine, *Good of Marriage*, 25 (my emphasis).
220. The term is borrowed from Coakley, *God, Sexuality, and the Self*.
221 Augustine, *Genesis Manichees* 2.15.
222. Augustine, *Genesis Manichees* 2.15.
223. Augustine, *Genesis Manichees* 2.16.
224. Augustine, *Genesis Manichees* 2.16.
225. Augustine, *Genesis Manichees* 2.16.

By the writing of *Literal Meaning of Genesis* (416), Augustine provides an answer to this troubling question by appealing to the *imago Dei*. Augustine argues that it is the creation of humans in the image of God which distinguishes them from animals. He identifies the *imago dei* with the human capacity of reason. He writes, "What gives the man his pre-eminence is that God made man to his image, in this respect that he gave him an intelligent mind, which puts him ahead of animals."[226] While the language used here is decidedly masculine, Augustine asserts that both males and females are created in the image of God. He asserts that "the female too, because it is simply in the body that she is female, is also being renewed in the spirit of her mind in the recognition of God according to the image of him who created that in which there is no male and female. . . . The woman of course also had her mind, a mind endowed with reason, with respect to which she too was made to the image of God."[227] While inequality exists in the physical abilities of the sexes, he contends, both men and women have rational abilities. Both are created in the image of God and are being renewed in that image. It must be remembered that for Augustine, the mental realm has dominion over the bodily realm. Therefore, the real differences between males and females are external, not internal.[228] While this nuanced position represents an improvement over his earlier work, the basic distinction is just internalized. The rational part of the human mind which engages in the "contemplation of eternal truth" is male while the part concerned with the "management of temporal affairs" is female.[229]

Perhaps the most robust display of Augustine's sexed anthropology is found in *On the Trinity* (419). Here, Augustine expands his understanding of the division of the human mind. He asserts that the higher and lower parts of the mind were designed to work together in fellowship. This harmony of mind, Augustine argues, is analogous to the first man and woman becoming one flesh.[230] Here, Augustine applies a version of a complementarian understanding of the sexes to what occurs within the human mind. He argues that "the woman together with her husband is the image of God, so that the whole substance is one image."[231] When the mind is unified and

---

226. Augustine, *Literal Meaning of Genesis* 6.21. See also Augustine, *Literal Meaning of Genesis* 3.16, 30.
227. Augustine, *Literal Meaning of Genesis* 3.34.
228. Roberts, *Creation & Covenant*, 46.
229. Augustine, *Literal Meaning of Genesis* 3.34.
230. Augustine, *Trinity* 12.3.
231. Augustine, *Trinity* 12.7.

it "contemplates the truth, it is the image of God."[232] However, when the mind is divided in function, the higher part which focuses on eternal things is the image of God, while the lower part which focuses on earthly things is not the image of God. He writes, "But when she (the woman) is assigned as a help-mate, a function that pertains to her alone, then she is not the image of God; but as far as the man is concerned, he is by himself alone the image of God, just as fully and completely as when he and the woman are joined together into one."[233] Augustine uses decidedly gendered language in this discussion. In this allegorical treatment of the human mind, the higher, masculine part of the mind must keep the lower, feminine part of the mind in check. Augustine qualifies this stance by asserting that both women and men have a rational mind and experience the renewal of Christ in that portion of the self. This is true because there is no sex in the rational mind. The strength of Augustine's position is that both men and women are assumed to possess a rational mind and the ability to think on eternal things. Both can experience regeneration of that rational mind. Yet, Augustine still associates the lower portion of the mind, which focuses on temporal things and seeks after pleasure, with the female gender.

In *City of God* (426), Augustine continues many of the themes discussed in his earlier work. He affirms that both men and women have reason.[234] However, he argues that woman is weaker in her rational abilities than man. In his discussion of the first temptation, Augustine writes, "He [Satan] began, that is, with the lower, lesser part of the human couple so that, by stages, he might reach them both presuming that the man would not be so easy to dupe and could not be deceived into erring himself but would fall prey to another's error."[235] Because of her weaker rational abilities, Augustine contends, Eve was deceived while Adam willfully chose to be disobedient to the divine command. Furthermore, pleasure and desire, which continually arouse Augustine's suspicion, are identified with femininity.[236] Male is equated with mind, soul, and spirit, while female is the desires of the flesh which oppose the spirit. Thus, throughout his career, Augustine weaves together a gendered social hierarchy with a gendered hierarchy within the self, resulting in the elevation of men and masculinity at the expense of women.

232. Augustine, *Trinity* 12.7.
233. Augustine, *Trinity* 12.7.
234. Augustine, *City of God* 2.19.
235. Augustine, *City of God* 14.11.
236. Augustine, *City of God* 5.20.

On the other hand, in several ways Augustine's work represents a theoretical advance toward the non-hierarchical vision that has become common sense for much of the modern, Western world. A cursory selection of passages from *The Good of Marriage* will illustrate this point. First, while Augustine upholds the rule of the husband over the wife, he does seem to soften that dominion. He describes marriage as "a kind of friendly and genuine union of the one ruling and the other obeying."[237] While his view is hierarchical, Augustine conceives of a hierarchy that is in "opposition to the hierarchies of the earthly city."[238] Second, Augustine also emphasizes the mutuality of the marriage relationship. For example, he argues that fidelity is owed equally to each partner. Pressing further in his discussion of fidelity, Augustine describes non-procreative sex as a debt of the flesh and a "mutual service" owed to assist both the male and female partners in times of weakness and to protect that partner from the sin of adultery.[239] Third, Augustine employs an equal distribution of sexual regulations. If a violation of fidelity occurs and leads to divorce, regardless of whether the guilty partner is a male or a female, the same rules apply: remarriage is not allowed. He writes, "But I do not see how a man can have freedom to marry another if he leaves an adulteress, since a woman does not have freedom to marry another if she leaves an adulterer."[240] Fourth, in his evaluation of the way individuals use marriage, Augustine criticizes both husbands and wives. He argues that few married people, regardless of gender, follow Scripture's teachings on marriage. However, he holds out hope that marriage will facilitate the spiritual growth of the couple so that both partners will learn to focus their attention solely on the things of God.

Furthermore, in multiple texts, Augustine demonstrates more leniency toward women than men. In chapter 4 of *The Good of Marriage*, rather than pronouncing an outright condemnation of an adulteress, Augustine extends forgiveness if the adulteress repents and commits to a life of chastity.[241] Again, in chapter 5, Augustine recounts the example of a man who lives with a concubine for a time and then discards her in order to take a wife. Both accounts appear to originate from Augustine's life. Prior to his conversion, Augustine cohabitated with a woman for roughly fourteen years and had a child from the relationship. He asserts that he was sexually

---

237. Augustine, *Good of Marriage*, 9.
238. Roberts, *Creation & Covenant*, 66.
239. Augustine, *Good of Marriage*, 17.
240. Augustine, *Good of Marriage*, 18.
241. Augustine, *Good of Marriage*, 14.

faithful to her throughout this period.[242] Eventually, Augustine acknowledges that he felt pressure to marry. His mother may have been the source of this pressure as she is the one who arranged the marriage with a young girl about the age of ten. Augustine's partner of fourteen years was "ripped from [his] side, being regarded as an obstacle to [his] marriage."[243] Augustine responded to this upheaval by taking another woman who was "in no sense a wife" as a sexual companion.[244] At first, it is unclear why Augustine could not have married his partner of fourteen years. Such a union would have fulfilled the requirements of a common-law marriage, and was considered acceptable in Augustine's day. Furthermore, the church had made provision for common-law marriages at the Council of Toledo in 400.[245] However, in *Confessions*, Augustine reveals two possible factors in the thought process behind his decision to dismiss his common-law wife. First, in his earliest description of his relationship with his partner, he writes, "I lived with a girl not bound to me in lawful wedlock but sought out by the roving eye of reckless desire.... This experience taught me at firsthand what a difference there is between a marriage contracted for the purpose of founding a family, and a relationship of love charged with carnal desire in which children may be born even against the parents' wishes."[246] Roman marriage law stated that marriage existed for the purpose of procreation.[247] It may be that Augustine and his common-law wife had no intention of having children, but engaged in the "relationship of love" solely for the purpose of assuaging sexual desire. This would bring the legal or "lawful" legitimacy of their relationship into question. Second, as Augustine discusses his struggles with the pleasures associated with sexual desire, he believes that he would gain a certain measure of dignity "if only the honorable name of matrimony were conferred upon these pleasures."[248] For Augustine, the connection between honor and marriage is twofold. First, marriage acts as a cover or pardon for lustful sex, bringing increased moral worth to the sexual encounter. Second, marriage allows children to be "born properly and decently."[249] It appears that both legitimacy and decency are important to Augustine's understanding of marriage. His common-law relationship did not meet these criteria and

---

242. Augustine, *Confessions* 4.2.
243. Augustine, *Confessions* 6.25.
244. Augustine, *Confessions* 6.25.
245. Augustine, *Confessions*, 156n84.
246. Augustine, *Confessions* 4.2.
247. Hunter, "Augustine," 75.
248. Augustine, *Confessions* 6.22.
249. Augustine, *Good of Marriage*, 33.

therefore putting away his long-term partner was deemed necessary. As he reflects on this situation some years later in *The Good of Marriage*, Augustine judges himself more harshly than the woman.[250]

In summary, while Augustine's description of gender relations is an affront to twenty-first-century notions of equality, it is unfair and anachronistic to judge a fifth-century individual by contemporary standards. Augustine's writings both contributed to and are resistant to our own views. Because of the depth of his theological vision and the lasting contribution Augustine has had on the tradition, it may be that our views on gender relations are merely rebalanced configurations of his thought. At the same time, the contemporary reader should avoid the tendency to read Augustine's writings as timeless truths by directly applying his teachings on gender to the contemporary setting. Augustine's writings on the relationship between the sexes were progressive for their times as he encouraged the church toward deeper visions of equality in Christ. As we learn from his writings and seek to listen to them in our attempt to address contemporary challenges, perhaps we should honor Augustine by appealing to the "mysterious difference" between his time and ours. He attempted to be faithful to Scripture and Christian tradition while speaking to the crises and issues of his day. The contemporary setting differs from that of Augustine, as do the issues that the church encounters. The church's answers to the challenges posed by the contemporary debate on sexuality will likely differ from the answers that Augustine provided. However, if the church follows Augustine's lead in its commitment to Scripture and tradition, then "only the difference in the times [makes] the works of [the contemporary church] diverse" from that of Augustine.[251]

Contemporary Challenges to Augustine: Desire

I now turn my attention to a second category that complicates attempts to bring Augustine's theology to bear on contemporary discourse on sex and marriage, namely, his account of desire. Throughout its history, the church has had a tenuous relationship with desire. Nietzsche once quipped, "Christianity gave Eros poison to drink: although he didn't die from it, he degenerated into a vice."[252] At times, Augustine has been accused of being the one who "single-handedly ruined sex for the western world" because of his

---

250. Augustine, *Good of Marriage*, 15–16.
251. Augustine, *Good of Marriage*, 33.
252. Nietzsche, *Beyond Good and Evil*, 53.

purportedly negative outlook on sexual desire.[253] This accusation is not without merit. While Augustine describes sexual intercourse as a good because it leads to children, he spends more space discussing the connection between intercourse and lust.[254] However, his account of desire must be understood against the backdrop of his wider theology. Augustine uses intercourse and human sexuality as a trope for discussing the sinful nature of human beings and as a mechanism to explain the transmission of original sin. Sexual desire serves as a mirror which displays the "contortions and distortions of human motivation."[255] This allows Augustine to argue that both intercourse and the body have a place in God's created order, but both must be viewed with suspicion because of the influence of sin.[256]

To better demonstrate Augustine's understanding of desire, it is necessary to discuss the place of affect in his anthropology.[257] According to Augustine, affections are a natural part of the human experience. All humans, Christians included, experience the whole gamut of the affections. For Augustine, affections are a response to something that an individual wills to occur or not occur. Based on this description, affections are neither good nor evil in themselves. For Augustine, what makes an affection good or evil is "the quality of a person's will. If it is perverse, these emotions [*adfectus*] will be corrupt, but if it is right, they will not only be blameless but even praiseworthy."[258] The quality of a person's will is determined by its orientation toward or away from God. Augustine describes this orientation of the will as two categories of affection, two loves: love of God and love of self. When an individual's love is directed toward God, she will experience affections

---

253. Burrus et al., *Seducing Augustine*, 2.

254. Kelly, "Sexuality and Concupiscence," 90.

255. Otten, "Augustine on Marriage," 388.

256. See Jungling, "Passionate Order," 324; Otten, "Augustine on Marriage," 387–88.

257. I deliberately refrain from using the non-theological term "emotion." This category has two major deficiencies. First, as Andrew Cameron has pointed out, "emotion" is a concept that lumps together "involuntary appetites, passions, and commotions of animal nature as well as moral sentiments and voluntary affections" ("Logic of Love," 59). To put it another way, this concept confuses categories of body and soul. By contrast, the concepts of "passions," referring to involuntary bodily appetites, and "affections," referring to voluntary movements of the soul, allow for proper distinction between the two. Second, many modern views of emotion tend to follow a Nietzschean logic, which argues that humans are responsible for their actions but not their emotions. Emotions are part of the human life, but they cannot be questioned or evaluated ("Logic of Love," 64–65). However, within the passions/affections distinction, affection is seen as the positive alternative to passion, thus allowing for judgment to be made among various feelings.

258. Augustine, *City of God* 14.6. I have preserved Babcock's translation, but maintain that *adfectus* would be better translated as "affect/affection."

rightly. Augustine argues, "Citizens of the city of God . . . because their love is right, they have all these emotions [*adfectus*] in the right way."[259] By contrast, when the individual's love is directed away from God, affections are experienced wrongly. Augustine argues that both love and hate are affections that can be experienced rightly or wrongly. For example, the individual who "lives according to God and not according to man must be the lover of the good, and it follows that he will hate the evil."[260] Thus, Augustine is not against affections. Furthermore, he denounces attempts to avoid the experience of affections altogether. Instead, he encourages Christians to direct their affections to appropriate ends by orienting the will toward God.

This general description of affections can be applied to Augustine's discussion of desire. To illustrate his view of desire, Augustine compares food with intercourse. Just as food is a necessary good that leads to the greater good of a person's health, so intercourse is a necessary good that leads to the health of the race through procreation. On the one hand, Augustine affirms that both food and intercourse are goods that can be used by humans. On the other hand, he is concerned with how those goods are used. Regarding the experience of using these goods, Augustine argues that both eating and intercourse "are not without carnal pleasure."[261] It is important to note that nowhere in *The Good of Marriage* does Augustine condemn pleasure as inherently evil; his understanding of pleasure in no way represents an affirmation of stoic ideals. For example, he argues that the patriarchs experienced a "natural delight" while engaging in sexual intercourse with their wives. However, that pleasure was "by no means given rein up to the point of unreasoning and wicked lust."[262] Thus, Augustine is not fundamentally against pleasure, but he does make a distinction between pleasure and the more negative category of passion based on two characteristics. First, the experience of pleasure must be moderated by a "controlling temperance."[263] As previously discussed, an ordered life is one where the body and affections are subject to the control of the will. A proper experience of pleasure is one regulated by the will. By contrast, passion would be characterized by lack of control, or a pleasure not regulated by the will. This distinction between pleasure and passion allows Augustine to argue that marriage serves a further purpose beyond the three primary goods of marriage. He asserts that marriage provides a limit to pleasure and desire. Both the marriage vow

---

259. Augustine, *City of God* 14.9.
260. Augustine, *City of God* 14.7.
261. Augustine, *Good of Marriage*, 32.
262. Augustine, *Good of Marriage*, 33.
263. Augustine, *Good of Marriage*, 32.

and the practice of continence in marriage "usually allows some freedom to these carnal desires, but it reins them in and keeps them under control. Not even in marriage are they let go with unlimited freedom."[264] Thus, marriage provides for a more tempered, ordered experience of desire.

Second, for the experience of using a good to be characterized as pleasure, the good must be attached to its "natural" or proper end.[265] By contrast, sinful passion occurs when a necessary good is used solely for the purpose of experiencing pleasure, thereby divorcing the good from its proper end. Augustine applies these two distinctions to the experience of eating and intercourse. For example, a proper pleasurable experience of eating is when one eats in moderation for the purpose of nourishment. Eating becomes a sinful passion when one eats for the sake of pleasure. When applied to sex, the pleasure of marital intercourse is good when it is a byproduct of engaging in intercourse for the purpose of procreation. This use of the necessary good of intercourse is moderated by the fidelity of marriage and is attached to its proper end of procreation. Thus, the issue for Augustine is not pleasure, but excessive indulgence which separates pleasure from its appropriate telos.[266] Pleasure of an activity is good, while separating pleasure from the activity's end is not good.

This discussion has important consequences for a theology of marriage. As we shall see in chapter 3, multiple contemporary theologians have constructed theologies of marriage by severing the Augustinian link between marriage and procreation.[267] However, if the telos of an activity is removed, it becomes impossible to define "passion" in Augustinian terms, thereby losing the distinction between positive experiences of affections and negative experiences of passions. As we venture into the contemporary debate, proper attention will be given to how various revisionists incorporate desire into their theologies of marriage.

---

264. Augustine, *Continence*, 212.
265. Augustine, *Good of Marriage*, 32.
266. Meilaender, "Sweet Necessities," 6.
267. For example, see Barth, *Church Dogmatics* 3/4:175–90. Barth maintains Augustine's marital goods of fidelity and permanence but rejects procreation as a necessary good of marriage. For Barth, the ultimate telos of marriage is the "life-partnership" of the couple (Barth, *Church Dogmatics* 3/4:182). Eugene Rogers (*Sexuality and the Christian Body*) follows Barth in this regard. For another revisionist example, see Thatcher, *Liberating Sex*.

Conclusion

In many ways, Augustine's writing on the dangers of sexual desire seem antiquated. His call to refrain from intercourse in marriage due to its connection with lustful sexual desire and his Greek understanding of the will controlling the emotions do have their weaknesses. Postlapsarian desire, for Augustine, bears little resemblance to the good desire that God created, thereby making it difficult to discuss postlapsarian desire in a positive way. Also, his belief that the will should control actions, desires, and affections, makes purely rational sex the ideal. Yet, intercourse can also be described as a release, a letting go, a moment of mutual bodily submission between married partners. While some of his arguments and conclusions may be insufficient to address many of the questions facing contemporary theologians, Augustine was progressive, if not radical for his time. While other writers assumed that sexual intercourse and the desire that accompany it were so marred by sin that they refrained from discussing the topics, Augustine investigated the views swirling around him. Rather than single-handedly destroying sex, he found a place in his theology for desire, intercourse, marriage, virginity, and continence. As Mathewes argues, Augustine "brought together, however imperfectly, what previous thinkers had kept asunder."[268]

---

268. Mathewes, "Original Sin," 38–39.

3

Contemporary Revisions of Augustine's Theology of Marriage

WHILE AUGUSTINE'S THREE GOODS of marriage have set the terms of the conversation on Christian sexual ethics, the cultural and social norms that influence definitions of the institution have shifted since the fifth century.[1] A detailed excursus on this topic from Augustine to present day is beyond the scope of this project. For the purposes of this chapter, I will provide a brief glimpse of the shift occurring in sexual mores since the sexual revolution. Over the last fifty years, sexual trends in the West have undergone a series of drastic alterations.[2] First, the advent of inexpensive, reliable, readily available birth control provided a way to sever the link between sex and procreation. This development brought about alterations to Western views on children, family, parenting, etc.[3] The church has not been immune to these changes. Where there was once cohesion for the church's sexual ethics, Stanley Hauerwas asserts that there is no longer any normative understanding of sex, marriage, and family among Christians. The church no longer knows what these entities are or for what purpose they exist.[4] Second, fewer people are choosing to marry. Between 1970 and 2010, there was a 50 percent decline in the number of marriages per 1000 people in the United States, as individuals are electing to cohabitate before, or instead of, marriage.[5] Marriage is no longer the norm in Western society. Third, premarital virginity is no longer widely practiced. Ninety-five percent of Americans engage in sexual intercourse before marriage.[6] Fourth, advances in technology caused the world to shrink. These new technologies are not mere tools that we use; they "fundamentally alter our perception of the self, the

---

1. Paris, *End of Sexual Identity*, 24.
2. See Davies and Loughlin, *Sex These Days*.
3. Davies and Loughlin, *Sex These Days*, 25–27, 35–46.
4. Hauerwas, "Moral Value of the Family," 155–57, 164–65.
5. Wilcox, *When Marriage Disappears*, 66.
6. Finer, "Trends in Premarital Sex," 73–78.

other, and the world."⁷ For example, the internet makes it easier for people to connect through online dating, while at the same time, providing a place for sexual expression behind a veil of anonymity. Finally, the influence of religion over sexual practice has diminished. Western society has shifted from a "religiously ordained natural order to a scientifically grounded secular framework."⁸ In many ways, the contemporary landscape bears little resemblance to the setting in which Augustine wrote.

In spite of these differences, I will argue that Augustine's three goods of marriage continue to hold a defining place in contemporary discourse on sexual ethics. The central components of Augustine's theology of marriage have guided Christian sexual ethics for centuries and as such are deeply imbedded in current theological discussions. Either explicitly or implicitly, contemporary authors are responding to the marital goods of procreation, fidelity, and permanence. In this chapter, I will examine the work of four contemporary authors who seek to revise the church's traditional theology of marriage. The authors surveyed in this chapter are responding to the changing sexual norms described above, as well as the more specific question of the place of same-sex-attracted individuals and their relationships within the church. I will begin with Elizabeth Stuart who argues that marriage is a patriarchal institution that should be rejected and replaced by friendship as the preferred model for relationship. In her criticism of marriage, Stuart rejects each of the three goods of marriage and supplies three goods of friendship in their place. Next, I will engage the work of Adrian Thatcher who argues that, contra Stuart, marriage should be revised, not abolished. As such, Thatcher maintains the importance of fidelity and permanence to Christian marriage but rejects procreation as a necessary good. Third, I will examine the work of Eugene Rogers who, like Thatcher, upholds fidelity and permanence, but reassesses the importance of procreation. Finally, I will analyze the work of Robert Song who defends Christian marriage as a creation good while exploring the importance of the advent of Christ for the possibility of new relational vocations grounded in eschatology. We begin with this set of authors because they provide distinct responses to questions regarding the nature of Christian marriage, the challenge presented by same-sex relationships, and the church's response to wider society.

The chapter will proceed by examining each author's theology of marriage/relationship and the implications of that theology for Augustine's three goods of marriage. As will become clear, the issue of procreation is of vital importance to contemporary revisionists' accounts of sexual ethics.

7. Ornella, "Posthuman Pleasures," 316–17.
8. Ernst, *Histories of the Normal and Abnormal*, 4.

Procreation is perhaps the greatest theological hurdle to the church's inclusion of same-sex relationships. Because each of the authors in this chapter seeks to make space for same-sex relationships, careful attention will be paid to how each author engages with the good of procreation. Finally, I will put each author in dialogue with the work of Augustine. My main interest in this exercise is not to judge the author based on his or her agreement with Augustine, but instead to see how Augustine might both challenge certain lines of thought and illuminate new pathways that might not be available to each author on his or her own terms.

Elizabeth Stuart: Theology of Friendship

Elizabeth Stuart's project, *Just Good Friends: Towards a Lesbian and Gay Theology of Relationship*, calls for a theology of relationship grounded on the relational category of friendship rather than marriage.[9] To present a new theological starting point from which to discuss relationships, she must first offer a thorough critique of the church's traditional position. My exposition of Stuart will begin with an examination of her criticisms of the church's traditional theology of marriage. Next, I will describe her theology of friendship and the impact of that theology on the three goods of marriage. Lastly, I will analyze points of agreement and areas of tension between Stuart's friendship and Augustine's theology of marriage.

Criticism of Marriage and Family

Stuart criticizes the institution of marriage in three ways. She begins with a genealogical critique. Stuart argues that the advent of marriage coincides with the rise of patriarchal societies.[10] According to this narrative, the invention of agricultural technology allowed men to take over the plant-gathering roles traditionally held by women. As men tended the soil and reaped a harvest, they assumed a place of ownership over the land and its fruits. To maintain control of their property, men developed the concept of male heredity. Through this mechanism, the patriarch's power and possessions were passed on to a male heir. To ensure that the heir belonged to the patriarch's bloodline, it became necessary to control the sexual activity of women. Thus monogamous marriage "was born to ensure a woman's

---

9. For other works reclaiming the importance of friendship as a relational category, see Hunt, *Fierce Tenderness*; Raymond, *Transsexual Empire*; Vasey, *Strangers and Friends*.

10. Stuart, *Just Good Friends*, 110–11.

faithfulness to her man."[11] In further support of this narrative, Stuart draws on the work of Engels. He writes, "The first class antagonism which appears in history coincides with the development of the antagonism between man and woman in monogamous marriage, and the first class oppression with that of the female sex by the male."[12] Though the church has attempted to disrupt this narrative through the use of theological language of equality, Stuart argues that, in practice, marriage has always been a labor relationship of inequality, designed by men for the purpose of economic control achieved through the oppression of women.[13]

Second, Stuart employs an empirical critique of marriage. She notes that throughout much of its history, the church has espoused a positive and robust theology of marriage. As previously seen, Augustine articulated three primary goods of marriage: procreation, fidelity, and sacrament. But he also pointed to the "friendly association [of the marriage couple]" as an important good.[14] Over time, the church further developed his theology of marriage. In the seventeenth century, The Book of Common Prayer asserted that marriage exists not only for procreation and a remedy against sin but also for "the mutual joy; for the help and comfort given one another in prosperity and adversity."[15] The writers of Vatican II spoke glowingly of the "unity of marriage . . . made clear in the equal personal dignity which must be accorded to man and wife."[16] In spite of the language of friendship, mutuality, and equality expressed in these documents, Stuart argues that the experience of most married people falls well short of the theological ideal. Citing a variety of statistics from the late 1980s and early 1990s, the author asserts that marriage is plagued by high rates of divorce and infidelity. She also argues that marriage is often a dangerous place for women. From marital rape to other cases of physical and emotional abuse, women bear the burden of this patriarchal institution.[17] Based on this data, Stuart concludes that the gap between professed theology of marriage and lived experience is wide. Quoting David Oliphant, "Any attempt by the Church or any other organization to hang on to old idealism about marriage has got to face and

11. Stuart, *Just Good Friends*, 111.
12. Engels, "Origin of History and the Family," 233.
13. Stuart, *Just Good Friends*, 107, 112.
14. Augustine, *Good of Marriage*, 22.
15. Rogers, "Celebration and Blessing of a Marriage," 46.
16. Flannery, *Vatican Council II*, 952.
17. Stuart, *Just Good Friends*, 107–8.

give account for this terrible reality."[18] Based on the experience of married people, Stuart declares that marriage is a failed ideal.

Finally, Stuart offers a hermeneutic critique of the church's use of Scripture in its theology of marriage. Stuart employs a feminist hermeneutic model which seeks to challenge traditional readings of dominant scriptural passages on sex and marriage, while reclaiming lesser-used passages which further problematize traditional positions.[19] She engages two key New Testament passages on marriage: 1 Corinthians 7 and Ephesians 5. Commenting on 1 Corinthians 7, she acknowledges that many interpreters emphasize the mutuality in Paul's commands to the married couple. For example, authority over the spouse's body and access to conjugal rights applies to both the husband and the wife (1 Cor 7:3–4). However, Stuart contends that any notions of mutuality found in 1 Corinthians must be read alongside the rest of Paul's theology. She argues that the term "authority" (*exousia*) is tied to "notions of slavery" and a "context of complete capitulation" for Paul.[20] In Pauline thought, she writes, "to have authority over another's body is to have complete power over it."[21] The language of domination becomes more complicated when considering the plight of women in Paul's context. Though Paul indicates that this power over one's spouse is reciprocal, Stuart argues it is both "naïve and foolish" to believe that one's experience of power in the marriage bed would differ greatly from one's experience of power outside the home.[22] Here, Stuart affirms a connection between the public and private spheres of life. She writes, "Whilst men retain primary control over women's bodies in society at large, men and women are never going to have equal authority over each other's bodies."

Stuart also sees a connection between slavery and New Testament marriage language in Ephesians 5. Wives, like children and slaves, are commanded to "'submit to,' 'be subject to,' 'obey' (all the meanings of *hypotassetai*) their husbands."[23] Wives are the property of husbands. Furthermore, the unequal relationship between husband and wife in Ephesians 5 is used as a metaphor for the inherently unequal divine/human

---

18. Stuart, *Just Good Friends*, 109. See Oliphant, "Modern Marriage," 19.

19. For other examples of this hermeneutic by feminist authors, see Ruether, *Sexism and God-Talk*; Trible, *Texts of Terror*; Trible, *God and the Rhetoric of Sexuality*. For a womanist example, see Thistlethwaite, *Sex, Race, and God*. For an example from queer theory, see Moore, *God's Beauty Parlor*.

20. Stuart, *Just Good Friends*, 123.

21. Stuart, *Just Good Friends*, 123.

22. Stuart, *Just Good Friends*, 123.

23. Stuart, *Just Good Friends*, 124.

covenant relationship.[24] While Stuart does not deny the importance of the covenant metaphor in Scripture, she argues that covenantal imagery should not be applied uncritically. This is an important criticism. Throughout the Bible and in the ancient Near East, covenants were made between unequal parties: God and humans, king and subjects, conqueror and conquered.[25] However, the majority of contemporary theology asserts that there exists an equality of being in men and women. Stuart argues that the proper application of a covenant between unequal parties to a marriage between equal, (traditionally) sexually differentiated beings must account for this disconnect. Problems arise from the fact that Scripture has failed to make this distinction. In summary, Stuart argues that in these dominant passages, marriage is defined in terms of power and submission. She writes, "At the heart of the metaphor, both in the Hebrew and Christian Scriptures, is an understanding of marriage very close to slavery," which does not account for the pain and suffering of women who enter that institution.[26]

Continuing her feminist reading of the Bible, Stuart turns her attention to a series of scriptural passages which challenge the church's traditional understanding of marriage through sexual subversion. She points to Tamar (Gen 38) who, in an effort to fulfill leverite marriage laws, violated the incest laws of Leviticus (Lev 18:16; 20:21) by having intercourse with her father-in-law. The situation is further complicated because Tamar was disguised as a prostitute. Yet, Stuart notes, this unusual relationship led to the birth of David.[27] In another example, Ruth flouts sexual law and custom by engaging in premarital sexual contact with Boaz (Ruth 3). As a Moabite, she would have been excluded from membership in the people of God (Deut 23:3–4). Yet, this non-traditional relationship led to the birth of David's grandfather, Obed. While Stuart uses Ruth as an example of breaking sexual law, it is important to note that Ruth's actions lead to her inclusion into the covenant, rather than the dissolution of covenant. Commenting on these examples, Stuart writes, "The Hebrew Scriptures are littered with stories that demonstrate Yahweh's purposes being forwarded by deliberate floutings of sexual convention and law—law which it was believed had come from the deity."[28] While emphasizing the importance of

---

24. Stuart, *Just Good Friends*, 125–26. "For the husband is the head of the wife as Christ is the head of the church, his body, and is himself its savior. As the church is subject to Christ, so let wives also be subject in everything to their husbands" (Eph 5:23–24).

25. Stuart, *Just Good Friends*, 133.

26. Stuart, *Just Good Friends*, 125.

27. Stuart, *Just Good Friends*, 127.

28. Stuart, *Just Good Friends*, 127.

sexual subversion in challenging the belief that Scripture presents a single, monolithic sexual ethic, she does qualify this position. She argues that certain elements of these stories, namely, "incest, adultery, or deception," should be rejected in Christian sexual ethics.[29]

Finally, Stuart surveys Jesus' teachings on marriage and family. She argues that Jesus challenged traditional familial relations in a variety of ways. First, Jesus' call of discipleship required immediate obedience, even if obedience required leaving family and other social obligations behind (Mark 1:16–20; Luke 9:59–62). Allegiance to the kingdom involves singular focus of one's affections, even requiring one to "hate" one's family (Luke 14:26–27). Second, Jesus redefined "family." When Jesus' family came to speak with him, he responded by elevating ties between members of the Kingdom of God over that of blood relatives (Mark 3:31–35).[30] Finally, Stuart examines Jesus' response to the Sadducees over the question of resurrection and marriage (Mark 12:18–27). Here, Jesus indicates that marriage will no longer exist in the eschaton. In response to these examples, Stuart concludes that, far from supporting pro-family rhetoric common in many contemporary churches, Jesus' teachings problematize family commitments.[31] Yet in spite of Jesus' teachings, Stuart asserts that both marriage and family have been elevated to the level of idolatry.[32] Based on these criticisms, Stuart concludes that marriage is unsalvageable, and therefore a new relational paradigm is needed.

Theology of Friendship

As a replacement for the church's harmful and outdated model of marriage, Stuart recommends a theology of relationship centered on friendship. The grounding for Stuart's theology of friendship relies heavily on her Christology. Her examination of the life, teachings, death and resurrection of Jesus results in two conclusions about the nature of friendship. First, friendship is lived in and expressed through the body. Throughout his ministry, Stuart argues, Jesus demonstrated great care for human bodies through acts of healing and through his concern for unloved bodies. His commitment to the worth of bodies was then transmitted to his followers. Stuart asserts

---

29. Stuart, *Just Good Friends*, 173.

30. For a detailed account which expands this argument, see Bennett, *Water Is Thicker than Blood*.

31. Stuart, *Just Good Friends*, 162–65. Stuart traces the rise of family at the expense of a theology of celibacy to the Protestant Reformation (*Just Good Friends*, 24).

32. Stuart, *Just Good Friends*, 109.

that Jesus' call of discipleship further illustrates the value of the body. Stuart writes, "Following him means literally getting up and walking off (Mark 1:16–20). It means standing with and among the non-persons; it means engaging in acted parables that draw attention to the presence and absence of God ... it means being prepared to be bodily tortured and killed."[33] Not only do the life and death of Jesus point to the importance of bodies, Stuart contends that his resurrection also indicates their worth. The bodily resurrection of Jesus signifies that humans do not escape the body in death. Humans were created with both body and soul and will exist in the eschaton as both body and soul.[34] Since the worth of bodies is affirmed by Jesus and human life is lived in the body, Stuart concludes that our relationships, including friendship, must be expressed in the body.

Second, friendship is passionate. Stuart argues that the gospels, especially Mark, portray Jesus as a "man of passion."[35] In Jesus, we see one who weeps at the death of a friend, angrily overturns tables in the temple, and experiences anguish in the garden. Stuart laments that the Christian tradition, with Augustine as the primary culprit, has had a wary and often negative understanding of passion. In response, she calls for "a fundamental revolution of the theological imagination" suggesting that theology "start from the revolutionary position that passion is good."[36] However, it is not always clear what the author means by "passion." While Stuart uses "passion" to refer to a variety of emotions, she also uses passion and love interchangeably.[37] For example, Stuart notes her experience of being reprimanded by individuals who understood her passion to be a "disability." She writes, "It became very clear that I was not actually supposed to love people. I was supposed to package away my passion for some future man."[38] The action of the first sentence (loving people) is the passion to be hidden away in the second, thereby equating love and passion. This tendency is found in her theology of friendship where friendship is defined as a passionate relationship of love for another.

A third characteristic of friendship is that it is a sexual relationship. According to Stuart, one of the key problems in discussions of sexuality is

33. Stuart, *Just Good Friends*, 148.

34. Stuart, *Just Good Friends*, 150–51, 191.

35. Stuart, *Just Good Friends*, 149.

36. Stuart, *Just Good Friends*, 192.

37. Stuart, *Just Good Friends*, 178. Stuart also recounts the story of a young woman who was instructed by teachers in her church to love everyone. The young woman "fell passionately 'in love'" with the people around her and was reprimanded for her passionate love.

38. Stuart, *Just Good Friends*, 178.

the attempt to determine the demarcation between sexual and non-sexual activity.[39] In practice, this division provides the foundation for differentiating between licit and illicit actions which occur between, for example, unmarried couples. Activity which is considered "sexual" is forbidden to unmarried couples while non-sexual activity is allowed. Stuart believes that this division between sexual and non-sexual activity is unhelpful and leads to compartmentalization of human relationships and the criteria by which those relationships are judged.[40] In response, Stuart asserts that sexuality is a broad term that refers to more than desire for genital contact. Sexuality, she contends, is fundamental to personhood and "has an effect upon the whole of a person's relating."[41] Based on this understanding, Stuart argues that all relationships are sexual. Thus, all of our actions in those relationships have a sexual dimension to them as well. Stuart argues that separating relationships into sexual and non-sexual categories, thereby failing to acknowledge the sexual dimension which all relationships contain, has two consequences. First, it leads to isolation as individuals are prohibited from discussing their sexual feelings. Stuart argues that isolation is the antithesis of friendship.[42] Second, the sexual/non-sexual division creates a double standard by which relationships are judged. For example, a (sexual) Christian marriage is judged on the basis of procreation, fidelity, and sacrament, while a (presumably non-sexual) friendship is judged by different criteria. By eliminating the distinction, she argues, all relationships can be judged by the same criteria. According to Stuart, honesty and justice are the standards by which all relationships should be judged.[43]

Fourth, Stuart asserts that friendship has an important place in salvation history. To expand this claim, it is necessary to briefly sketch some of Stuart's wider theological convictions, starting with her understanding of the relationship between creation and sin. Stuart writes, "We are called to relate to the world in friendship. . . . In other words, we are called to delight in the world around us, to approach it in a positive rather than negative manner. We are called to engage with it, not fly from it; we are called to

---

39. Stuart notes that penetration and orgasm have been the two primary dividing lines between sexual and non-sexual acts. As penetration is connected to psychological desires to dominate and orgasm is concerned with a male desire "to bolster the male ego," both are defined in the terms of patriarchy and should be disregarded (*Just Good Friends*, 77–79).

40. Stuart, *Just Good Friends*, 84.

41. Stuart, *Just Good Friends*, 72.

42. Stuart, *Just Good Friends*, 84

43. Stuart, *Just Good Friends*, 86.

work for justice within it."⁴⁴ Stuart has a positive view of the doctrine of creation. Creation, both in its created state and as it is now, is good. At the same time, the call for individuals to work for justice hints at Stuart's hamartiology. While she does not provide a comprehensive definition in this work, several statements reveal her understanding of sin. For example, in her discussion of the limits of friendship, Stuart argues that humans cannot befriend everyone because we are "broken-hearted people, formed by our previous relationships."⁴⁵ Here, the internal brokenness that individuals experience is somehow connected to external relationships, rather than to one's inherent sinfulness. In another passage, Stuart further clarifies her understanding of sin. She writes, "It is the tragedy of the human condition that we are socially constructed, that we are all (no matter how subversive) formed by our environment."⁴⁶ Here, sin has a clear social dimension that forms and constructs human life, ordering social relations through norms of sex, gender, class, etc.⁴⁷ Finally, she writes, "We live out our relationships in a context of structural sin and we are formed by that context. It is our 'original sin' stamped onto us at a frighteningly early age."⁴⁸ This quote is the only mention of original sin in her book. Here, she makes clear that, in her theology, sin is societal structure that is external to human beings.

According to Stuart, friendship is the means by which wholeness is restored, both to individuals and to the world. Friendship accomplishes this aim in several ways. First, friendship is a subversive fight against the evil powers of this world. Because it is a relationship of equality and inclusion, friendship allows humans to "break rank" with the societal structures of sin that encourage isolation and inequality.⁴⁹ Continuing the militaristic theme, Stuart argues that "every friendship we make is a triumph over the forces of sin."⁵⁰ Second, friendship represents a return to the relational ideal which God created. When bonds of friendship are formed, Stuart argues that "we are recovering creation as God created it to be."⁵¹ Third, friendship is the means of individual sanctification. It is the relationships "in which we become most fully what God intends us to be."⁵² Fourth, friendship is

44. Stuart, *Just Good Friends*, 214.
45. Stuart, *Just Good Friends*, 216.
46. Stuart, *Just Good Friends*, 194.
47. Stuart, *Just Good Friends*, 231–33, 180.
48. Stuart, *Just Good Friends*, 219.
49. Stuart, *Just Good Friends*, 43.
50. Stuart, *Just Good Friends*, 220.
51. Stuart, *Just Good Friends*, 44.
52. Stuart, *Just Good Friends*, 220.

an example of eschatological witness. Through these relationships, humans experience "a tantalizing foretaste of what life could be like."[53]

Based on these characteristics, Stuart defines friendship as "positive mutual encounter and influence which results in transforming behavior."[54] The individuals in this kind of relationship are, according to Stuart, like two pieces of clay coming together and mutually pressing on the other. Both pieces of clay remain forever changed by the encounter. While Stuart appeals to a variety of biblical stories to support her theology of friendship, her primary text is John 15:12–17, where Jesus calls his disciples "friends." According to Stuart, in these verses Jesus rejects the master/slave language found throughout Scripture in favor of the mutuality of friendship. Stuart argues that this master/slave dichotomy is foundational for discussions of marriage throughout the New Testament. Because Jesus rejects this model of relating, it is clear to Stuart that marriage should be rejected and replaced by the superior relational model of friendship.[55]

Friendship and the Three Goods of Marriage

Criticism of Procreation

Stuart's project represents a replacement for a traditional theology of relationship grounded in marriage. As such, her relational paradigm criticizes traditional understandings of the three goods of marriage: procreation, fidelity, and sacrament. Regarding the first good, Stuart argues that the church has tended to identify procreation as the primary telos of marriage to the detriment of other goods. This tendency takes a variety of forms. Some church traditions have made openness to procreation necessary for a marriage to be considered legitimate. Others have stated that procreation is the only permissible reason for sex. Stuart sees this singular focus on procreation as a denial of the goodness of the body and enjoyment of bodily existence.[56] In the church's traditional theological system, she argues, sexual intercourse is not a good in itself, but is good only in its ability to produce

---

53. Stuart, *Just Good Friends*, 44.
54. Stuart, *Just Good Friends*, 170.
55. Stuart, *Just Good Friends*, 170.
56. Stuart does acknowledge that this understanding of procreation and its relationship to marriage has been altered in some church traditions. The Book of Common Prayer asserts that marriage exists not merely for procreation (or lust aversion) but also for "mutual society, help, and comfort" for the marriage partners. Stuart also cites examples of theologians who are working to revise the church's stance on procreation (see Williams, "Toward a Theology," 130–43; Thatcher, *Liberating Sex*).

offspring. One's partner in marriage is not a person to whom sacrificial love is directed. Instead, he becomes an instrument by which the proper telos of marriage is accomplished. According to Stuart, this instrumentalization of sex and one's partner is an example of works-based righteousness. In response to this harmful theology, she argues that Christians need "theologies of sexuality which begin with genuine belief in the goodness of bodies, passion and sexuality in themselves, rather than 'works-justification' theologies which justify the existence and enjoyment of these things only if they produce children or some other 'goods.'"[57]

According to Stuart, the propensity to focus on the procreative telos of marriage has made it difficult for the church to discuss sexuality in a coherent way. She argues this difficulty occurs because the church has attempted to assign an inherent meaning to an activity where none exists. Stuart supports this claim by appealing to the relationship between actions and meaning. She argues that actions have no meaning in themselves. Instead, actions can only be understood "in the course of interactions and over the course of time [as] individuals and societies spin webs of significance."[58] In other words, specific actions are given meaning in a specific context. It is the relational context, not the act itself, which is key to interpreting and understanding the action.[59] Stuart argues that by giving sex one universal meaning or telos, the church is unable to recognize positive characteristics such as mutuality or justice in relationships that do not fit the one universal meaning ascribed to the one permissible sexual relationship: marriage. Many church traditions have no place for loving cohabitation or intentionally non-procreative marriages which display a plethora of other goods. As an additional consequence to its focus on procreation, the church has struggled to recognize and denounce various forms of violence that can and do exist in some procreative marriages.[60] If the primary purpose of marriage is procreation, then various forms of abuse are, at best, of secondary importance.

Through these criticisms, Stuart severs any necessary link between licit sexual relationships and procreation. As this chapter will demonstrate, Stuart is not alone in making this move. Judgment concerning the efficacy of such an argument, as well as an examination of the doctrinal concerns at stake in removing the theological link between procreation and a couple's sexual relationship, will be examined in detail later in this chapter.

57. Stuart, *Just Good Friends*, xviii.
58. Stuart, *Just Good Friends*, 73.
59. Stuart, *Just Good Friends*, 80, 190.
60. Stuart, *Just Good Friends*, 73–74.

Criticism of Fidelity

In her support of friendship, Stuart also criticizes and redefines fidelity. She argues that the language associated with traditional understandings of faithfulness is problematic. Stuart offers two examples. First, fidelity in marriage is often connected to the concept of covenant: a binding commitment to remain faithful to one's partner. However, as previously noted, covenants were made between unequal parties: king and subject, divine and creature, conqueror and vanquished. Stuart argues that this inequality, perpetuated in marriage covenants, has no place in a theology of relationship between two equal parties. Second, the inequality of covenantal partners is often accompanied by language of servitude. In his influential chapter on marriage, the Apostle Paul described marital fidelity in terms of bodily ownership. Stuart acknowledges that marriage covenants have also included language of love in their wording, but this love "was always one-sided and referred to respect and obedience: the vassal or conquered was commanded to 'love' the lord or conqueror."[61]

Because Stuart's theology of friendship seeks to replace relational models built on the language of power and submission with a model grounded in mutuality, fidelity must be redefined. In this new paradigm, faithfulness has several characteristics. First, it is a relationship-specific term. As previously mentioned, actions have no inherent meaning in Stuart's theology. Instead, actions are given meaning in a relational context. Therefore, fidelity is unique to each relationship and is defined by the friendship partners.[62] Stuart adds an important clarification to this understanding of fidelity. She argues that allowing the relationship partners to set the parameters of fidelity is not mere liberal consent dressed in theological language. Whatever its benefits, consent still functions in a society of unequal power where relationships are based on ownership and debt. In this context, two adults can consent to engage in an act of prostitution. By contrast, Stuart argues that the rules of friendship prohibit the use of another's body solely for selfish enjoyment, whether or not consent is granted.[63] In response, she asserts that friendship requires partners to meet a higher standard. She writes, "Consent is not a firm enough moral basis to build a sexual ethic upon. Free love is not liberation: justice is liberation."[64] Thus, while partners can and must define

---

61. Stuart, *Just Good Friends*, 133.
62. Stuart, *Just Good Friends*, 224.
63. Stuart, *Just Good Friends*, 224–25.
64. Stuart, *Just Good Friends*, 193.

what fidelity means in the context of their relationship, that definition must coincide with justice and mutuality.

Stuart's emphasis on the contextual nature of fidelity has an important consequence for the category. While keeping commitments to one's partner is vital to fidelity in friendship, the meaning of those commitments is defined by the given relationship or occasion. Because relationships and the settings of those relationships change over time, Stuart argues that we are always free to make new commitments when new circumstances arise. Based on this logic, commitments which rely on prior circumstances for their validity are not necessarily binding. This move allows Stuart to argue that monogamy is not a necessary component of relational faithfulness. For Stuart, monogamy is problematic because it places a limit on the expression of love and passion. By contrast, friendship is characterized by openness; it is not "a relationship that can only be achieved with one or two people at a time."[65]

The openness of friendship is grounded in the doctrine of God. Stuart argues that Scripture presents a complex picture of God. Throughout the Bible, images of a faithful God are placed side by side with images of "God as the promiscuous lover who loves everything and everyone created—an idea which has constantly grated with many Jews and Christians who would prefer their God to be strictly monogamous."[66] Stuart argues that the universal God of universal love, rather than the tribal God, is the basis for expressing universal sexual love in human relationships. Stuart writes, "Christians are called to be promiscuous with their love. The message of the gospels is that our love is called out beyond our families, into the world. Nor is love something 'merely spiritual' or intellectual—it is embodied, it involves us taking our bodies to other people's bodies."[67] Thus, the faithfulness of friendship does not require or expect monogamy.

For those concerned about the potential negative consequences posed by the ongoing opportunity to renegotiate one's commitments paired with a reading of Scripture that encourages an ever-expanding expression of love, Stuart is quick to point out that this view of fidelity is not a license for sexual freedom. While the expression of love should be ever-widening, it is possible to be unfaithful to one's partner. She writes, "The sin of friendship is betrayal."[68] Thus, fidelity is redefined as trust between friendship partners. In this system, honesty is the only limit to fidelity. Stuart makes clear that friendship is not a relationship without boundaries;

---

65. Stuart, *Just Good Friends*, 48.
66. Stuart, *Just Good Friends*, 190.
67. Stuart, *Just Good Friends*, 213.
68. Stuart, *Just Good Friends*, 219.

there exist "soft boundaries" open to negotiation and renegotiation by the friendship partners.[69] She acknowledges the risk associated with soft boundaries, compared to the relative security of firm rules governing traditional relationships. However, her project is concerned with overcoming the tendency to categorize relationships and apply different standards to the various relational groupings. She asserts that friendship, with its necessarily soft boundaries, has the advantage of requiring individuals to "take full responsibility for all [their] relationships."[70]

Despite her criticism of traditional views of fidelity and the move toward a single, relational category with fluid boundaries, Stuart's theology of friendship does have an elevated category. As friends journey together and grow in their level of trust and self-giving, she argues, they may reach a place of "radical vulnerability."[71] She defines this category as a relationship where friends shed all pretense and reveal themselves entirely to each other. Such intimacy is only achieved over time and relies on confidence that one's partner will remain steadfast throughout that process. What is important for this analysis of Stuart's understanding of fidelity is her conviction that, due to the existence of sin in social systems which discourage both honesty and self-giving, it is "virtually impossible" to have more than one relationship of radical vulnerability at a time.[72] Deeper levels of trust and vulnerability require a hardening of Stuart's loose boundaries and a narrowing of the pool of persons with whom love and vulnerability are shared.

Criticism of Permanence

A theology of friendship presents a direct challenge to the permanence of marriage precisely because friendship is a category of relationships that is not intended to be permanent. Stuart notes that friendships terminate for a variety of reasons. Their conclusion may come about because one partner "finds . . . empowering love elsewhere" or because "the relationship is suffocated by social structure" or simply because over time "people change."[73] Beyond this empirical evidence, Stuart offers a theological reason for her rejection of permanence based on her doctrine of God. Stuart rejects theories of divine immutability and, consequently, asserts that God is a being who is impacted by humans just as humans are impacted by the divine. Because

---

69. Stuart, *Just Good Friends*, 225.
70. Stuart, *Just Good Friends*, 225.
71. Stuart, *Just Good Friends*, 220–21.
72. Stuart, *Just Good Friends*, 222.
73. Stuart, *Just Good Friends*, 229.

God's relationship with creation is dynamic and open to change, human friendships also share this characteristic. Once the possibility for change enters the equation, "nothing is permanent."[74]

While affirming the importance of keeping commitments to one's friendship partner, Stuart argues that there are times when it is beneficial and healthy for a relationship to end. She writes, "When a covenant becomes a positively oppressive force in people's lives, causing misery to all involved, then people should be allowed out of the tomb into the possibility of resurrection. It seems to me that perhaps the ultimate test . . . is knowing when to let go of the covenant and each other and when to attempt to ride out the inevitable storms of relationships. Relationships do end, passion does die, hearts do turn cold."[75] Here, Stuart takes seriously the experience of individuals in traditional covenantal relationships. Many individuals, often women, have experienced violence at the hand of a marriage partner. It is possible for churches to sanction such violence through appeals to the permanence of marriage. In such cases, Stuart argues that divorce is not the ultimate relational sin and can be a source of new life for the victim. The quotation also reveals an important qualification of Stuart's understanding of passion. Though she advocates for passion as one of the key qualities of friendship, Stuart acknowledges that passion is not a stable category. Since "passion does die" and "hearts do turn cold," relationships built on the foundation of passion will not stand the test of time.

While denying permanence as a necessary element of friendship, Stuart does make two caveats. First, she is open to friends making lifelong commitments to each other.[76] Because the relationship partners determine the parameters of the relationship and there are endless possible configurations of such an agreement, lifelong commitments are a theoretical option. Second, Stuart argues that childrearing changes the complexion and expectations of a relationship. Children assume lifelong commitments from their parents. If two friends intend to conceive or adopt a child, "they have a right to expect of each other life-long commitment to and responsibility towards that child."[77] While this statement does not preclude some level of change in the trust and self-giving toward one's friendship partner, the commitment to maintaining a "loving, stable, passionate environment" for the child does require affirmation of relational permanence.[78]

---

74. Stuart, *Just Good Friends*, 41.
75. Stuart, *Just Good Friends*, 229.
76. Stuart, *Just Good Friends*, 221.
77. Stuart, *Just Good Friends*, 222.
78. Stuart, *Just Good Friends*, 222.

Three Goods of Friendship

In summary, Stuart rejects marriage because she believes it is grounded in patriarchal ideas of domination and submission. Each of the three goods of marriage stems from male readings of Scripture which should be rejected as well. In place of patriarchal marriage, Stuart suggests friendship as an appropriate model of relationship. Friendship is based on mutuality and equality, not domination and submission. As such, Stuart offers three new goods which better reflect her theology of relationship. Such relationships are "based upon mutual acceptance, respect and delight."[79]

Stuart & Augustine

As has become evident through this analysis of her work, Stuart is in direct dialogue with Augustine and the subsequent tradition that bears his name. It is now necessary to tease out the doctrinal concerns at stake in some of the key moves that she makes. To that end, I will now examine a series of questions and issues that arise when Stuart's work is placed alongside Augustine's thought.

The first issue for discussion is the origin of marriage. While Stuart traces the beginning of the institution of marriage to the rise of patriarchy, Augustine would go further back in primeval history. According to Augustine, God declared that it was not good for the first human to be alone (Gen 2:18). In response, God provided a partner for the first human. The creation of these two beings for the purpose of "friendship" and "companionship" is the origin of marriage in Augustine's theology.[80] From an Augustinian perspective, tracing the origin of marriage to the rise of patriarchy leads Stuart to an incorrect analysis of marriage. The result is that Stuart confuses criticism of some manifestations of marriage with criticism of the institution itself. This theological difference between Augustine and Stuart points to a larger source of theological disagreement between the authors. Experience is the starting point for Stuart's theological reflection. Her three primary criticisms of marriage outlined earlier in this chapter (genealogical, empirical, and even hermeneutical) rely on experience as their foundation. Stuart elevates experience over Scripture because she is wary of power and control involved in biblical interpretation. From the formation of the canon in the first century CE to the subsequent church councils formed to define orthodoxy, Stuart asserts that the interpretation

---

79. Stuart, *Just Good Friends*, 80.
80. Augustine, *Good of Marriage*, 1; *City of God* 12.22.

of Scripture has been presided over by powerful men. If patriarchy is woven into the fabric of scriptural interpretation, then feminist theologians, as well as queer theologians, need to begin their theological reflection from a place other than that which is controlled by "the winners of past struggles . . . white, Western, male prelates."[81] Therefore, Stuart begins with experience because "it is in our interaction with life around us that revelation occurs."[82] By contrast, Scripture is not only the starting point for Augustine's theological reflection, it is also the element that is given the most weight. Augustine does not deny the important role that experience plays in the interpretation of Scripture. In *Confessions*, Augustine wrestles with his life experience. Yet, throughout the book, he continually points to the limits of his experience. For example, he notes that he does not remember his birth or anything that came before that event.[83] Pressing further, due to the effect of sin on perception, Augustine asserts that his understanding of his experience is always incomplete.[84] This problem of memory and perception forces him to turn to Scripture for answers that experience cannot provide. This disagreement between Augustine and Stuart highlights an important characteristic of theological reflection. The point from which one begins one's theological inquiry impacts not only the answers discovered, but also the shape of the questions themselves.

Second, Stuart's doctrine of sin has implications for her theology of relationships. According to Stuart, sin is primarily a social, external force that works on humans to obstruct their capacity to love openly and vulnerably.[85] Augustine would agree with the existence of social, structural sin. However, he would also argue that sin must be understood in terms of its impact within the individual. Per Augustine's reading of Scripture, sin is the result of the human will's turning from God and to the self. Whereas in Eden, the first humans experienced a unity of body and soul/will, the will no longer governs the body after the fall.[86] The result is that sin effects the entire human, both body and soul. According to Augustine, humans are born into a "body that is doomed to die. There is never a time when death is not at work in him."[87] Sin has a totalizing effect on human nature. If Stuart were to incorporate the personal dimension of sin, as seen in Augustine,

81. Stuart, *Just Good Friends*, 11.
82. Stuart, *Just Good Friends*, 12.
83. Augustine, *Confessions* 1.43.
84. Augustine, *Confessions* 4.103.
85. Stuart, *Just Good Friends*, 220, 227.
86. Augustine, *City of God* 13.12–15.
87. Augustine, *City of God* 13.10.

this move would impact the theological structure of her argument in several ways. For example, she asserts that friendships are passionate. Throughout her work, passion is always a positive category. However, if the self has been corrupted by sin, then the passions are not excluded from corruption as well. While passion may be a positive force in interpersonal relationships, it can also be damaging and destructive. Including an account of sin's impact on the individual might also lead Stuart to qualify the expectations she places on friendship. According to Stuart, friendship is the means by which wholeness is restored to the individual and to the world. Human friendship becomes a means of salvation. However, if sin has corrupted humankind, then this description asks friendship to solve a problem it is incapable of solving. Stuart's description places weight on friendship that the category was never meant to bear. If human nature has been compromised, then salvation must be offered from outside human nature. A more robust account of sin would enable Stuart to say that friendship is a good gift from God, while acknowledging that it is fallen because humans are fallen. Therefore, humans are encouraged to enjoy friendship as a limited good without placing undue expectations on the relationship.

Third, it is necessary to discuss the impact of Stuart's revision of Augustine's three goods of marriage. Stuart's new three goods of relationships, mutual acceptance, respect, and delight, do highlight an Augustinian theme that is often overlooked in his theology of marriage. Augustine argues that both marriage and sex exist, in part, for the good of the couple.[88] For Augustine, marital sex contributes to the couple's friendship.[89] So, there is an internal telos in his theology of marriage. However, in order to keep the relationship from becoming a self-seeking quest to fulfill one's desire for pleasure, Augustine argues that marriage requires a telos beyond the couple. Thus, procreation is a necessary good of marriage and marital sex. Beyond procreation, Augustine would also question Stuart's definition of fidelity. Stuart emphasizes the importance of the relational context in determining licit/illicit activity. This move allows her to argue that the relational partners determine the definition and parameters of faithfulness. While Augustine would agree with emphasizing the context of the relationship rather than focusing on specific genital acts, he would argue that the appropriate relational context for sexual activity is marriage. And the parameters of marriage, including definitions of faithfulness, are given in Scripture, rather than decided upon by the couple.[90] Allowing partners the opportunity to

---

88. Augustine, *Good of Marriage*, 22.
89. Augustine, *Good of Marriage*, 9.
90. Augustine, *Good of Marriage*, 13; *Commentary*, 52.

continually redefine fidelity based on ever-changing circumstances seems to mean that one's commitments are never broken. They are simply renegotiated. The result is that prior commitments are given no weight when deciding whether or not to make new commitments. Stuart's attempt to redefine fidelity results in the elimination of permanence as a relational good. According to Stuart, the only occasion where permanence still applies is when the relationship brings forth or adopts children. From a theological perspective, however, it is not clear how children change the nature of the relationship. The late addition of permanence when there are children is insufficiently integrated into Stuart's account. By contrast, Augustine argues that for Christian marriages, permanence is of the utmost importance. It is the one good that remains in effect regardless of whether the goods of procreation or fidelity are fulfilled.[91]

A final issue for examination is the impact of Stuart's doctrine of God on her theology of relationships. As previously mentioned, Stuart rejects monogamy by appealing to the universal love of God. She argues that the universal love of God is the basis for expressing universal sexual love in human relationships. This logic works because she rejects the image of a covenant God who chooses a people and remains steadfastly faithful to that people. When the image of a faithful God is removed from the equation, Stuart is able to provide a theological rationale for accepting the termination of friendships. Friendships can end because friendship does not rely on the God of the covenant for its rationale. However, based on her appeal to the universal love of God, it is unclear how Stuart can assert that "the sin of friendship is betrayal."[92] Betrayal relies on the logic of faithfulness seen most readily in the God of the covenant. Furthermore, Stuart's appeal to the God of universal love is brought into question by her inclusion of the relational category of "radical vulnerability," the pinnacle to which growing friendships aspire. Stuart believes that radical vulnerability can only be experienced with one person at a time, thereby limiting the sharing of love within human relationships. This limit is inconsistent with the ever-expanding love of the universal God in which Stuart grounds her theology of relationship. By contrast, Augustine consistently appeals to the God of the covenant. From the choosing of Abram to the rescue of the Hebrews from Egypt, to the release of Israel from exile, God consistently demonstrates fidelity to the covenant people.[93] While Augustine affirms the expanding nature of God's covenant seen

---

91. Augustine, *Good of Marriage*, 18; *Adulterous Marriages* 1.4–7.

92. Stuart, *Just Good Friends*, 219.

93. Augustine, *City of God* 10.312–14. See also Augustine, *City of God* 15.140–16.332, where Augustine recounts the history of God's faithfulness to Israel.

in the inclusion of the Gentiles, Augustine asserts that this event represents the culmination of God's promise to Abram, further demonstrating faithfulness to the covenant. The image of the covenant God provides Augustine with the logic to affirm the fidelity and permanence of marriage. Augustine argues that leaving a living spouse to marry another is akin to rejecting "the one God" so that one might serve other Gods.[94]

Despite these criticisms, Stuart's work serves an important pedagogical function for the church. She invites the church to consider the gap between the lived experience of parishioners and the relational theology that is professed by a specific church or denomination. She also reminds a predominantly male clergy of the power inherently involved in biblical interpretation and the devastating effects that women have experienced under the guise of the authority of Scripture. Finally, she asks whether the church has overemphasized the link between procreation and sex, resulting in sex and one's partner becoming means to ends rather than ends themselves. With an eye to these patriarchal challenges and to the question of the necessity of procreation to marriage, I now turn my attention to the theology of Adrian Thatcher.

Adrian Thatcher: Theology of Progressive Relationship

Thatcher's work represents a second attempt to revise the church's theology of marriage. While Thatcher shares many of Stuart's concerns about the relationships between patriarchy and marriage, he arrives at a different conclusion about the institution. Thatcher acknowledges and takes seriously the disparity between the ideal of marriage affirmed by the church and the experience of many married couples.[95] At the same time, he argues that while the dominant form of contemporary marriage may exhibit patriarchal tendencies, the institution is not inherently patriarchal.[96] The combination of these two convictions leads Thatcher to argue that, contra Stuart, marriage should not be abolished, but instead the church's theology of marriage needs revision. This section will begin with a description of Thatcher's theology of marriage found in his *Liberating Sex: A Christian Sexual Theology*.

---

94. Augustine, *Good of Marriage*, 49.
95. Thatcher, *Liberating Sex*, 114.
96. Thatcher, *Liberating Sex*, 91.

Theology of Marriage

Thatcher's theology of marriage is grounded in three Christian doctrines. The first is a particular type of Trinitarian theology called the "social" model.[97] According to Thatcher's description, social Trinitarianism describes God as "a community of persons-in-relation."[98] Thatcher highlights three features of this definition. First, the triune God exists as three distinct persons: Father, Son, and Spirit. Second, although they are distinct, the persons exist in undivided unity. Finally, each divine person "is constituted by its relation to the other."[99] For example, the Father is the Father because of the existence of the Son to whom he is Father. In the same way, the Son is the Son because of his relationship to the Father. According to Thatcher, the Spirit exists, in part, so that the love between the Father and Son might be celebrated and shared more widely. Based on this description, Thatcher argues that the triune God is characterized by "interdependence, interrelation, and communion."[100] Thatcher applies this social Trinitarian model to human relations by appealing to the *imago dei*. He argues that since humans are created in the image of God, there is an "overlapping" of the "being or nature of God with the being or nature of people."[101] Because of this overlapping of natures, humans are able to reflect the characteristics seen in the Trinity, albeit in a limited and finite way. Thus, humans are relational beings whose relationships are also characterized by "interdependence, interrelation, and communion."[102]

To better understand Thatcher's application of social Trinitarianism to human relations, it is necessary to discuss his epistemology. For Thatcher, Trinitarian relationality is the grounding for a theory of human relationality. But if that is the case, how does one come to know the particulars of

---

97. For a brief history of the social-trinitarian model, see Gresham, "Social Model of the Trinity," 325–43. An early analogy comparing the Trinity to human persons was made by the Cappadocian Fathers. In the fifth century, Augustine proposed a psychological model of the Trinity, with the human soul as the primary analogate. The Trinity was compared to the activities of remembering, knowing, and willing. While the social model received attention in the twelfth century by Richard St. Victor, Aquinas followed Augustine in appealing to the psychological model. The twentieth century brought with it a resurgence of the social model in Hodgson, *Doctrine of the Trinity*. Preeminent contemporary examples include Moltmann, *Trinity and the Kingdom*, and Zizioulas, *Being as Communion*.

98. Thatcher, *Liberating Sex*, 55.
99. Thatcher, *Liberating Sex*, 53.
100. Thatcher, *Liberating Sex*, 54.
101. Thatcher, *Liberating Sex*, 53.
102. Thatcher, *Liberating Sex*, 53.

the inner life of the Trinity? To address this question, Thatcher appeals to his understanding of incarnational Christology. He argues that Christ is the "revelation of divine love in [a] human, embodied, relational being."[103] In Christ, the second person of the Godhead, Trinitarian love is revealed and made available to the world. Thus, we have knowledge of the Trinity through the life, teachings, death, and resurrection of Christ. However, Thatcher argues that Christ is not the only source of knowledge of Trinitarian relationality. He makes two moves to expand this point. First, because Christ's revelation of God occurred in the flesh, Thatcher asserts that knowledge of God is learned in and through the body.[104] Revelation is experienced in the body. Second, Thatcher argues that the Incarnation is both a unique event in the person of Christ and the ongoing way through which God relates to the world. According to Thatcher, Incarnation is "re-enacted to different degrees and in different ways in all human bodily life."[105] According to this view, Incarnation is "the chief paradigm or exemplification of what God does, that is, the normal and most usual way of knowing God is in the body. . . . It is through human flesh that God became supremely known, and through the body that God continues to be known."[106] When these two moves are combined, human experience becomes the basis of one's knowledge of God. Thatcher writes, "In loving, embodied relationships we discover the nature of God."[107] Therefore, the various characteristics of the Triune God are revealed in the context of human relationships.

From his description of incarnational Christology, Thatcher deduces another characteristic of both divine and human love. He asserts that the love which exists between the persons of the Trinity is completely self-sufficient. However, in the Incarnation, God's love was revealed and shared with the world in the person of Jesus Christ. From this, Thatcher reasons that divine love, and, by extension, human love are meant to be shared.[108] One of the ways that human love is shared is through sexuality. Thatcher argues that sexuality is connected to our God-given nature and is therefore good.[109] He defines sexuality as "the way of being in, and relating to, the world as a *male* or *female* person."[110] Pressing further, Thatcher asserts

---

103. Thatcher, *Liberating Sex*, 27.
104. Thatcher, *Liberating Sex*, 43–44.
105. Thatcher, *Liberating Sex*, 2.
106. Thatcher, *Liberating Sex*, 40.
107. Thatcher, *Liberating Sex*, 2
108. Thatcher, *Liberating Sex*, 41, 89.
109. Thatcher, *Liberating Sex*, 104, 138.
110. Thatcher, *Liberating Sex*, 48.

that it is through sexuality that humans "experience and express the incompleteness of their individualities as well as their relatedness to each other as male and female."[111] According to this statement, sexuality has an outward orientation, revealing that humans are not meant to be alone. It is through sexuality that God invites humans into relationship with others, so that love might be shared. When the divine call to share love through sexuality is applied to the marriage relationship, Thatcher argues that married love exists, in part, for the good of the couple. But marital love, because it is based on divine love, "contains a dynamic which reaches beyond the couple in its drive to share itself more widely."[112] Therefore, marriage has an internal and an external telos grounded in the sharing of love.

Thatcher's incarnational Christology is closely tied to his theology of the Eucharist. He argues that the paradigmatic sharing of divine love occurs in the Eucharist, literally the "gift of the body," where Christ's body is broken, given for, and received by church.[113] Thatcher compares this sacrificial giving of oneself for the purpose of being received by another to the act of love-making between married partners. He writes, "The God incarnate in the Christ who gives his body in the supreme act of self-giving love for the world is the same God who is incarnate in the love which married partners share and in the physical way that love is expressed."[114] For Thatcher, both marriage and marital love-making are sacramental acts which facilitate "human participation in divine love."[115]

In summary, these three doctrines provide the foundation for Thatcher's sexual theology, and more specifically, his theology of marriage. The social Trinity discloses the relational nature of the divine, which is characterized by equality and interdependence. This relational nature is shared in a limited way by humans who are created in the image of God. The Incarnation discloses that divine love is meant to be shared and that grace is experienced through flesh. Thus, human relationships are characterized by the sharing of love. Finally, the Eucharist reveals the tangible, bodily way in which divine love is shared. In marriage, humans mirror this bodily giving and receiving of love in the act of love-making. Thus, Thatcher argues that marriage is a sacrament, where couples can potentially "experience the holy

---

111. Thatcher, *Liberating Sex*, 48
112. Thatcher, *Liberating Sex*, 89.
113. Thatcher, *Liberating Sex*, 41.
114. Thatcher, *Liberating Sex*, 89–90.
115. Thatcher, *Liberating Sex*, 92.

in and through the flesh."[116] Here, sacrament refers to a place where the eternal and the temporal touch.

Marriage as Progressive Relationship

One of the key features of Thatcher's theology is his assertion that the relationship of a couple should be viewed as a journey. From their initial meeting to dating, engagement, and marriage, Thatcher argues that the couple is on an excursion of growth from limited levels of commitment toward lifelong commitment. Throughout this journey, couples reevaluate their relationship and decide whether to proceed to the next stage of commitment or to go their separate ways. This process of discernment and evaluation continues until the marriage of the couple, at which point the couple is committed to each other for life. Thatcher likens this growth model of relationships to the process undertaken by a prospective monk or a nun when deciding whether to take their vows.[117]

The view that marriage is the result of the progressive journey of the couple toward deeper levels of commitment leads Thatcher to challenge what I will call the "ceremonial" theory of marriage. According to this view, the exchange of vows at a public wedding ceremony constitutes the beginning of a couple's marriage, establishing a clear temporal point from which to discuss pre-marital and post-marital activity.[118] Traditionally, this is also the point from which determinations are made about the legitimacy of sexual activity. Thatcher believes this approach is insufficient for three reasons. First, he argues that this view conflates the personal, religious, and legal meanings of marriage. While marriage does have certain legal dimensions through which marital rights are conferred on the couple by the state, the church can speak to other relevant meanings like the holiness or sanctity of marriage. Both of these may differ from the meaning that couples give to their dynamic marital relationship. Examples include belonging, security, fulfillment, etc. Second, if marriage is constituted solely by the public consent of the couple, then consummation is not necessary. However, this view runs contrary to Jesus' teachings where he describes marriage as two people becoming "one flesh" (Mark 10:6–8). Based on this passage, the church has asserted that consummation is necessary for marriage. Third, in Western church tradition dating back to Aquinas, it is the couple, not the minister, who administers the sacrament of marriage. The

---

116. Thatcher, *Liberating Sex*, 88.
117. Thatcher, *Liberating Sex*, 98.
118. Thatcher, *Liberating Sex*, 83–84.

"sacramental moment" occurs when consent is exchanged.[119] Thatcher argues that in order for a couple to give consent in front of family and friends at the wedding ceremony, it is temporally necessary for the couple to have previously consented to each other. Because the couple administers the sacrament through the exchange of mutual consent, it is possible to discuss the marriage of a couple prior to the public ceremony. Based on this logic, the wedding ceremony is not the beginning of a marriage. It is the public recognition of a marriage that already exists. When applied to a discussion of licit versus illicit sexual activity, Thatcher argues that is more helpful to speak of "pre-ceremonial" rather than pre-marital sex.

The importance of this distinction becomes evident as Thatcher pairs the idea that a wedding does not constitute a marriage with the assertion that having sex is not the same thing as intercourse.[120] Thatcher argues that the tendency to equate sex with intercourse is the result of a patriarchal construction that relies on two assumptions. The first is that procreation is the primary telos of sex. To address this concern, Thatcher argues that while humans provide a variety of meanings to sexual activity, including "exploration, recreation, expression, and procreation,"[121] the church has asserted that procreation is the primary purpose of sex. This development led to the construction of a "sexual repertoire" which encouraged couples to "[discharge] semen into the vagina as quickly, sinlessly, and productively as possible."[122] Thatcher argues that the focus on procreation through the placement of male seed into the vagina led to a definition of sex centered on male pleasure and male orgasm. Thus, male sexual experience became normative in defining sex as intercourse. A second patriarchal assumption is that there is an essential connection between pleasure and reproduction. Thatcher asserts that the sex-as-intercourse definition takes an anatomical connection between pleasure and procreation which exists in men's bodies and applies it to the sexual experience of women. For men, pleasure, orgasm, and the means of reproduction (sperm) are intimately connected in the sexual act. By contrast, women's bodies are created in such a way that it is possible to experience pleasure and orgasm through the clitoris, apart from the reproductive function of the vagina. In response to the patriarchal assumptions built into our understanding of sex, Thatcher argues that a new definition of sex along with a new sexual repertoire is needed that accounts for the sexual experience of women.

119. Thatcher, *Liberating Sex*, 82–83.
120. Thatcher, *Liberating Sex*, 99.
121. Thatcher, "Postmodernity and Chastity," 131.
122. Thatcher, *Liberating Sex*, 100.

Combining the convictions that because marriage is viewed as a progressive journey, rather than a ceremony, and having sex is not necessarily intercourse, Thatcher sets forth a set of three progressive categories of sexual experience. The first is sexual recreation. This category covers a wide range of activities from pubescent sexual exploration of the self to the sexual petting of a partner. Thatcher argues that both activities provide "essential sexual experience in the process of sexual awakening and curiosity to sexual maturity."[123] Three convictions lie behind this category. First, while sexuality is good because it is created by God, the desire associated with our sexuality is prone to distortion. Second, sinful sexual desire cannot be tamed. Thatcher argues that it is a "consuming power that will not be denied."[124] A third conviction is that continence is not a viable option for most people.[125] In our modern context, individuals are marrying later in life, increasing the number of years from puberty to marriage. Thatcher argues that requiring individuals to keep powerful lustful urges at bay for decades is both untenable and unpastoral. Based on these assertions, Thatcher concludes that the category of sexual recreation is needed. The author makes clear that he is not advocating an ethic whereby all sexual urges should be gratified. Instead, he is inviting the church to consider a new standard by which sexual activity is judged. The criterion that Thatcher uses to judge between licit and illicit sexual activity is the principle of proportionality. According to this principle, "the level of sexual expression should be commensurate with the level of commitment in the relationship."[126] When a couple's desire for sexual activity does not coincide with the appropriate level of commitment, he advocates a "theology of waiting."[127]

The second of Thatcher's progressive relational categories is sexual intercourse. Here, Thatcher distinguishes between penetrative and non-penetrative sex. Appealing to the teachings of Jesus, Thatcher asserts that intercourse adds a new dimension to the sexual relationship. He argues that prior to engaging in penetrative sex, the couple has not consummated the relationship and has therefore not yet become "one flesh."[128] Though not directly stated, presumably new responsibilities and expectations are placed on the couple at this stage of relationship. While Thatcher argues that intercourse is "experienced most profoundly when it is an expression

---

123. Thatcher, *Liberating Sex*, 103.
124. Thatcher, *Liberating Sex*, 69. See also Thatcher, *Liberating Sex*, 117.
125. Thatcher, *Liberating Sex*, 99–100.
126. Thatcher, *Liberating Sex*, 173.
127. Thatcher, *Liberating Sex*, 104–5.
128. Thatcher, "Postmodernity and Chastity," 136–37.

of love between married partners," he does make room for pre-ceremonial intercourse.[129] In order to make this move, Thatcher introduces a category of relationship called betrothal. Citing the work of John Spong, Thatcher defines betrothal as "a relationship that is faithful, committed, and public, but not legal or necessarily for a lifetime."[130] Because this relationship is characterized by a high level of commitment, sexual intercourse is considered licit. In essence, betrothal replaces the marriage ceremony as the temporal point of commitment from which sexual intercourse becomes licit. Thatcher insists that betrothal is a distinct type of relationship. Betrothal requires that the couple declare their intent to marry. This intention is what separates betrothal from cohabitation. And while they share several characteristics, betrothal also differs from marriage. Marriage is a lifelong commitment, where betrothal may or may not lead to the couple making permanent commitments to each other. Once the couple declares their intent to marry, betrothal allows the couple space to ascertain whether they should make lifelong marriage vows. Thus, Thatcher describes betrothal as a time of testing for the couple.[131] A further distinction is that while marriage is a relationship that may be open to children, procreation is denied to betrothed couples.

The third category of sexual relationships is the procreative relationship. Thatcher asserts that while unmarried couples can engage in sexual recreation and may have sexual intercourse while betrothed, procreation is an activity that is reserved only for marriage.[132] This is true, he contends, because children fundamentally alter the relationship of the parents to each other. At birth, the child brings with her new demands on the parent's time, priorities, etc. While acknowledging that children can grow and thrive whether or not they are raised by two parents, Thatcher argues that marriage is the context in which children are most likely to excel.[133] The reason for this flourishing is the congruency between the child's expectations and parent's commitment to permanent fidelity. Thatcher argues that children expect lifelong commitments. In marriage, "partners have made unbreakable promises to each other . . . and their commitment to each other is able to provide the stability and steadfast love their children require."[134] Drawing on the work of Aquinas, Thatcher

---

129. Thatcher, *Liberating Sex*, 101.
130. Thatcher, *Liberating Sex*, 105. See also Spong, *Living in Sin?*
131. Thatcher, *Liberating Sex*, 123.
132. Thatcher, *Liberating Sex*, 101.
133. Thatcher, *Liberating Sex*, 91. See also Thatcher, *Marriage after Modernity*, 142–49.
134. Thatcher, *Marriage after Modernity*, 153.

argues that having a child outside of wedlock is "against the interests of that child."[135] Because parents are responsible not only for having children but also for raising those children, Thatcher asserts that Christian ethics must only allow sexual practices which safeguard the interests of the child.

Thatcher's progressive relationship theory and his three categories of sexual experience challenge what he sees as a negative trajectory in church, namely, the tendency to overemphasize the importance of sexual activity and, by extension, sexual sin. If sexual activity is the church's principal focus and sex can only be licitly expressed in marriage, then a primary pastoral objective is to encourage couples to get married. Here, Thatcher worries, marriage becomes a means of avoiding sexual sin and might be advocated whether it is in the best interest of the individuals in question or not. Thatcher does not deny the importance of sexual activity, nor does he reject the existence of sexual sin. However, Thatcher does seek to alter the conversation. He advocates for a progressive relational system in which varying degrees of sexual expression are allowed so long as they are coupled with concordant degrees of commitment. Relationships are viewed as a series of progressive commitments culminating in the lifelong commitment of marriage. A lifelong commitment, not the opportunity for sexual expression, is the goal. The result of such a view, Thatcher contends, is that the marriage covenant is given more weight than sexual activity.

Appropriation of Augustine's Three Goods of Marriage

To this point in our discussion of Thatcher's work, we have examined the doctrines that support his theology of marriage and his conviction that relationships and their various levels of sexual expression are progressive in nature. We will now investigate the ways in which the revisions Thatcher makes to the church's traditional theology of marriage impact his articulation of the three goods of marriage.

Procreation

Thatcher regards procreation as a good of marriage. There are three key features of his understanding of procreation. First, procreation is a way that humans image God. According to Thatcher, humans are called to reflect the characteristics of the Trinitarian God in whose image they are created. Humans image God by reflecting God's relational qualities. Thus, humans image God by sharing love with others. Humans are also capable

---

135. Thatcher, *Marriage after Modernity*, 153.

of mirroring God's creative power. Through procreation, Thatcher argues, parents "participate in God through the experience of the mingling of the life-providing physical powers of the lovers' bodies," which he describes as a "surging intimation of the creative presence of God."[136] Through procreation, parents participate in the "creating and sustaining" of the world.[137] Second, Thatcher asserts that physical procreation is a possible telos of marriage, but not a necessary one. The advent of contraception through technological means has allowed for the separation of sex from its procreative telos. After noting the positive and negative impacts of such technology, Thatcher appeals to the "virtually unanimous [public] support" and use of birth control as evidence that a Christian sexual ethic must account for such a development. He provides an extended theological case in support of the use of technological contraception, which is beyond the scope of this chapter.[138] The important point for this discussion is Thatcher's conviction that "marriage need not be procreative in the physical sense."[139] Parents are free to "lovingly choose to bring children into the world" or to refrain from doing so.[140] At the same time, Thatcher wants to maintain the theological link between marriage and procreation. To accomplish this aim, he affirms an allegorical understanding of the command to be fruitful and multiply. Thatcher contends that non-procreative, "fruitful possibilities" exist in the relationship of the couple as they grow toward each other.[141] This possibility is clearly on display in the relationship of heterosexual couples who are unable to procreate. He argues that these childless couples serve as a reminder that the "fruitfulness and creativity of marriages is neither defined by, nor exhausted by, having children."[142] His allegorical reading of the divine command to be fruitful and multiply will be an important move in Thatcher's discussion of lesbian and gay relationships. Third, while Thatcher is keen to distance physical procreation from marriage, he does not completely divorce the two. He acknowledges that at some stage, most married couples will want to have children. He does not mention whether he thinks that this desire is the result of genetic predisposition or socialization. Nor does he present a theological account of this desire, where the longing to procreate is intrinsic to the concept of marriage. Instead, he states that when couples

---

136. Thatcher, *Liberating Sex*, 113.
137. Thatcher, *Liberating Sex*, 91.
138. Thatcher, *Marriage after Modernity*, 171–208.
139. Thatcher, *Liberating Sex*, 113.
140 Thatcher, *Liberating Sex*, 91.
141 Thatcher, *Liberating Sex*, 87.
142. Thatcher, *Liberating Sex*, 145.

desire to have children and choose to procreate, the child represents the "fulfillment of the couple's love" for each other.[143]

Fidelity

Thatcher also affirms fidelity as a good of marriage. For Thatcher, marital fidelity is grounded in the concept of covenant. He argues that Scripture describes God's covenantal faithfulness to "the world, the church, and all humanity."[144] Marital fidelity points to God's unwavering faithfulness to the world. Thatcher defines marital fidelity as a "life-long commitment to the [couple's] joint flourishing."[145] This definition includes sexual fidelity to a single partner for a lifetime. Thus, there is a connection between faithfulness and permanence in marriage. At the same time, the appeal to "joint flourishing" in this definition affords Thatcher room to discuss the existence of marriages that are harmful to one or both parties. Again, he highlights the gap between the church's ideal of marriage and the experience of married couples. While marriage can be a relationship of mutual encouragement and support, it can also be a locale for violence and degradation. This is the reason Thatcher refrains from using Paul's language of having "power over" the body of one's spouse in his discussion of fidelity.[146] When Thatcher's definition of fidelity is taken to its logical conclusion, two important implications arise regarding the relationship between faithfulness and permanence. If marital fidelity is a commitment to the flourishing of oneself and one's partner, fidelity can be broken by more than sexual unfaithfulness. Pressing further, if there are a variety of ways to be unfaithful, then it is theoretically possible for some examples of infidelity to be so egregious that they violate the permanence of the marriage bond.

Permanence

Thatcher holds permanence to be a necessary good of marriage. He asserts that it is the lifelong quality of a couple's commitment that "makes a marriage a marriage."[147] While a couple may renegotiate their level of commitment from the time of dating through betrothal, once they exchange consent to marry and become one flesh, they are permanently bound to each other.

---

143. Thatcher, *Liberating Sex*, 113–14.
144. Thatcher, *Liberating Sex*, 91.
145. Thatcher, *Liberating Sex*, 90.
146. Thatcher, *Liberating Sex*, 64.
147. Thatcher, *Liberating Sex*, 147.

CONTEMPORARY REVISIONS OF AUGUSTINE'S THEOLOGY OF MARRIAGE   107

At the same time, Thatcher does qualify this position. In surveying the various New Testament texts on the permanence of marriage, Thatcher asserts that divorce is forbidden by Jesus in Mark 10:11–12. However, Thatcher also notes an exception found in Matthew and Luke which permits divorce and remarriage if sexual fidelity has been broken (see Luke 16:18; Matt 5:31–32; 19:9). Thatcher's hermeneutic method takes the exceptions to be more normative than the rule forbidding divorce in Mark 10. To support this claim, Thatcher asserts that since Mark was written prior to the other gospels, it is probable that the writers of Matthew and Luke interpreted and modified Jesus' command in Mark in an effort to apply Jesus' teachings to their communities. Thatcher argues that the early church's practice of interpreting and applying the teachings of Jesus, exemplified by Matthew and Luke, is afforded to Christians today. Based on this logic, Thatcher writes, "The fornication exception generates other exceptions."[148] He does not provide a detailed list of the various activities which he believes violate fidelity and, by extension, the permanence of marriage. However, he points to marital violence as one such exception. In such a case, "divorce is simply demanded"[149] and remarriage is permissible.[150] Throughout this discussion of permanence, Thatcher is attempting to balance a delicate tension. On the one hand, marriage is meant to be a permanent commitment. On the other hand, marriage vows are made by sinful people living in a sinful world. Thatcher addresses this tension by encouraging the ideal of marriage while refusing to condemn those who do not fulfill their marriage vows.

Application to Lesbian and Gay Relationships

While Thatcher's primary aim is to articulate a theology of relationship, sexuality, and marriage for a heterosexual context, he also seeks to extend this theology to lesbian and gay relationships. He believes this move is necessary for three reasons. First, he asserts that sexuality and sexual orientation are gifts from God and are therefore good. Sexuality, he writes, "does not need to be renounced, concealed, pronounced sick, or regarded as deficient. . . . To do this is to disown what God has given."[151] While sexuality is distorted by sin and must be regulated, requiring lesbian and gay individuals to be celibate results in denying them the opportunity to express their sexuality. Thatcher argues that such a stance amounts to denying that the sexual part of a person

---

148. Thatcher, *Liberating Sex*, 121.
149. Thatcher, *Liberating Sex*, 118, 125.
150. Thatcher, *Liberating Sex*, 118, 125.
151. Thatcher, *Liberating Sex*, 137.

is created good by God. Second, Thatcher asserts that sexuality cannot be abstracted from personhood. He writes, "Sexuality is too much a part of a person's totality for it to be separated out from the rest of him or her, and repressed."[152] Finally, since humans were created by God to be lovers who participate in divine love and share love with others, and sexuality is the way that humans "experience and express the incompleteness of their individualities as well as their relatedness to each other as male and female," then the opportunity to share love through sexuality must be extended to lesbian and gay couples.[153] The result of these moves is that sexuality and its expression become essential to personhood in Thatcher's theology.

It is unclear how Thatcher is able to sustain the claim that sexuality need not be "renounced" or "repressed" when this claim is placed alongside his affirmation of faithfulness and permanence in marriage. Faithfulness, which Thatcher defines partly in terms of sexual exclusivity to one's partner, requires denying the fulfillment of sexual desires which are not directed toward one's partner. Also, Thatcher's qualified affirmation of permanence extends the denial of extra-marital sexual activity for the duration of the partners' lives. Furthermore, sexual renunciation is not only applicable to married or betrothed couples in Thatcher's theology of relationship. Prior to betrothal, he argues that a couple's level of sexual expression should correspond to the partners' level of commitment to the relationship. This commitment assumes relational fidelity. Based on Thatcher's account, Christian sexual ethics requires varying levels of sexual renunciation for both married and unmarried couples. This renunciation applies to both heterosexual and same-sex couples.

Extending the goods of Christian marriage to lesbian and gay couples requires Thatcher to make three moves. First, he must discuss the church's traditional conviction that the creation accounts indicate that sexual differentiation is a requirement for Christian marriage. To address this concern, he appeals to social Trinitarian theology. As stated above, the triune God, who is a community of equal persons in perfect relationship, is the grounding for Thatcher's theology of human relationships and marriage. More specifically, he argues that the "sharing in divine love" between Trinitarian Persons is the "basis for thinking about and having sex."[154] However, Thatcher writes, "In God each of the Persons transcends gender difference. The love between them is clearly not heterosexual."[155] If Trinitarian love is

---

152. Thatcher, *Liberating Sex*, 138.
153. Thatcher, *Liberating Sex*, 48.
154. Thatcher, *Liberating Sex*, 27.
155. Thatcher, *Liberating Sex*, 146.

the basis for the expression of human love, and divine love is not defined by sexual differentiation, then the expression of human love, specifically in marriage, need not be limited to sexually differentiated relationships.

Second, Thatcher addresses the belief that the Genesis command to "be fruitful and multiply" indicates a necessary connection between marriage and procreation. As previously mentioned, Thatcher asserts that procreation is a good of marriage and that the divine command to be fruitful still applies. Yet, he asserts that "fruitfulness . . . is neither defined by, nor exhausted by, having children."[156] Thatcher finds evidence for this statement in the existence of heterosexual childless couples and in the marriages of those who are beyond childbearing age. He argues that the church can respond to these groups in one of two ways. Either childless couples and the elderly are not married because of their inability to procreate, or fruitfulness must be understood to include more than physical procreation. Thatcher chooses the latter option and appeals to an allegorical interpretation of the divine command. He argues that lesbian and gay couples can fulfill the goods of fidelity and permanence in the same way that heterosexual couples satisfy these goods. However, regarding the command to be fruitful, same-sex couples engage in a different kind of reproduction than that of heterosexual couples. Thatcher maintains that both kinds of reproduction are legitimate ways of being obedient to the divine command. In this way, gay and lesbian couples can be compared to childless heterosexual couples, whose marriages are affirmed by the church.

Third, after addressing the two primary theological hurdles to the acceptance of lesbian and gay relationships, Thatcher discusses the differences that exist between heterosexual and same-sex couples. It is difficult to determine the importance that difference plays in Thatcher's theology. On the one hand, he emphasizes the similarities that exist between heterosexual and same-sex couples. For example, he describes the difference of sexual orientation by asserting that being gay is like "being left-handed in a right-handed culture."[157] The aim of this statement is to displace the homophobic fear that heterosexuals have toward lesbian and gay people by downplaying the differences between the two groups. To further emphasize what the two groups have in common, he argues that, regardless of orientation, all are susceptible to sexual sin and are in need of redemption and sanctification. Because of these similarities, Thatcher asserts that lesbian and gay relationships should be "subject to the same standards of self-discipline and personal holiness as

---

156. Thatcher, *Liberating Sex*, 145.
157. Thatcher, *Liberating Sex*, 137.

everyone else, no greater, no less."¹⁵⁸ Thus, because the differences between heterosexual couples and lesbian and gay couples are not exceedingly great, the goods of the institution of marriage should be made available to same-sex couples. On the other hand, Thatcher also asserts that gay and lesbian relationships are empirically different than heterosexual relationships. In a later work, Thatcher asserts that lesbian and gay partnerships are a different type of union. The difference between marriage and same-sex relationships is the biological ability to procreate. Thatcher holds that this difference is important precisely because it manifests itself biologically, which is "the most basic level of our being."¹⁵⁹ Because heterosexual marriage and same-sex unions differ on this foundational point, Thatcher argues that same-sex couples should be afforded the goods and privileges that accompany marriage, but that their unions should not be called marriage. In *Liberating Sex*, he refers to committed, monogamous, permanent same-sex relationships as "lifelong unions," while in *Marriage after Modernity*, he prefers the term "covenanted love."¹⁶⁰ Regardless of the label that is given to these monogamous, permanent relationships, Thatcher believes that same-sex couples should be afforded the same rights and privileges that married heterosexual couples experience. Through this argument, Thatcher seeks to strike a balance between elevating and diminishing the importance of difference.

Thatcher & Augustine

Two issues arise when Thatcher's work is placed alongside Augustine's thought. The first involves Thatcher's progressive relationship theory and his three categories of sexual experience. The system has several commendable elements. First, it recognizes the advent of readily available contraception and seeks to address its widespread use. It is no longer self-evident that sex leads to procreation. As such, the traditional sexual repertoire concluding in orgasm from vaginal intercourse and the very definition of what counts as sex needs reassessment. Second, Thatcher's relational theory emphasizes the context of the relationship over specific sexual actions. This context is defined, in part, by the couple's level of commitment, resulting in an emphasis of covenantal marriage over a preoccupation with sexual activity. Third, Thatcher invites the church to wrestle with the existence of a faithful, committed sexual relationship that is not a marriage. In spite of these contributions, difficulty arises in Thatcher's description of betrothal. According to Thatcher, betrothal is a

---

158. Thatcher, *Liberating Sex*, 138.
159. Thatcher, *Marriage after Modernity*, 299.
160. Thatcher, *Liberating Sex*, 144; *Marriage after Modernity*, 302.

non-procreative, sexual relationship defined by faithfulness, commitment, and a publicly-declared intent to marry. Prior to betrothal, sexual intercourse is not allowed. In effect, betrothal is a relational category which replaces marriage as the point at which intercourse becomes licit. Thatcher asserts that his approach has "clear advantages" to the traditional system.[161] For example, it emphasizes that procreation belongs to marriage and that marriage is a permanent commitment. However, it is unclear how much betrothal adds to a theology of relationship. Previous questions surrounding pre-marital, now pre-ceremonial, sex would now be replaced by discussions of pre-betrothal sex. While there may be merit to Thatcher's progressive theory of relationship and its accompanying sexual paradigm, it appears that the introduction of betrothal moves up the temporal point of discussion rather than altering the discussion in a substantive way.

The second issue for discussion is Thatcher's attempt to navigate the difference and similarity between same-sex couples and heterosexual couples. As mentioned above, he seeks to minimize the differences between these groups while acknowledging the difference in their experience. According to Thatcher, the key difference between these groups is the ability to procreate, which he describes in biological, rather than theological terms. His solution is to afford the same goods and privileges to heterosexual and same-sex couples under different labels: marriage versus lifelong union or covenanted love. Two questions arise from this proposal. First, is the ability to procreate the only substantive difference in the experience of sexually differentiated and same-sex couples? Second, does Thatcher's solution undermine the unique/different experience of gay and lesbian individuals? Marriage and "lifelong unions" or "covenanted love" are relationships defined by monogamy and permanence. They share the same goods and privileges. Based on Thatcher's description, these relationships appear to diverge in name only. The use of different labels to describe identical relationships may not adequately preserve the difference espoused by lesbian and gay individuals, but instead may result in homogenizing same-sex and heterosexual couples.[162]

---

161. Thatcher, *Liberating Sex*, 105.

162. O'Donovan, *Conversation Waiting to Begin*, 15. See also Song, *Covenant and Calling*, 89, where he writes, "Same-sex marriage on the liberal egalitarian model, whereby all difference is erased, might end up ironically being the most conservative of options, and the particular gifts that lesbians, gays, transsexuals and intersex people, as well as heterosexual couples wishing to explore forms of non-procreative vocation, might bring to the Church and to wider society would be suffocated in a smog of conformity."

Eugene Rogers: Sexuality and the Christian Body

I now turn my attention to the work of a third author seeking to revise the church's traditional theology of marriage. In his work *Sexuality and the Christian Body*, Eugene Rogers presents a defense of Christian marriage which seeks to provide a rationale for that institution which is broad enough to include both heterosexual and same-sex couples.[163] He also works to recover a theology of monasticism and celibacy for Protestants.[164] This section begins with a description of Rogers' theology of marriage. According to Rogers, Christian marriage mirrors God's election, reflects Trinitarian love, and sanctifies the body and sexual desire. Following a detailed examination of each of these emphases and the author's application of their logic to same-sex couples, I will assess the impact of Rogers' theology on Augustine's three goods of marriage. Particular attention will be directed toward Rogers' reassessment of procreation. Finally, I will examine several questions that arise when Rogers' work is placed alongside Augustine's theology of marriage.

Theology of Marriage

Rogers argues that the church has determined that marriage serves two primary purposes. Employing a broad generalization, he asserts that these teloi divide along Catholic/Protestant lines. The Roman Catholic Church tends to value procreation as the primary telos of marriage, while Protestants hold that marriage exists to control lust.[165] Rogers puts forth two criticisms of these views. First, he argues that the advent of readily available birth control has severed the self-evident link between marriage and procreation highlighted by Catholic doctrine. It is no longer obvious that marriage exists for and leads to procreation. Furthermore, the use of a partner for procreation or the proper channeling of one's sexual desire highlighted in Protestant thought risks reducing that partner to a tool. For these reasons, Rogers asserts that the traditional purposes espoused by Catholic and Protestant teaching are insufficient to sustain a robust theology of marriage. Therefore, a different foundation is needed. In response, he argues that Christian marriage is a "means of anticipating God's catching human beings up into that wedding feast that God celebrates in the life of the Trinity, an elevation that the tradition has

---

163. Rogers, *Sexuality and the Christian Body*, 3, 11.
164. Rogers, *Sexuality and the Christian Body*, 67.
165. Rogers, *Sexuality and the Christian Body*, 74.

had the wisdom to call consummation."[166] From this definition, Rogers argues that marriage serves three purposes: mirroring God's election, reflecting Trinitarian love, and sanctifying the body and sexual desire. Let us examine the ways that Rogers unpacks each of these claims.

Mirroring God's Election

First, marriage mirrors God's election. Rogers argues that in the Hebrew Scriptures, God freely chose a specific people and established a covenant with them. Broadly speaking, access to God was connected to membership in this chosen people group. Among males, circumcision was the sign that one was a member of God's covenant people. This covenant distinguished between Abram's family, who would eventually be known as the Jews, and the rest of the peoples of the earth. God promised to remain faithful to Abram's family, to bless them, and to bless the world through that family. God's election took a dramatic turn in the New Testament as Gentiles were grafted into the covenant by grace through faith in Christ. This engrafting or adoption of the Gentiles is attributed to the work of the Holy Spirit.[167] Rogers highlights that Gentiles, who have no claim to God, are brought into the covenant "as Gentiles, that is, uncircumcised, not keeping the law."[168] As we shall see, it is this move which propels much of Rogers' theology.

The acceptance of Gentiles as Gentiles has three important implications for Rogers. First, it allows him to pair election with a discussion of gender and sexuality. He writes, "Both sex and circumcision . . . involve the very highest work of Christ in dying for the community he loves—as well as the same part of the body."[169] Through this androcentric claim, Rogers argues that election of the Jews and adoption of the Gentiles are both concerned with the body, more specifically the penis. Thus, election and salvation involve maleness, (and hopefully) femaleness, and how one lives one's sexual differentiation. The move from talk of the body to that of sexual orientation requires further justification. The link between the two will be examined later in this chapter. Second, Rogers brings together the two doctrines of election and marriage by appealing to Christology. He argues that the God who initiates the covenant with Israel is made manifest in Christ, who is the bridegroom of the church.[170] In Christ, the covenant of election

---

166. Rogers, *Sexuality and the Christian Body*, 27.
167. Rogers, *Sexuality and the Christian Body*, 48–53.
168. Rogers, *Sexuality and the Christian Body*, 48–49.
169. Rogers, *Sexuality and the Christian Body*, 144.
170. Rogers, *Sexuality and the Christian Body*, 153.

becomes grounds for the covenant of marriage. This claim is summarized in a succinct quote from Karl Barth, "In that the election of God is real, there is such a thing as love and marriage."[171] Third, the inclusion of Gentiles in their Gentileness affords Rogers theological room to discuss the inclusion of lesbian and gay marriages into the church's theology of marriage. To make this move, Rogers offers an analysis of two chapters of Paul's letter to the Romans. In Romans 1, Paul argues that the Gentiles saw evidence of God in the created world, but refused to respond appropriately by giving thanks to God. Instead, they engaged in idolatry.[172] In response, God "gave them up to degrading passions" and "unnatural" same-sex relationships (Rom 1:26). Thus, idolatry led to same-sex behavior. The word "unnatural" is the Greek phrase *para phusin* which Rogers translates as "contrary to nature." Paul then makes a rather startling rhetorical move. This same phrase from Romans 1 is used in Romans 11:24 to describe God's activity of grafting the Gentiles into the covenant.[173] Commenting on these verses, Rogers writes, "In saving the Gentiles, God shows solidarity with something of their nature, the very feature that had led the Jew Paul to distinguish himself from them: their excessive sexuality."[174] Gentile nature, which Rogers identifies with sexuality, was not a barrier to salvation.[175] From this analysis, Rogers argues that if God can bring Gentiles into the covenant through the Spirit, thereby committing an unnatural act by accepting what was previously defined as unnatural, then the overwhelmingly Gentile church must hold open the possibility that the Spirit can do a new thing by bringing lesbian and gay individuals into the church without requiring a change in their sexuality.[176] Rogers equates failure to demonstrate openness to God's freedom to potentially include lesbian and gay individuals and their marriages with resisting Christ and refusing to celebrate the Spirit's work.[177]

171. Rogers, *Sexuality and the Christian Body*, 27, 153. See Barth, *Church Dogmatics* 3/1:318.

172. "For though they knew God, they did not honor him as God or give thanks to him, but they became futile in their thinking, and their senseless minds were darkened. Claiming to be wise, they became fools; and they exchanged the glory of the immortal God for images resembling mortal human beings or birds or four-footed animals or reptiles" (Rom 1:21–23).

173. "For if you have been cut off from what is by nature a wild olive tree and grafted, contrary to nature [*para phusin*], into a cultivated olive tree, how much more will these natural branches be grafted back into their own olive tree" (Rom 11:24).

174. Rogers, *Sexuality and the Christian Body*, 65.

175. Rogers, *Sexuality and the Christian Body*, 53.

176. Rogers, *Sexuality and the Christian Body*, 65, 178, 238–39.

177. Throughout his work, Rogers issues a series of strong warnings against those who deny the possibility of same-sex marriage. Those in the church who refuse to be

Reflection of Trinitarian Love

Not only does marriage mirror God's election, Rogers also asserts that the institution reflects Trinitarian love. Contra Stuart and Thatcher who argue that human experience is the starting point for theological reflection on love and sexuality, Rogers offers a different theory of analogy. He asserts that sinful human experience is too "fickle" and "unreliable" to be the primary point of reference.[178] A more stable analogue is needed. Therefore, theology must begin with the faithful God of the covenant, as described by Scripture and tradition.

Rogers' theory of analogy requires us to begin by examining his Trinitarian theology. He asserts that God exists as three distinct, yet unified, persons. Love exists in the godhead, Rogers contends, because there exists a distinction between the persons of the Trinity. Stated succinctly, "Because the three persons are distinct from one another, God can 'be' love."[179] Thus, this distinctness within the Trinity is the basis of divine love. This claim leads to Rogers' second assertion about the Trinity. He describes the triune life as "a wedding feast, the love of two celebrated by a third."[180] In this framework, the Father loves the Son, the Son returns love to the Father, and the Spirit both witnesses and celebrates that love. From this description, Rogers asserts that love requires an object, and love necessitates a witness or a third party. Following his theory of analogy, Rogers' understanding of Trinitarian life relies on his interpretation of Scripture. He argues that knowledge of the Triune life is seen most clearly in the gospels at the Baptism, Transfiguration, and Resurrection of Jesus.[181] In the Baptism, the Father is pleased with the Son, who is declared to be his "beloved," while the Spirit descends in the form of a dove (Matt 3:16–17; Mark 1:10–11; Luke 3:21). A similar scene unfolds at the Transfiguration. Here, Rogers follows an Eastern Orthodox interpretation which locates the Spirit in the cloud that descended upon Jesus and the disciples (Matt 17:5; Mark 9:7; Luke 9:34–35).[182] Finally, the

---

open to this possibility risk resisting the work of Christ (*Sexuality and the Christian Body*, 254) and refusing to celebrate the Spirit's work (245). To illustrate the seriousness of this inhospitable posture toward same-sex unions, Rogers cites Jesus' statements comparing those who reject his disciples to the inhabitants of Sodom and Gomorrah (258). The result of this posture, exhibited by the outright refusal to celebrate same-sex marriage, is that one "cuts him or herself off from the work of the Spirit and the life of God" (196).

178. Rogers, *Sexuality and the Christian Body*, 234, 239.
179. Rogers, *Sexuality and the Christian Body*, 198.
180. Rogers, *Sexuality and the Christian Body*, 195.
181. Rogers, *Sexuality and the Christian Body*, 220, 229.
182. For an Eastern Orthodox interpretation of this passage, see Ware, "God as

Spirit raises the Son at the Resurrection, thereby "[reuniting] the Father and the Son" (Rom 8:11).[183] From these events in Scripture, Rogers concludes that the Trinity, made up of distinct, unified persons, "is a public celebration of a fluid or perichoretic three, 'a dancing day.'"[184]

Rogers applies his theory of Trinitarian love to humans by appealing to the doctrine of creation. While the love between Trinitarian persons is completely sufficient, not lacking in any way, God freely chose to create. Thus, creation exists as an outpouring of Triune love. Rogers asserts that it is "deeply *characteristic* of God to create, to give to another."[185] This is true because Triune love is characterized by an eternal "dance" of giving, responding, and celebrating among the divine persons.[186] Rogers illustrates this claim by appealing to the mission given to the Son by the Father. In the Trinity, the Father eternally sends the Son and receives him back. The Son responds by going out from the Father, and, by doing so, returns to the Father in obedience to the Father's will. All the while, the Spirit bears witness and celebrates. Rogers applies the giving and responding in the Trinitarian life to his doctrine of creation. Creation allows for the possibility of the continual reciprocation of giving and responding in gratitude expressed in the Triune life to be embodied in time and space.[187]

Rogers notes that applying characteristics of the relational Trinity to human relationships requires two distinctions. First, whereas there is both distinction of persons and unity in the Trinity, distinction becomes difference when applied to human relationships. Here, difference does not have a negative connotation, referring to a relational barrier which hinders love of neighbor. Instead, difference is a God-given part of finite existence, or what Rogers calls the "appropriate condition of creaturely intimacy."[188] Second, where Trinitarian love has no spatial or temporal limits, Rogers argues that creaturely love requires both time and space. Bodily boundaries allow the possibility for touch and embrace, while time allows for mutual self-giving which can only occur in consecutive moments in time. Rogers asserts that it is in the finite realm of time and space that humans, persons created in the image of the Divine Persons, are invited to "participate in the love by which

---

Trinity," in *Orthodox Way*, 27–42.

183. Rogers, *Sexuality and the Christian Body*, 220, 196.
184. Rogers, *Sexuality and the Christian Body*, 197.
185. Rogers, *Sexuality and the Christian Body*, 197.
186. Rogers, *Sexuality and the Christian Body*, 197–98.
187. Rogers, *Sexuality and the Christian Body*, 200.
188. Rogers, *Sexuality and the Christian Body*, 201.

God loves God."[189] Following this logic, it is creation that makes possible the vocations of monasticism and marriage, where Triune love is expressed in time and place. Rogers writes, "The formation of Christian households and corresponding monastic vows of stability honor the ties of love to place. The bonds of marriage and corresponding monastic vows of constancy honor the ties of love to time. Creaturely love involves making space, and taking time."[190] Thus, it is in faithfulness to a specific location and a commitment to permanence that marriage and monasticism mirror Trinitarian love.

Defining human love as a bodily expression which takes place in time and space allows Rogers to introduce the category of sexual orientation. He asserts that sexual orientation is "in part a special appreciation for the particular delights of spatial finitudes, or bodily forms."[191] This appreciation for bodily forms is intimately connected to the concept of desire. This leads us to Rogers' third telos of marriage, which addresses the place of bodily desire within his theology.

Sanctification of Desire

As was discussed in chapter 2, the Christian tradition has maintained an ongoing wariness of sexual desire. Several early theologians seemed to believe that the category is beyond saving. By contrast, Rogers describes marriage as a "means of redemption" or as the location where the sanctification of the body and desire takes place.[192] In order to make this statement, Rogers must first reclaim a theological rationale for bodily desire as a positive theological category. Rogers makes three arguments in pursuit of this goal. The first relies on his doctrine of God. According to Rogers, God desires to bring creation to fulfillment. Election is God's method for achieving this aim. Rogers writes, "For the consummation of creation God chooses Israel."[193] The covenant God, whom Scripture describes as both Father and Lover, has an "implacable desire for consummation."[194] Thus, Triune love for creation is a specific kind of love characterized by desire or yearning for fulfillment. Second, Rogers appeals to Christology. He asserts that when Christ took on flesh, he also assumed *eros* or bodily desire. The result of the Incarnation is that bodily desire is redeemed and transformed

189. Rogers, *Sexuality and the Christian Body*, 45.
190. Rogers, *Sexuality and the Christian Body*, 201.
191. Rogers, *Sexuality and the Christian Body*, 201.
192. Rogers, *Sexuality and the Christian Body*, 27.
193. Rogers, *Sexuality and the Christian Body*, 203.
194. Rogers, *Sexuality and the Christian Body*, 204, 221.

into a spiritual "yearning" for the consummation of creation in the person of Christ. Thus, Rogers contends, *eros* is given a spiritual dimension "without ceasing to be erotic."[195] Rogers makes clear that it is God's desire for humans as seen in Jesus Christ, not sinful human *eros*, that is the starting point for theological reflection on desire.[196] This means that human love must be normed by "the love by which Jesus pleases the Father," a love which results in "goodness, righteousness, holiness, and the fulfillment of the Trinitarian purpose."[197] Third, Rogers appeals to the relationship between the Father and the Son described in the Baptism, Transfiguration, and Resurrection. Baptism and Transfiguration reveal that the Father is pleased with the Son. Rogers argues that the Father is pleased with the Son, in part, because of the Son's enactment of Triune love in time and space. He writes, "It is God's own erotic love of us human beings that God approves when God loves the Beloved."[198] To further illustrate the kind of love God demonstrates toward humans, Rogers points specifically to the Son's "*philanthropia*."[199] Rogers believes that there is "more than a little of *eros* in the *philanthropia*, in the love of God for the human being."[200] In the Resurrection, Rogers argues, the Son's erotic *philanthropia* for humankind is vindicated by the "good pleasure of the Father."[201] Thus, Trinitarian love cannot be fully defined in terms of *eros*. However, based on the Father's election, Christ's *philanthropia*, and the vindication of the Son's love of humankind by the Father, Rogers asserts that erotic love can be considered a "subset of the love of the Son for human beings and the love for which the Father loves the Son, the love in which the Holy Spirit delights."[202]

While God's love within the Trinity may or may not be described as *eros*, Rogers asserts that God's love for humans is erotic. He writes, "The love by which God loves human beings is *eros*, if *eros* is a love that yearns for union with the other, yearns for the flesh of the other, is made vulnerable and passionate for the other."[203] While God's sufficient nature precludes yearning and need, God chose to take on need in the humanity of Jesus,

---

195. Rogers, *Sexuality and the Christian Body*, 204.
196. Rogers, *Sexuality and the Christian Body*, 226–27, 234.
197. Rogers, *Sexuality and the Christian Body*, 222.
198. Rogers, *Sexuality and the Christian Body*, 225.
199. Rogers, *Sexuality and the Christian Body*, 221.
200. Rogers, *Sexuality and the Christian Body*, 221.
201. Rogers, *Sexuality and the Christian Body*, 222.
202. Rogers, *Sexuality and the Christian Body*, 222.
203. Rogers, *Sexuality and the Christian Body*, 225.

which Rogers identifies as "God's humanity."[204] Scripture reveals that God's *eros* for humanity is directed toward two groups: Israel and the church. Rogers argues that God's love for Israel is erotic because "Israel is the flesh of Jesus, God's own flesh."[205] In similar fashion, God loves the church with erotic love because she is Christ's body, as well as Christ's bride, two descriptors that become "one flesh" in marriage.[206] Because of God's yearning desire to bring creation to fulfilment through election, Christ's erotic *philanthropia*, and God's pleasure at the Son's *philanthropia*, Rogers asserts that *eros* can be considered a positive theological category.

Rogers must now connect God's erotic love for humans with the *eros*, or bodily desire, that humans experience for each other. This requires explicating the relationship between desire and the body in Rogers' theology. As previously stated, human love requires time and space. In this framework, bodies honor love's tie to space. Rogers argues that it is through the body that humans learn of God's love for them, a love characterized by yearning and desire. It is also through the body that humans experience perhaps their deepest desire, the desire to be wanted. Rogers calls this longing to be wanted sexual desire. Rogers writes, "Sexual desire is a bodily manifestation of my desire to be wanted, which is finally satisfied only by God's desire for me."[207] Thus, the purpose of sexual/bodily desire is to teach humans that God loves them. Rogers argues that God uses bodily desire to achieve this aim in two ways. First, God can use one's bodily desire, mediated through a community, to learn of God's love for him or her and guide his or her bodily desire directly toward God. In this situation, Rogers argues, such divine action results in the vocation of celibate monasticism. Second, God can teach an individual of God's love by directing his or her bodily desire toward another human. Though God may not be the primary object of one's bodily desire in this instance, Rogers asserts that knowledge of God's love can be attained through loving and being loved by one's spouse in the vocation of marriage.

From this description, Rogers asserts that monasticism and marriage have three characteristics in common. First, both are vocations into which humans are called by God. Like monasticism, marriage is not a foregone conclusion for lesbian and gay individuals, let alone heterosexual individuals. Second, God uses sexual desire to draw humans into the vocations of marriage and monasticism, allowing desire to become a positive theological category. It is important to note that Rogers does not argue that *eros*,

---

204. Rogers, *Sexuality and the Christian Body*, 225.
205. Rogers, *Sexuality and the Christian Body*, 234.
206. Rogers, *Sexuality and the Christian Body*, 224.
207. Rogers, *Sexuality and the Christian Body*, 83.

as such, is good. After sin, *eros* has become a source of temptation which attracts humans to each other. In a postlapsarian world, this attraction is often divorced from good. Yet Rogers also argues that concupiscence, or "the eros appropriate to material human beings," is more than sinful sexual desire.[208] The term also "names the incompleteness or yearning or desire that humans suffer—or enjoy—on account of being material creatures."[209] Bodily desire is part of what it means to be a finite creature. Furthermore, Rogers asserts that while desire is a source of sin, it is also the means of redemption. To support this claim, Rogers also appeals to human finitude. He writes, "As spatio-temporal beings, humans cannot dispose of themselves all at once, in a single, ultimate action. Rather, when they choose, they choose incompletely."[210] All human choices are partial in scope. When this understanding of finite existence is coupled with the reality of sin, one's partial choices are always a complicated mixture of good and evil. This move provides the logic for affirming a positive side of concupiscence. Choosing to sin by following concupiscence can result in the experience of regret, a yearning for wholeness or restored relationship. In turn, this yearning creates the opportunity for repentance. Thus, concupiscence is more than a sinful force within humans, it is also the appropriate creaturely desire, a desire to be wanted, that ultimately leads to repentance and redemption. For Rogers, "Concupiscence is God's way into human creatures, and the human creature's way into God."[211]

Third, both monasticism and marriage are forms of community in which sexual desire is transformed. Rogers argues that *eros* is a God-given impulse that draws humans to each other in community. Through bodily desire, God ensures that humans "cannot escape from the neighbor, and from the neighbor's claim."[212] Community allows for the possibility of being challenged and transformed by another who "like the Spirit will not leave us alone."[213] It is within communities of monasticism and marriage, where one commits to live with another for the duration, that God transforms *eros* into *agape*. Rogers describes this work of sanctification as one of the primary purposes of these vocations. Rogers admits that monasticism is more readily associated with sanctification than is marriage. However, he

---

208. Rogers, *Sexuality and the Christian Body*, 227.
209. Rogers, *Sexuality and the Christian Body*, 227.
210. Rogers, *Sexuality and the Christian Body*, 227–28.
211. Rogers, *Sexuality and the Christian Body*, 228.
212. Rogers, *Sexuality and the Christian Body*, 227.
213. Rogers, *Sexuality and the Christian Body*, 270. See also Rogers, *Sexuality and the Christian Body*, 78.

argues that marriage is a kind of monasticism due to the shared telos of sanctification of desire accomplished through bodily practices.[214]

According to Rogers, the transformation of *eros* into *agape* is accomplished through asceticism. He defines asceticism as a "discipline of denial and restraint that liberates the human being for sanctification."[215] At this point, Rogers makes an important caveat. The purpose of asceticism is not finally negation through the denial of self and one's desire. Drawing from Evdokimov, Rogers asserts that "the most ascetic act is not renunciation of self but total self-acceptance."[216] Asceticism, he contends, exists to teach humans to accept that they are "occasions of joy, that God desires them as if they were God."[217] When applied to marriage, asceticism becomes a "practice of and for the community by which God takes sexuality up into God's own triune life, graciously transforming it so as to allow the couple to model the love between Christ and the Church."[218] The community to which Rogers refers in this statement not only includes the one flesh community of the couple, but also the church. Therefore, asceticism not only exists for the good of the couple, but also for the wider faith community. Rogers argues that God can cause marriage to transcend itself, where it becomes an eschatological witness of the Kingdom and of God's love. Here, Rogers addresses the traditional Protestant telos of marriage: the control of lust. If marriage exists to sanctify desire through denial and restraint for the good of the church, then marriage is not primarily concerned with the fulfillment of selfish desire.[219]

Rogers' assertion that the call to ascetic living applies to all Christians, regardless of their sexual orientation or specific bodily vocation, has two implications for his theology of marriage. First, the statement is a rhetorical move that seeks to diminish the gulf between lesbian, gay, and heterosexual individuals, uniting all three groups under the call to asceticism. The underlying assumption is that the disagreement taking place over the validity of same-sex marriage occurs between committed believers who are already united by Christ . . . not between Christians and non-Christians. Second, if asceticism can be lived in a number of vocations (marriage, celibacy, and monasticism) and vocation is a God-given

---

214. Rogers, *Sexuality and the Christian Body*, 80–81. The move to equate the ascesis of monasticism with that of marriage is borrowed from Evdokimov, *Sacrament of Love*.

215. Rogers, *Sexuality and the Christian Body*, 70.

216. Rogers, *Sexuality and the Christian Body*, 231. See Evdokimov, *Sacrament of Love*, 100.

217. Rogers, *Sexuality and the Christian Body*, 27. See Wiliams, "Body's Grace," 309–21.

218. Rogers, *Sexuality and the Christian Body*, 73.

219. Rogers, *Sexuality and the Christian Body*, 71, 196.

calling, then one's vocation cannot be predetermined based on membership to a specific people group.[220] Rogers has in mind the ecclesial practice of requiring gay and lesbian individuals to assume a celibate life in order to be admitted into the church. Rogers rejects forced celibacy based on one's sexual orientation because it represents a conflation of body and soul. This requirement assumes that one's genetic bodily composition determines one's vocation.[221] Rogers argues that such genetic determinism rejects the importance of particularity. Put more specifically, "It proceeds as if the shape, color, or desire of one's body predetermines one's vocation without any need for considering cases or interior discernment."[222] Rogers argues that the practice of forced celibacy for lesbian and gay individuals has two problems. First, it infers that the desire experienced by lesbian and gay individuals is inherently evil and must be renounced. The comparative example would be that of an alcoholic giving up drinking. However, unlike sobriety where the alcoholic abstains from alcohol to become a more complete individual, Rogers argues that the renunciation of one's sexual desire is not directed toward the good. Instead, this renunciation is toward "nothing, a negation of human fulfillment."[223] Perhaps the more critical problem of forced celibacy is that it denies lesbian and gay individuals the opportunity for bodily asceticism. Rogers argues that if sexual desire is deeply connected to identity/personhood, more specifically if it is God's way into the individual and the individual's way into God, then "sexuality cannot be passed by; it must be assumed, transfigured" through asceticism.[224]

Appropriation of Augustine's Three Goods of Marriage

I now turn my attention to the impact of Rogers' theology on Augustine's three goods of marriage. As previously mentioned, Rogers presents a defense of Christian marriage that seeks to be broad enough to include both heterosexual and same-sex couples. By addressing Christian marriage, Rogers has chosen to work within the parameters of the Christian

---

220. Rogers, *Sexuality and the Christian Body*, 22, 55, 62.

221. Rogers compares this argument to other historical examples of genetic determinism. He specifically highlights the negative ways in which arguments from genetic determinism were used in Jew/Gentile, male/female, and free/slave debates to suggest the existence of an innate moral defect in the latter groups which makes them incapable of following God's commands (*Sexuality and the Christian Body*, 54).

222. Rogers, *Sexuality and the Christian Body*, 22.

223. Rogers, *Sexuality and the Christian Body*, 231.

224. Rogers, *Sexuality and the Christian Body*, 230.

tradition. While my work is interested in Augustine and the legacy of his theology in the Western Christian world, Rogers leans primarily on Eastern sources. In *Sexuality and the Christian Body,* he directly cites Augustine's *The Good of Marriage* only once.[225] Other references to Augustine are primarily concerned with Augustine's Trinitarian theology as it relates to the issue of procreation.[226] Thus, on the surface, it does not appear that Augustine is a primary conversation partner for Rogers. This preference for Eastern sources at the pivotal moments in his argument leads to questions of the appropriate method for integrating the two authors. However, in his defense of marriage Rogers relies on Aquinas and Barth, thus demonstrating his knowledge of and willingness to work within the Western tradition. Furthermore, it is clear that he is aware of Augustine's three goods of marriage. As the following section will demonstrate, Rogers' theology upholds the goods of faithfulness and permanence while rejecting procreation as a necessary good of marriage. Because Rogers makes only passing references to faithfulness and permanence, I will offer a brief synopsis of his appropriation of those goods. More attention will be devoted toward his effort to separate procreation from marriage.

Faithfulness & Permanence

Rogers offers three arguments to support his affirmation of faithfulness and permanence as necessary goods of Christian marriage. The first relies on his covenantal theology. He argues that God chose the Israelites and established a covenant with them. The Scriptures tell the story of God's continued faithfulness to the covenant with Israel, and the engrafting of Gentiles further demonstrate God's faithfulness to that covenant. The God who initiates the covenant with Israel is made manifest in Christ, who is the bridegroom of the church. In Christ, Rogers asserts, the covenant of election becomes grounds for the covenant of marriage. Thus, the intelligibility of covenantal marriage relies on God's continuing faithfulness to the covenant with Israel.

Rogers' definition of faithfulness is clarified and linked to permanence through his appeal to the ascetic telos of marriage. He argues that Triune love is the primary analogate for human love. Unlike eternal, divine love, creaturely love requires time and space. After the fall, the creaturely gift of time and space devolves into a "burden."[227] Because of sin, time is associated with the threat of death, and space becomes separation. Bodily

---

225. Rogers, *Sexuality and the Christian Body,* 74.
226. Rogers, *Sexuality and the Christian Body,* 169, 197, 205, 245–46.
227. Rogers, *Sexuality and the Christian Body,* 249.

desire, once intended for mutual fulfillment, has devolved into a quest for self-fulfillment, separated from seeking the good of others. In this setting, marriage is a vocation of denial and restraint which brings desire into ascetic practice in order to transform that *eros* into *agape*. According to Rogers, this transformation is accomplished over an extended amount of time through relationship with a faithful, committed, monogamous partner. For *eros* to become *agape*, married partners "need somebody who loves them to call them on their faults from whom they cannot easily escape . . . the experience of living with someone, the neighbor, who won't leave one alone (agape)."[228] Thus, the transformation of desire through ascetic practice requires the faithfulness and permanence of marriage.

Finally, Rogers' commitment to the permanence of Christian marriage is strengthened by his appeal to the gospel. He argues that marriage receives its "rationale" from God's love as expressed in the gospel.[229] In the gospel, conditional love is rejected in favor of God's eternal, unqualified love. Rogers asserts that marital love follows this pattern of gospel love by declaring to remain faithful to one's partner "for better or worse, for richer or poorer, in sickness and in health."[230] Based on these arguments, Rogers asserts that Christian marriage requires faithfulness and permanence.

Procreation

While Rogers affirms the necessity of faithfulness and permanence for marriage, the same cannot be said of procreation. In order to sever the link between marriage and procreation, Rogers must criticize the claim that procreation is a necessary telos of marriage. Rogers builds his case by appealing to the doctrines of creation and Christology. He challenges the necessity of procreation in three ways. First, he argues that making procreation a necessary telos of marriage implies that God's act of creation was necessary.[231] Leaning on the work of Aquinas, Rogers provides an interpretation of the doctrine of creation which argues that humans are created in the image of God "as God wills and acts . . . rather than as God is *in se*."[232] Because God wills to create, humans image God through the creative nature of *proles*. Since humans are command to image God, a task accomplished through procreation, procreation is therefore necessary to human existence. Within

---

228. Rogers, *Sexuality and the Christian Body*, 83.
229. Rogers, *Sexuality and the Christian Body*, 235.
230. Rogers, *Sexuality and the Christian Body*, 235.
231. Rogers, *Sexuality and the Christian Body*, 207.
232. Rogers, *Sexuality and the Christian Body*, 204.

this framework, refusing to procreate amounts to refusing to image God. Rogers argues that by making procreation necessary, God's act of creation becomes necessary by extension. However, he contends, creation has already been described as an overflowing of Trinitarian love; it is a grace. If procreation images God's act of creation, Rogers argues that procreation "must be recovered as a matter of non-necessity, of grace, of prayer. Even within a fertile marriage."[233] In place of the procreative metaphor, Rogers argues that the marriage covenant is a better metaphor for God's love in creation. It is the marriage covenant which "adds to love time and space for exchanges of mutual gift, with procreation or without."[234] Second, borrowing from Aquinas, Rogers asserts that procreation exists for the good of the species, not the individual. Therefore, not every marriage is required to bring forth children. Rogers argues that this move is necessary for Aquinas to explain the celibacy of Jesus, while also making room for infertile marriages.[235] If the good of the species does not require every marriage to be procreative, then procreation is not a necessary good of marriage. Finally, Rogers argues that the inability to procreate does not diminish one's ability to image God.[236] He argues that this is true because procreation is not the proper telos of both sex and marriage. Marriage and sex have a sacramental quality whose "chief end . . . is not to make children of human beings, but to make children of God."[237] For Rogers, sex and marriage exist for the sanctification of the couple. Children may contribute to sanctification, but they are not necessary to the task.

Next, Rogers employs Christology to criticize the necessity of procreation for marriage. In the Incarnation, God became human in the person of Jesus. According to the Gospels, Jesus was conceived by the Holy Spirit and born of the Virgin Mary (Matt 1:18–23; Luke 1:26–35). Jesus was not conceived through procreative sex between a male father and a female mother.[238] Pressing further, Jesus did not procreate, but instead made the command to be fruitful relative to obedience to God.[239] According to Rogers, both Jesus' birth and his life problematize the necessity of physical procreation.

---

233. Rogers, *Sexuality and the Christian Body*, 207.
234. Rogers, *Sexuality and the Christian Body*, 207–8.
235. Rogers, *Sexuality and the Christian Body*, 129, 205–6.
236. Rogers, *Sexuality and the Christian Body*, 209.
237. Rogers, *Sexuality and the Christian Body*, 206.
238. Rogers, *Sexuality and the Christian Body*, 262. Elsewhere, Rogers appeals to Eve being brought forth from Adam's rib rather than through procreative means to criticize the necessity of procreation (*Sexuality and the Christian Body*, 209).
239. Rogers, *Sexuality and the Christian Body*, 210.

In response to these criticisms of procreation, Rogers invites Christians to consider an alternative model for understanding how humans image God. If Trinitarian love, rather than creation, is the primary analogate for marriage, then procreation is not necessary. Therefore, Rogers argues, "Christians best imitate God's relation to them as children not when they bear and beget [children], but when they *adopt* them."[240] He provides the following evidence to support the claim. First, adoption is a reminder that a child, like creation, is a gift of grace rather than a necessity or an achievement. Here, Rogers compares marriage to God's covenant with Abraham. Abraham and Sarah were past the age where bringing forth children was a possibility through human achievement. Yet, Sarah gave birth to Isaac. Rogers argues that "as marriage represents God's covenant with Abraham . . . children are understood as in some sense unnecessary and the gift of grace."[241] Second, Rogers asserts that adoption is a better representation of God's engrafting of the Gentiles than physical procreation. Israel participates in the covenant through election and by holding to God's promise that the world will be blessed through the physical procreation of Israel. By contrast, Gentiles participate in the covenant through adoption, an act of God described as "contrary to nature,"[242] not through procreation. Third, adoption witnesses to Jesus, the embodiment of the covenant between God and humans. Jesus was not born of a human father but was raised by Joseph. Jesus also fathered no children but welcomed children to himself.[243] Based on these arguments, Rogers concludes that adoption best represents the welcome that Jesus received and extended to others.

It is important to note that while Rogers supports adoption as a way for married couples to mirror Trinitarian love, he argues that it is not necessary for couples to adopt in order to fulfill the command to be fruitful and multiply. He writes, "It is sufficient for them to be: consider the lily of the field, how it grows. It neither spins nor sews. It grows wild, without purpose, except to glorify God and give joy to human beings."[244] Thus, marriage can fulfill its ultimate purpose of witnessing to God's glory with or without producing children. Here Rogers hints at an allegorical reading of the command to be fruitful. Indeed, Rogers asserts that glorifying God is a different kind of production to which all marriages can aspire.

240. Rogers, *Sexuality and the Christian Body*, 206.
241. Rogers, *Sexuality and the Christian Body*, 261.
242. Rogers, *Sexuality and the Christian Body*, 263.
243. Rogers, *Sexuality and the Christian Body*, 261–62.
244. Rogers, *Sexuality and the Christian Body*, 217.

Commonalities for Same-Sex and Heterosexual Christians

Throughout his work, Rogers defended Christian marriage. His method has been to reduce the distance between heterosexual and same-sex couples by focusing on the theological characteristics of heterosexual marriage which can be extended to same-sex couples. I will end this analysis by highlighting the areas of overlap. First, the call to asceticism applies to all Christians. It is through asceticism, either in marriage or celibacy, that Christians are called to continue "their witness to the kingdom, which is participation in God's own Trinitarian life."[245] Second, the theological tradition has allowed the vocations of marriage and celibacy to represent Christ's union with his bride, the church. Where celibates glorify God through their bodies directly, married people glorify God in their sex with another.[246] Rogers asserts that the vocation of marriage represents a more straightforward analogy than that of celibacy for Christ's relationship with his bride (the church). However, the church's inclusion of celibacy as an analogate reflects the "flexible" nature of that analogy.[247] Due to the flexibility of the analogy, it is theoretically possible for gay and lesbian marriages to also reflect Christ's relationship with the church. Finally, all Christians are called to edify the church. Rogers writes, "Weddings, gay or straight, build up the eucharistic community both by contributing the institutional stability of marriage, and because weddings represent the Trinitarian life."[248] Wedding ceremonies encourage the church to witness and celebrate the love of the couple and the love of the Trinity concurrently.

Rogers & Augustine

Three issues arise when Rogers' work is placed alongside Augustine's thought. The first involves the theological weight that Rogers gives to sexuality. Next, I will query marriage as a means of redemption. Finally, I will examine Rogers' handling of procreation.

First, it is necessary to consider the theological weight given to the category of sexuality. From his writings, Rogers deems sexuality to have great significance in relation to identity. Two moves make this clear. One of the key

---

245. Rogers, *Sexuality and the Christian Body*, 80.

246. Rogers, *Sexuality and the Christian Body*, 242, 246–47.

247. Rogers, *Sexuality and the Christian Body*, 242. On a separate note, Rogers also points to the irregular sexual relationships found throughout Scripture which God uses to bring about salvation history (*Sexuality and the Christian Body*, 243–44).

248. Rogers, *Sexuality and the Christian Body*, 244.

arguments that Rogers makes in favor of the inclusion of same-sex marriage involves the grafting of the Gentiles into the covenant. The argument is constructed so that the salvation of the Gentiles by the work of the Spirit is analogous to the inclusion of same-sex marriage within the church's theology. The Gentiles are engrafted as Gentiles, i.e., without having to change their nature, a nature which Romans 1 identifies with idolatry resulting in excessive sexual expression. Rogers argues that if no change is required of the Gentile's sexual nature, lesbian and gay relationships should be accepted by the church without requiring any alteration of their sexual nature. Sexuality becomes the lynchpin of the analogy. By this construction, the acceptance of same-sex relationships is given weight similar to the salvation of Gentiles. The importance of sexuality in Rogers' theology of marriage becomes more apparent when this move is coupled with the warnings that he issues to his opponents. It should be noted that Rogers begins his work with calls for charity toward one's opponents.[249] He argues that the issue of sexuality should not divide the church.[250] However, Rogers is unable to sustain his benevolent tone. As Rees argues, Rogers engages in "the worst dimensions of identity politics" by creating a linguistic opposition between those who support his claims about the inclusion of same-sex marriage and those who do not.[251] Through his appeal to the parable of the wedding banquet from Matthew 22, Rogers threatens violence and exclusion for those who reject the validity of same-sex marriage. He argues that refusing to celebrate the expression of sexuality exhibited in these relationships amounts to denying the work of the Spirit and results in removing oneself from the redemption of God. Thus, sexuality is given salvific importance in Rogers' theology.

The elevation of the category of sexuality to the level of salvific significance is built on two assumptions about human nature. First, according to Rogers, sexuality is a fundamental characteristic of one's identity. Sexuality enables humans to express love in time and space. It also serves as the seat of desire, which is God's way into human creatures and humans' way into God.[252] Therefore, it cannot be removed or bypassed in the discussion human identity. Second, the salvific importance of the category is grounded on the conviction that sexuality is a fixed reality, understood by Rogers in binary terms. It is through sexuality that the body is understood and the self is unified. Throughout his work, Rogers accepts the hetero/homosexual binary as given. He does this by appealing to the "fit of gay and

---

249. Rogers, *Sexuality and the Christian Body*, 33.
250. Rogers, *Sexuality and the Christian Body*, 14, 35, 47, 267.
251. Rees, *Romance of Innocent Sexuality*, 117.
252. Rogers, *Sexuality and the Christian Body*, 201, 228.

lesbian bodies into the body of Christ."[253] The pairing "gay and lesbian" with "bodies" represents "the affirmation of the presence of the sex that makes those bodies intelligible."[254] To put it another way, Rogers assumes that one's sexuality is a stable category that gives intelligibility to the body. The body receives intelligibility through the performance of one's sexuality in one's bodily vocation. Therefore, the performance of a fixed, intelligible sexuality is central to identity, and that intelligibility is necessary for bodies to "fit" into the "body of Christ."

According to Rogers, self-unity is achieved through the performance of one's sexuality in the vocations of marriage or monasticism. However, the requirement that one's sexuality must be performed or lived presents a challenge to the stability of the category. Based on this construction, Rees argues that, for Rogers, sexuality is "not something people do, nor is it something people are. It is something that people become."[255] Because continual performance of one's sex is required to prove its intelligibility, the unity achieved through sexuality can only ever be partial and unstable in nature. This, in turn, would destabilize the necessity of presenting a unified sexual self in order to fit into the body of Christ. From an Augustinian perspective, it is not clear that one can achieve unity of the self through sexuality, or through any other means in this life. Self-unity is precisely the thing that was destroyed in the fall.[256] Unity is restored not through human accomplishment, i.e., the performance of one's sexuality, but by turning to God, the source of knowledge of one's self. Any unity that one experiences in this life will be partial, and final restoration of self-unity will only occur in the eschaton. If unity of the self through sexuality is not possible in this life, it is not clear that sexuality should be granted the weight that Rogers ascribes it.

Second, a series of questions might also be posed to the theological expectations that Rogers places on marriage. This can be illustrated by examining Rogers' theological rationale for the inclusion of lesbian and gay marriage. He makes the theological claim that marriage is a "means of redemption."[257] Since all people are in need of redemption, Rogers contends, redemptive marriage should be available to heterosexual and same-sex couples. However, redemption must always be considered in a narrative context.[258] Therefore, the question must be posed to Rogers, from what is one

---

253. Rogers, *Sexuality and the Christian Body*, 27.

254. Rees, *Romance of Innocent Sexuality*, 116.

255. Rees, *Romance of Innocent Sexuality*, 49. See also Rees, *Romance of Innocent Sexuality*, 58.

256. Augustine, *City of God*, 13.12–15.

257. Rogers, *Sexuality and the Christian Body*, 27.

258. Rees, *Romance of Innocent Sexuality*, 112–14.

redeemed through marriage? Because Rogers frames this redemption in terms of ascetic practice which redeems and transforms bodily desire, presumably marriage redeems one from barriers to relationship with God which are exhibited most readily by sinful *eros*: possessiveness, lust, objectification, etc. Rogers argues that excluding same-sex couples from the vocation of marriage as a means of redemption results in denying those individuals the opportunity to sanctify *eros*. According to Rogers, the sanctification of *eros* through the asceticism of marriage leads humans to total self-acceptance. Self-acceptance is achieved through the knowledge that humans are desired and loved by God "as if we were God."[259] When the question of the narrative context of redemption is applied to same-sex couples, "from what are they being redeemed?" Rogers' answer seems to be that they are redeemed from exclusion from the redemptive possibilities of marriage.

If the first question this chapter posed to Rogers was concerned with the ability to achieve a unified self, the second challenges his claim that marriage as a means of redemption is the proper vehicle for achieving unity of the self for either heterosexual or same-sex couples. From an Augustinian perspective, it is not clear whether marriage can bear the weight that Rogers ascribes to it. Augustine readily defended marriage as a good. He supported this claim not only by articulating the three primary teloi of his theology of marriage, but also by referring to the positive impact that marriage was created to have for the couple. These include a strengthening of the bond of friendship,[260] and a deepening of the companionship of the couple.[261] However, after the fall, Augustine argues that the bond of friendship has devolved into a chain, the couple's companionship is now a source of mutual temptation, and the institution brings distress. In the current age, Augustine describes marriage as a good, but a limited good. Placing redemptive significance on marriage, i.e., hope of redemption through union with another person, places undue expectations on the institution and one's partner that they were never intended to bear.[262] The outcome of such misplaced hope will end in dissatisfaction for marriage and one's partner. By contrast, asserting that marriage is a limited good allows for proper enjoyment of the institution of marriage, and the opportunity for marital partners to experience appropriate mutual enjoyment of the other.

Finally, I will examine Rogers' handling of procreation. While Rogers briefly references the Augustinian goods of faithfulness and permanence,

---

259. Rogers, *Sexuality and the Christian Body*, 27, 231.
260. Augustine, *Good of Marriage*, 9, 22.
261. Augustine, *Good of Marriage*, 12.
262. Rees, *Romance of Innocent Sexuality*, 12.

his main concern is to sever the necessary link between procreation and marriage. He rightly recognizes procreation as a key barrier to the inclusion of same-sex relationships into the church's theology of marriage. The rejection of procreation as a necessary good affords Rogers space to construct a new foundation for marriage on the goods of faithfulness and permanence alone. Thus, the marital covenant for both heterosexual and same-sex couples can be sexual without being procreative.

Two questions arise regarding the efficacy of this move. First, the claim that procreation is unnecessary to marriage is made by appealing to a variety of doctrines: trinity, incarnation, Christology, election, and sanctification to name a few. However, his use of the doctrine of creation requires more attention. In order to sever marriage from its procreative telos, Rogers appeals to an allegorical reading of the Genesis command to be fruitful and multiply. He argues that both monasticism and marriage participate in the sanctifying work accomplished in community, whether or not children are produced.[263] Referring specifically to marriage, he asserts that God is honored when children are present, regardless if they are of biological origin or adoption. He further argues that the sanctification of marriage and monasticism brings glory to God, which is the ultimate telos of human life. Rogers refers to glorifying God as a different kind of producing.[264] By equating adoption with begetting children, and by his appeal to sanctification as a kind of production, Rogers reveals his preference for an allegorical reading of the Genesis command. The question is whether such an approach can support a sufficiently robust doctrine of creation. Augustine wrestled with this question throughout his career. In his early work, he interpreted the creation account allegorically. Toward the middle of his career, Augustine preferred a more concrete interpretation. In his more mature work, Augustine decided that both a literal and allegorical interpretation of Genesis, and more specifically the command to procreate, is needed to make sense of the biblical text. In the next chapter, I will examine what is at stake in how one reads the Genesis creation narratives, along with how an Augustinian approach might enhance Rogers' account.

Robert Song: Covenant and Calling

Quoting Evdokimov, Rogers argues that "should God cause marriage to transcend itself, it can become 'the eschatological representation of the

---

263. Rogers, *Sexuality and the Christian Body*, 84.
264. Rogers, *Sexuality and the Christian Body*, 217.

kingdom.'"[265] I now turn my attention to a fourth author who investigates the theological implications of eschatology for a theology of marriage. Robert Song offers an important revision of the church's traditional theology of marriage in his work, *Covenant and Calling*. Like Rogers, Song presents a defense of Christian marriage with an eye toward creating space for same-sex relationships. However, the starting place, methodological choice of doctrines used, and prescription for addressing the challenge that same-sex relationships pose to the church vary widely between these two authors. Whereas Rogers relies primarily on a robust account of the doctrines of the trinity and election, which lead him to the conclusion that marriage exists primarily for the sanctification of desire for both heterosexual and same-sex couples, Song's work depends on a tension between the doctrines of creation and eschatology understood through Christology. The central theme that Song pursues is the "significance of the advent of Christ for sexuality" and the vocational possibilities that result.[266] Traditionally, the church has allowed for the relational vocations of celibacy and marriage. However, Song presses the logic of Christ's advent further by suggesting the possibility of a third, distinct vocation: covenantal partnership. This section will examine Song's theology of marriage, where he affirms Augustine's three goods of marriage, tracing their origin to creation and election. Special attention will be given to Song's conviction of the necessity of sexual difference and procreation for Christian marriage. Next, I will assess Song's claim that the coming of Christ reveals different trajectories of the three goods of marriage, thus allowing for the possibility of covenantal partnerships. Finally, I will examine several questions that arise when Songs' work is placed alongside Augustine's theology of marriage.

Theology of Marriage

According to Song, the doctrine of creation is the appropriate starting point for articulating a theology of marriage. The reason for this methodological choice is twofold. Not only does Scripture begin with the stories of creation, but also when Jesus taught about marriage, he referred to the creation stories.[267] When speaking on marriage and divorce, Jesus said, "But from the beginning of creation, 'God made them male and female.' 'For this reason a man shall leave his father and mother and be joined to his wife,

---

265. Rogers, *Sexuality and the Christian Body*, 196. See Evdokimov, *Sacrament of Love*, 169.

266. Song, *Covenant and Calling*, x.

267. Song, *Covenant and Calling*, 1–2.

and the two shall become one flesh'" (Mark 10:6–8). In this passage, Jesus brings together the two creation accounts of Genesis 1 and 2. The reference to humans being created male and female points to Genesis 1:27–28, where sexual differentiation is connected to the *imago dei*. As male and female, the two humans are blessed and commanded to be fruitful and multiply and to fill the earth and subdue it.[268] Jesus' reference to the man leaving his parents and clinging to his wife comes from the second creation account where God creates a human from dust and deems that this human should not be alone. In response, God creates woman out of the human's rib to be a "helper" and a "partner" (Gen 2:18). From this analysis, Song concludes that creation provides the initial grounding for marriage.

From the creation accounts, Song draws three preliminary conclusions about marriage. First, he asserts that marriage is a "*created* good."[269] From a theological perspective, marriage is not a social construct or merely a naturally occurring empirical reality. The institution receives its shape and definition from a theological account of creation, and as such, resists definitions supplied by non-theological sources. Thus, Song argues, marriage is not defined primarily by contemporary manifestations of the institution, often exhibited by patriarchy and heterosexism. Instead, to affirm that marriage is a created good indicates that the various manifestations of marriage "do not exhaust the meaning of marriage, [and] they cannot of themselves determine what marriage as a created ordinance is."[270] Second, Song argues that marriage is a "created *good*."[271] Marriage is a gift from God designed for the good of humankind. It exists to serve "the good of the partners, of their children and wider family, and . . . society as a whole."[272] Third, marriage has a definitive structure. According to Song, this structure is revealed in the two creation accounts. In Genesis 1, humans are created male and female with what Song refers to as "an intrinsic mutual relationality" characterized by "the faithful and permanent relationship of the partners."[273] The male/female relationship takes further shape in Genesis 2:24 where the text says that the man and woman become "one flesh." Here, the relationship of the

---

268. "So God created humankind in his image, in the image of God he created them; male and female he created them. God blessed them, and God said to them, 'Be fruitful and multiply, and fill the earth and subdue it; and have dominion over the fish of the sea and over the birds of the air and over every living thing that moves upon the earth'" (Gen 1:27–28). See Song, *Covenant and Calling*, 2.

269. Song, *Covenant and Calling*, 3.

270. Song, *Covenant and Calling*, 3.

271. Song, *Covenant and Calling*, 3.

272. Song, *Covenant and Calling*, 3.

273. Song, *Covenant and Calling*, 4.

couple takes on a sexual component. However, Song argues, the relationship of the man and the woman does not exist merely for the couple. As Genesis 1:28 indicates, humans are created male and female for the purpose of completing a specific task: having dominion over the earth. Dominion is accomplished through obedience to the command to be fruitful and multiply. And procreation is the result of the sexual relationship of the sexually differentiated couple. From these passages, Song asserts that marriage has a twofold structure. As creation good, marriage requires sexual differentiation and procreation. Let's examine these claims in greater detail.

In his effort to create space for same-sex relationships within the church's theology of sexuality, Song takes a different route from that of Thatcher and Rogers regarding the importance of sexual difference. Thatcher denies the importance of sexual difference to marriage by appealing to Trinitarian love, the non-sexually differentiated divine love which serves as the basis for human love in marriage. Rogers asserts that marriage is a vocation that exists for the purpose of asceticism and as such should be available to same-sex and heterosexual Christians. For these authors, vocation and sanctification supersede the Christian tradition's insistence on sexual difference in marriage. By contrast, Song asserts that the move to deny the importance of sexual difference represents a specific type of argument for contemporary theological projects that support same-sex relationships. In a variety of ways, these proposals conclude that "the sex of the partners does not intrinsically matter. . . . And this assertion of the unimportance of the sex of the partners is then read back into creation, so that no significance can be attributed to the creation of human beings as male and female."[274]

In response to this tendency amongst some revisionists, Song argues that the denial of the importance of sexual difference to marriage suffers from three problems. First, the argument borders on the gnostic tendency of "denying the goodness of the material creation."[275] He contends that the Scriptures and Christian theology have consistently affirmed creation as good. That goodness applies not only to created material, but also to the form God has given creation. Song extends this logic to the form of human bodies. There is something good in the creation of humans as male and female. Song is quick to note that determining the exact meaning and shape of the goodness of humans created male and female, as well as the application of that knowledge to wider human relations is not a straightforward enterprise. He denounces attempts to read gender roles from the pages of Scripture and efforts to subjugate or relativize bodies that do not conform to traditional

---

274. Song, *Covenant and Calling*, 24.
275. Song, *Covenant and Calling*, 24.

gender norms. However, Song argues that "to abandon the notion of sexual differentiation entirely . . . is to run the risk of denying any meaning at all to the phrase 'male and female he created them.'"[276] Second, by rejecting the importance of sexual difference, Song asserts, the argument severs its connection to the doctrine of creation and thereby risks "losing its proper theological shape."[277] By removing or weakening the doctrine of creation for a discussion of marriage and sexuality, one is in danger of making claims that are not sufficiently theologically grounded. Song argues that without the teloi that creation provides, marriage can easily serve other ends. For instance, marriage can be described as merely a social contract that exists for utilitarian purposes. Benefactors of such an arrangement can include the couple, the state, or members of the legal profession to name a few. When the connection between creation and marriage is removed, Song claims, one's theology of marriage also loses access to other theological resources. For example, creation is part of a larger theological narrative which includes election, incarnation, redemption and eschatology. Creation points to its consummation in the eschaton. Removing the doctrine of creation from the discussion results in losing access to a robust eschatology. Third, Song argues that denying the importance of sexual difference results in obfuscating the link between marriage and procreation in creation.[278] In the first creation account, humans are created and instructed to have dominion over the earth. Dominion is accomplished through filling the earth, i.e., procreation, which is the result of the one-flesh relationship of the sexually differentiated couple. Creation ties marriage to procreation, which currently can only be accomplished through sexual differentiation. Thus, the necessity of sexual difference to marriage must be maintained if marriage is to be grounded in a robust doctrine of creation.

This discussion of sexual differentiation leads to the second prong of Song's theology of marriage: procreation. While sexual differentiation is a requirement for marriage, Song argues that it is only necessary because of its link to procreation. He writes, "Sexual differentiation is therefore justified within marriage, but it is only justified because marriage is oriented to procreation. There are no other grounds that can provide the theological weight needed to require that marriage be sexually differentiated."[279] For Song, the discussion of whether same-sex couples should be affirmed and the manner of their inclusion hinges not on gender or sexual differentiation,

---

276. Song, *Covenant and Calling*, 25.
277. Song, *Covenant and Calling*, 25.
278. Song, *Covenant and Calling*, 26.
279. Song, *Covenant and Calling*, 48–49.

but on whether the relationship has the ability to be procreative or not.[280] This move is a distinct break from the much of the contemporary discussion which tends to focus on sexual difference. Song asserts that heterosexual relationships differ from same-sex relationships precisely because the former is procreative and the latter is not. He notes that same-sex couples can embody the goods of faithfulness and permanence, but not procreation as understood in the Genesis account. For Song, this is a "morally relevant difference" which calls into question attempts to make same-sex and heterosexual relationships analogous.[281] Song writes, "Procreation is not the only good of marriage as a created ordinance, let us be clear, but it is an intrinsic and inseparable good of it."[282] Procreation has been and continues to be an essential part of the church's understanding of marriage. Thus, if space is to be created for same-sex relationships, it must rely on a logic different from that of marriage as a good of creation.

Song argues that procreation is essential, in part, because it provides an external telos for marriage in the form of children. He writes, "Children symbolize, and in their demands on their parents they actualize, an openness to hospitality that prevents marriages collapsing into an egoistic and complacent coupledom."[283] Yet, Song does qualify this position. He notes that there are instances where procreation is not an option for a married couple. In this case, presumably marriage would need an alternative external telos to physical procreation. Song uses the example of an infertile couple as a test case. He argues that while infertile couples cannot satisfy the marital good of physical procreation, their marriage is open to various forms of allegorical fruitfulness. Infertile couples might engage in adoption or fostering. Pressing further, they might also discover "other ways of channeling the love and instincts for parenting than immediately through care for children."[284] Thus, infertile couples present a challenge to the connection between marriage and procreation, while they also provide an opportunity for instruction. From these couples the church discovers the possibility of a marriage relationship for which procreation is not normative and for whom "sexual intimacy must mean something that is separable from its procreative norm."[285]

---

280. Song, *Covenant and Calling*, xi, 37.
281. Song, *Covenant and Calling*, 27.
282. Song, *Covenant and Calling*, 31.
283. Song, *Covenant and Calling*, 34–35.
284. Song, *Covenant and Calling*, 35–36.
285. Song, *Covenant and Calling*, 36.

In summary, from the creation accounts Song asserts that marriage is a creation good which requires sexual differentiation and procreation. Procreation, which is accomplished through a sexually differentiated relationship, is the means by which humans fulfill the divine command to have dominion over the earth. While sexually differentiated marriage that is open to procreation is the norm, exceptions exist which challenge and inform the church's position regarding the necessity of physical procreation to marriage.

Not only does Song ground his theology of marriage in protology, he also relies on the doctrines of election and covenant. He asserts that Scripture compares marriage to the relationship between God and Israel and between Christ and the church. Marriage reflects and embodies the covenant of God with the people of God in which "God chooses to be the God of Israel, and in Christ to take as his covenant partner first Israel and then through the Church the whole of humankind, Jews and Gentiles alike."[286] Song is clear that the analogy functions in a top-down manner, with the Triune God as the primary analogate. In a limited and finite way, marriage reflects God's covenant with human beings, which reflects the relationship between the Trinitarian Persons. Through this analogy, marriage becomes "in some small part a participation in that divine covenant relationship."[287] The "small part" of God's covenant with humans in which marriage participates is embodied in the faithfulness and permanence of the marriage partners. Just as God has been unwaveringly faithful to God's people, marriage partners are called to embody continual faithfulness to each other. To put it another way, election and covenant provide the grounding for the necessary marital goods of faithfulness and permanence. According to Song, faithfulness and permanence are intrinsic goods, in that their necessity to marriage are not contingent on achieving other ends. For example, it can be argued that faithfulness and permanence are good for the upbringing of children, for the wellbeing of the couple, or for the stability of society. While there may be truth to these statements, Song argues, permanence and faithfulness are not contingent on whether a marriage achieves these ends. He writes, "It is one thing to say that I pledge my troth so long as it suits our well-being, and that of our children and of wider society, another to say that I pledge my troth *because that is what marriage is.*"[288]

Here, Song has chosen to employ a specific understanding of covenant: covenant by analogy. According to this type of covenantal theology, what is

---

286. Song, *Covenant and Calling*, 10.
287. Song, *Covenant and Calling*, 10.
288. Song, *Covenant and Calling*, 12.

true of God's inner relationship is also true in a limited way in creation and in human relations.[289] As mentioned above, marriage reflects God's covenant with Israel. Thus, covenant is defined as a commitment to relationship. The burden of the argument relies on a description of a God who loves humans faithfully and applies this description to human relationships. Righteousness, or right relationship, is achieved when an individual embodies God's kind of faithful love for his or her partner. It should be noted that this is not the only understanding of covenant presented in Scripture. Another example would be God's covenant with Israel at Sinai. This asymmetrical covenant was established by God and required Israel's obedience to the God of the covenant. In this setting, obedience to the word of God defines righteousness. Song does not indicate why he chose the former example of covenantal theology rather than the latter. Perhaps, like Stuart, Song is wary of the patriarchal tendency to apply Israel's obedience to the divine to the marriage relationship, thereby requiring a wife's submission to her husband. Song also refrains from providing specific scriptural examples of human relationships which embody his understanding of covenant. Are the relationships between David and Jonathan or Ruth and Naomi examples of the covenant that Song proposes? Providing a more robust account of the logic grounding his methodological choices supporting his covenant theology would have furthered Song's argument.

Not only does election and covenant provide the basis for the marital goods of faithfulness and permanence, Song contends, the doctrines also provide a link between creation and Christology in salvation history. He indicates that Christian theology cannot speak of creation as such. Creation is not a doctrine that operates independently from other doctrinal concerns. Instead, creation must be connected to "its context in the story of God's dealing with all that is not God."[290] This story begins with creation as an outpouring of Trinitarian love. Humans are created and are instructed to have dominion over the earth, a task accomplished through procreation. Thus, from the first command given to humans, there is a sense in which creation is moving toward a telos. The story proceeds through God's covenant with Abraham and God's continued faithfulness to Abraham's descendants from whom God's incarnate Son is born. It is in his use of Christology where Song makes a unique contribution to the debate regarding the church's response to same-sex individuals and their relationships.

---

289. Song, *Covenant and Calling*, 10.
290. Song, *Covenant and Calling*, 8.

Christology

According to Song, creation is theologically connected to Christology. More specifically, he argues that "the doctrine of creation is theologically inseparable from an understanding of Christ."[291] As evidence for this claim, Song cites Colossians 1:15–18 and John 1:1–3 which indicate that creation has its origin and coherence in Christ.[292] Based on these passages, Song suggests a qualified use of the categories of "nature" and "natural law." He states that the created world reveals "something of the glory of God and the nature of the good for human beings."[293] While supporting a limited use of these categories, he argues that the advent of sin has compromised human reason so that knowledge from nature no longer points humans to the good. This situation cannot be rectified except through grace. Therefore, nature and natural law can only be explicated by reference to the grace of Christ. Song writes, "Nature itself is graced . . . In the divine economy [it] is always related to Christ who is the one in whom it coheres. Natural law is known in and through Christ who is its origin and fulfillment."[294] Thus, Christ reveals the nature of creation and brings about creation's fulfillment.

Song defines this fulfillment not as restoration of creation, but as its transformation. As relates to his theology of marriage, two aspects of this transformation of creation are pertinent. First, Christ fulfills and transforms the divine command to have dominion over the earth. According to Genesis 1, humans were created in the image of God, male and female, and commanded to have dominion over the earth. Dominion was to be accomplished through procreation by sexually differentiated partners. Therefore, procreation and sexual difference were connected to what it means to be in the image of God. After the fall, Adam was no longer able to exercise dominion over creation. Yet, where Adam failed, Christ succeeded. Key for Song's account is that Christ's dominion is not accomplished through procreation. Christ did not marry or bring forth children. Yet, despite Christ's decision to refrain

---

291. Song, *Covenant and Calling*, 8.

292. "He is the image of the invisible God, the firstborn of all creation; for in him all things in heaven and on earth were created, things visible and invisible, whether thrones or dominions or rulers or powers—all things have been created through him and for him. He himself is before all things and in him all things hold together. He is the head of the body, the church; he is the beginning, the firstborn from the dead, so that he might come to have first place in everything" (Col 1:15–18); "In the beginning was the Word, and the Word was with God, and the Word was God. He was in the beginning with God. All things came into being through him, and without him not one thing came into being" (John 1:1–3a).

293. Song, *Covenant and Calling*, 9

294. Song, *Covenant and Calling*, 9.

from having children, Paul asserts that Christ has "all things in subjection under his feet" (1 Cor 15:27).[295] Because Christ has fulfilled the command to have dominion over creation, Song asserts that it is no longer necessary for humans to accomplish dominion through procreation. Therefore, procreation has different theological value after Christ.

Song expands this point by appealing to Jesus' teaching on marriage in the eschaton.[296] For Jesus' Jewish audience, procreative marriage was essential to the continuation of one's family after one's death. It was also a sign of God's continued blessing as described in the Abrahamic covenant. To this audience, Jesus speaks of a new age where God's people "neither marry nor are given in marriage" (Matt 22:30). Song expounds the logic of the text. At the resurrection of the dead, death will no longer be a threat. If there is no death, humankind will not need to sustain itself through procreation. If procreation is no longer necessary, then marriage loses its telos and reason for existence. Therefore, marriage will no longer exist in the eschaton. Commenting on this passage, Song writes, "What was crucial to the whole creation understanding of human beings, namely the nexus of marriage and procreation, will in the eschatological fulfilment of creation become redundant. The entire edifice of human relationships built around the becoming one flesh of man and woman and the expression of this in the one flesh of the child will no longer be integral to human existence."[297] Both the Incarnation and Jesus' teaching point to an alteration in the theological value of procreation and, by extension, marriage.

Song's assertion that the advent of Christ "resituates" the creation account and what it means for humans to image God has three implications for his theology of marriage.[298] First, because Christ accomplished the task of dominion, thus relativizing the necessity of having children, procreation has a new meaning. After the advent of Christ, procreation is no longer an essential part of human identity tied to what it means to image the divine. Instead, children are "a sign of God's continuing goodness . . . a sign of the divine gratuity."[299] In support of the claim that procreation is no longer a necessity, Song notes that the New Testament does not encourage Christians

---

295. Song, *Covenant and Calling*, 16–17.

296. "Those who belong to this age marry and are given in marriage; but those who are considered worthy of a place in that age and in the resurrection from the dead neither marry nor are given in marriage. Indeed they cannot die any more, because they are like angels and are children of God, being children of the resurrection" (Luke 20:34–36; cf. Matt 22:23–44; Mark 12:18–27).

297. Song, *Covenant and Calling*, 15–16.

298. Song, *Covenant and Calling*, 16.

299. Song, *Covenant and Calling*, 20–21.

to have children, nor is procreation given as a reason for Christians to marry.[300] Instead, Christians are encouraged to welcome and train children who already exist. Therefore, it is no longer necessary for humans to image God through procreation.

Christ's resituating of creation leads to a second implication, namely, that the advent of Christ points to an eschatological age and a new vocation that bears witness to that time. Where participation in the Old Testament covenant required procreation, Song argues, life in the church does not. Because of the Incarnation, "full humanity, full participation in the imaging of God, is possible without marriage, without procreation, indeed without being sexually active. Celibacy, in other words, has become an appropriate stance for those who wish to live in a new age."[301] Celibacy has become a sign of the age to come. Song is quick to note that the coming of Christ does not nullify the goods of creation; marriage is still an option for Christians. Furthermore, both Jesus and Paul defend marriage as a licit possibility. Though Jesus enables his followers to practice celibacy, he also defends the permanence of marriage against hasty attempts at divorce (Matt 19:1–12). And while Paul exhorts Christians to celibacy, he is clear that marriage is not sinful (1 Cor 7:28). This textual evidence leads Song to assert that the coming of Christ and the eschatological future to which it points is the "fulfilment of creation, but it is not its denial."[302] Marriage is still good, but it does not have the "aura of inevitability" it once had.[303]

Finally, Song argues that the advent of Christ reveals divergent logics and trajectories of the three goods of marriage. Procreation is grounded in creation as evidenced by Jesus' appropriation of the creation stories in Mark 10:6–8. However, the purpose of procreation (dominion) has been fulfilled by Christ. Therefore, procreation has "become redundant, theologically speaking, for those who are in Christ."[304] Because Christ brings about the fulfillment of creation, Song asserts that procreation remains a good of creation that is connected to marriage. Thus, contemporary marriages must be open to procreation. However, he contends that because Christ has fulfilled the purpose of procreation (dominion), procreative marriage is no longer necessary for Christians. Celibacy, a vocation which is embodied without genital sexual expression and procreation, is a calling

---

300. Song, *Covenant and Calling*, 19. The one exception to this would be 1 Tim 5:14, where the author encourages young widows to marry and have children so that their witness to the gospel might not be compromised.

301. Song, *Covenant and Calling*, 18.

302. Song, *Covenant and Calling*, xvi.

303. Song, *Covenant and Calling*, xvi.

304. Song, *Covenant and Calling*, 27.

available to Christians. As a result, celibacy witnesses to the eschaton, a time when there will be no need for marriage or procreation. By contrast, the marital goods of faithfulness and permanence differ from procreation in that they are grounded in the covenant rather than creation. As covenantal goods, they witness to the relationship between God and humans which will be brought to fullness in the eschaton.[305] According to Song, the separate theological groundings of creation and eschatology provide the logic for the divergent trajectories of the three goods of marriage, a logic that is revealed by the coming of Christ. *Proles* points to creation while faithfulness and permanence witness to the eschaton.

In summary, Song has argued that the coming of Christ has fundamentally altered our understanding of marriage and sexuality. Procreative marriage is no longer a given, as Christ reveals the vocation of celibacy as an option for Christians. While marriage witnesses to creation, celibacy witnesses to the eschaton where marriage will be no more. Traditionally, Christian theology has argued that marriage and celibacy are the two licit vocations for the embodiment of sexuality. However, Song pursues further the implications of the advent of Christ for sexuality, asking whether there is room for a third vocation that receives its logic from eschatology but exists for the "time between the times" in which humans now live.[306]

Covenant Partnerships

Song calls this third relational vocation *covenant partnership*, which he defines as "non-procreative committed [relationships]" that have the potential to "function as a kind of eschatological witness."[307] This definition indicates that covenant partnerships share some characteristics with marriage. For example, both marriage and covenant partnership witness to God's covenant with humankind. As such, both relationships are characterized by faithfulness demonstrated through sexual exclusivity and through actively seeking the good of one's partner. Marriage and covenant partnership are also marked by their commitment to permanence exemplified by lifelong, mutual vows to remain faithful until death. Finally, both relationships are vocations to which individuals are called. Song says of marriage and covenant partnership that "each has a particular gift from God, one having one kind and another a different kind (1 Cor 7:7; cf. Eph 4:7; 1 Pet 4:10); where there is a call, so also will there be the gift to

---

305. Song, *Covenant and Calling*, 27–28.
306. Song, *Covenant and Calling*, xi.
307. Song, *Covenant and Calling*, 28.

fulfill it."[308] As vocations, both relationships are directed to discipleship and training in holiness.

Though they share these characteristics, marriage and covenant partnerships also have important theological differences. While marriage is grounded in creation and is therefore directed toward procreation, covenant partnership is grounded in the eschaton where there will be no death and therefore no need for procreation. Thus, Song asserts that covenant partnership is a genitally expressed sexual relationship that, unlike marriage, is not open to physical procreation. Yet, as Song removes one external telos from these relationships, he hints at another. While procreation is precluded, he contends, the relationship is characterized by its openness to "other forms of fruitfulness" for the good of the Kingdom of God.[309] To support this claim, Song argues that the relationship of the covenant partners may enable a depth of fruitfulness that cannot be accomplished by individuals alone. Examples of this kind of fruitfulness may include certain works of charity, caring for children through adoption or fostering, environmental work, missional work in contexts which might preclude children, etc.[310] There are a number of ways in which covenant partners might use their relationship to bear fruit for the kingdom. At the same time, Song makes clear that the shape of a couple's fruitfulness is not based solely on the choice of the couple. He writes, "The precise forms of fruitfulness each couple [is] called to would depend on their times and circumstances."[311] Because covenant partnership is a vocation, the relationship's fruitfulness will depend on a certain level of givenness associated with the divine call upon the couple.

The definition of covenant partnership as a non-procreative relationship leads to a second key difference between marriage and covenant partnership. As previously mentioned, Song argues from the creation accounts that marriage exists for the purpose of procreation. Procreation is accomplished through intercourse between sexually differentiated partners. Thus marriage, by definition, requires sexual differentiation. Song writes, "Sexual differentiation is therefore justified within marriage, but it is only justified because marriage is oriented to procreation. There are no other grounds that can provide the theological weight needed to require that marriage be sexually differentiated."[312] On the one hand, this statement highlights the theological link between marriage and sexual difference

---

308. Song, *Covenant and Calling*, 29.
309. Song, *Covenant and Calling*, 28.
310. Song, *Covenant and Calling*, 28–29.
311. Song, *Covenant and Calling*, 29.
312. Song, *Covenant and Calling*, 48–49.

based on the doctrine of creation. On the other hand, it enables Song to provide a different logic for covenant partnerships. Such relationships are not grounded in creation and are therefore not oriented toward procreation. Instead, these relationships are grounded in eschatology. Song writes, "Baptism and the new identity in Christ take us beyond the creation categories of male and female in a way that renders them no longer of defining importance"[313] Thus, the theological grounding required to necessitate sexual differentiation in covenant partnerships is nullified. Based on this logic, covenant partnerships are open to both heterosexual and same-sex couples.

Sex and Procreation

Song has argued that the advent of Christ has nullified the necessity of procreative marriage. Thus, celibacy, characterized by non-genitally expressed sexual embodiment, is an option for Christians. At the same time, he insists that marriage, a genitally expressed sexual relationship, exists for the purpose of procreation. This argument results in the existence of a necessary link between the couple's sexual relationship and procreation. In both cases, the embodiment of one's sexuality is directed toward an external telos, preventing sexuality from being used merely to satisfy one's selfish desires. Yet, covenantal partnerships are genitally expressed sexual relationships that are not directed toward physical procreation. In order to make this move, Song must argue that genitally expressed sexual relationships serve goods beyond procreation.

Song makes three arguments in support of this claim. First, he appeals to Scripture. He points to Paul's teaching on sex and marriage in 1 Corinthians 7. In this passage, Song argues, Paul does not make a connection between sex and children. Instead, Paul says that a husband "should give to his wife her conjugal rights, and likewise the wife to her husband" (1 Cor 7:3). Here, marital sex exists to help the couple avoid sexual immorality. Commenting on this passage, Song suggests that Paul is referring to "having sex for its own sake rather than for the sake of having children."[314] Song also points to Genesis 2, where the couple's sexual love results in them becoming one flesh. He also highlights Song of Songs where a couple's sexual love is on full display apart from any reference to children. Song argues that these passages "imply or suggest sexual love without clear

---

313. Song, *Covenant and Calling*, 49.
314. Song, *Covenant and Calling*, 55.

reference to procreativity."³¹⁵ He does qualify this line of argumentation. He notes that Scripture was written prior to the advent of reliable birth control. It may be that the biblical writers could not imagine sex apart from its procreative potential, and therefore they did not feel the need to mention procreation in these passages. However, for Song's purposes, this caveat does not undermine his argument that these passages point to teloi of sex beyond procreation.

Second, Song draws on the long-running discussion of the ethics of contraception. The Roman Catholic Church asserts that marriage exists for both unitive and procreative ends, but the two cannot be separated from each other. *Humanae Vitae* states that "each and every marriage act must remain open to the transmission of life."³¹⁶ Thus, the Catholic position privileges each sex act. In response to this stance, Song argues that sexual intercourse receives meaning within a relational context. He writes, "The primary unit for moral consideration is not the individual 'marital act,' but the marriage itself as a whole."³¹⁷ This statement allows him to argue that a marriage must be open to new life, but it does not mean that every sexual act must be connected to procreation or that contraception is wrong in every situation. This argument leads Song to conclude that if the use of contraception is deemed licit, then "one also concedes that sex is characterized by a good which is independent of and additional to its orientation to procreation."³¹⁸

Finally, Song provides an example of a non-procreative good of sex. He argues that there can be a connection between sex and one's knowledge of God. Just as marriage and covenant partnerships bear witness to the covenant between God and the people of God, sex "embodies and points to the nature of our relationship with God."³¹⁹ The reciprocal desire and joy of the sexual encounter bears witness in a limited way to "the intimacy of communion one will experience with God . . . a glimpse into the inner life of God."³²⁰ Thus, sex can become a finite human symbol which points beyond itself toward love within the Godhead and God's love for creation.

Based on these arguments, Song concludes that sex has multiple meanings in the relationship of a couple. If sex has meaning beyond procreation, then non-procreative sex need not necessarily be characterized as an effort to fulfill one's selfish bodily desire. It is theoretically possible to

---

315. Song, *Covenant and Calling*, 55.
316. Paul VI, *Humanae Vitae*.
317. Song, *Covenant and Calling*, 58.
318. Song, *Covenant and Calling*, 58.
319. Song, *Covenant and Calling*, 59.
320. Song, *Covenant and Calling*, 60.

conceive of the sexual relationship of the couple being oriented to goods that do not include procreation. This opens the door to discussing the virtues of sexual relationships that are not directed toward children, i.e., covenant partnerships.

Song & Augustine

Throughout his work, Song makes a variety of moves that are reminiscent of Augustine. Two key examples are his choice to interpret creation through a christological lens and to acknowledge the importance of sexual difference for marriage. Yet, he extends these ideas beyond what was articulated by the Latin Father. It is important to examine the cogency of Song's use of these concepts. With that in mind, we will discuss three questions that arise when Song's work is placed alongside Augustine's thought. The first question addresses the origin of Song's third vocation as it relates to its continuity with Christian tradition. The second two questions are related to Song's approach to sexual difference.

Throughout his work, Song acknowledges that Christian tradition has held marriage and celibacy to be the two licit vocations through which one embodies one's sexuality. Yet, Song proposes the possibility of a third vocation. This tension between what the church has believed to be true for centuries and Song's novel proposition brings with it a series of questions. Where did this new vocation originate? Why is it available now? These questions are summarized by Christopher Roberts. According to Roberts, Song sets forth a "hidden logic of the tradition . . . an option that he concedes this same tradition has managed to overlook for two thousand years," thus encouraging Christians "to entertain seriously the possibility that our own moment in time has uniquely privileged access to God's true intentions for human sexuality."[321] While Roberts' criticism and subsequent dismissal of Song's work is too hasty, Roberts does hint at an important issue for discussion. Song's account relies on an interpretation of salvation history as a hermeneutic key for reading biblical passages concerned with sexuality. He argues that creation has been fulfilled by Christ, whose coming opens the eschatological vocations of celibacy and covenant partnership that were previously unavailable.[322] The underlying assumption of such an account is that these vocations have been available since the advent of Christ. To state it another way, Song asserts that both celibacy and covenant partnership have been true to the overarching witness of the New Testament, even if

---

321. Roberts, review of *Covenant and Calling*, 116.
322. Song, *Covenant and Calling*, x.

Christians are only now becoming aware of the implications that Christ's advent has for sexuality. Two historical parallels for this argument are the abolition of slavery and the role of women in the church and wider society.[323] In both cases, there was a strong theological case made in favor of the status quo. Proponents of slavery and those in favor of denying women equal social standing called attention to biblical texts that supported their cause. Such proponents also pointed to the long historical gap between the writing of the New Testament and their present time as evidence in favor of maintaining the status quo. To overcome these considerable barriers, abolitionists and activists for women's rights were forced to undertake the rigorous task of devising thick theological arguments that demonstrated how their claims concorded with the whole of the biblical witness.[324] One of the reasons that Augustine's theology of marriage continues to hold weight in contemporary discourse is that he wrestled with the entirety of the biblical witness alongside the queries and challenges of his day and articulated a position of extraordinary theological depth and cohesion. There is much to commend in Song's revisionist account of sexual ethics, specifically his attention to creation and Christology. Yet, his approach would benefit from further detailed biblical analysis to see if covenant partnership is a relational vocation that is true to the whole story of Scripture.

A second issue for discussion is Song's approach to sexual difference. Song argues that procreation is the only theological justification for requiring sexually differentiated partners in marriage. Therefore, relationships that are not oriented toward procreation need not be sexually differentiated. Stated succinctly, "Baptism and the new identity in Christ take us beyond the creation categories of male and female in a way that renders them no longer of defining importance."[325] Two questions arise from Song's approach to sexual difference. First, does procreation exhaust the importance of sexual difference in the creation accounts? While there is a clear link between the two categories in Genesis 1, the connection is not as clear in Genesis 2. In the latter passage, God places the human in the garden to till and keep it. In verse 18 God declares, "It is not good that man should be alone; I will make him a helper as his partner." From Genesis 2, it is conceivable that the creation of a sexually differentiated partner for the human relates to helping the human complete the task of tilling the garden. Sexual difference could also relate to companionship. Based on Genesis 2, it is not clear that sexual

---

323. Song, *Covenant and Calling*, 72–74.
324. For a survey of these arguments, see Webb, *Slaves, Women & Homosexuals*.
325. Song, *Covenant and Calling*, 49.

difference is merely a functional distinction that is necessary only for the purpose of procreation.

Moreover, Song has stated that sexual difference is connected to creation. He has also argued that creation is moving toward a telos, specifically its eschatological fulfillment in Christ. This fulfillment is described as a transformation of creation. For Song, Christ's transformation of creation has rendered sexual difference no longer of defining importance. From an Augustinian perspective, Christ has altered the modes in which men and women relate to each other, in that celibacy is now an option alongside marriage. Also, the promises of Christ are available to both men and women. Yet for Augustine, "Despite the two sexes having common heirship to God's promises, their visible, sexual differences still retain significance."[326] In his later work, Augustine argues that God created humans as sexually differentiated beings before the fall, and as such maleness and femaleness is good. Though sin has negatively impacted maleness and femaleness in a variety of ways, sexual difference is neither the culprit for sin nor something to be cast aside. Augustine is so committed to the goodness of bodies and their specific form as male and female, he argues that sexual differentiation will remain in the eschaton. This is true even as Christ resituates the telos of sexual difference from procreation to something else that has yet to be revealed. Christopher Roberts argues that for Augustine, "if sexual difference had one significance at creation, which was relativized *post Christum natum*, then there is no reason why it cannot adapt for heaven."[327] The question that this Augustinian logic poses to Song is if Christ has transformed creation to the extent that sexual difference is no longer of defining importance for Christians, what importance does the category have both now and in the eschaton?

Finally, Song's project relies heavily on Christology, specifically the impact of the advent of Christ for sexuality. One of Song's key arguments is that Christ reveals the divergent logics of the three goods of marriage. Procreation is grounded in and witnesses to creation while faithfulness and permanence receive their logic from covenant, and as such, bear witness to the eschaton. It is these divergent trajectories that allow Song to argue that the vocation of marriage points to creation while celibacy and covenant partnership witness to the eschaton. The question that must be presented is, what becomes of Song's argument in favor of divergent trajectories if it can be demonstrated that all three goods of marriage can be grounded in a doctrine of creation? Augustine agrees with Song that procreation is tied to creation. However, Augustine also finds logic for

---

326. Roberts, *Creation and Covenant*, 58.
327. Roberts, *Creation and Covenant*, 63.

faithfulness and permanence in creation. He asserts that there existed in the first couple a "faithful partnership of genuine love, and alertness of minds and body in true concord."[328] Furthermore, Augustine grounds the unbreakable marriage bond in the creation of the woman out of the man's rib. He argues that this event emphasizes the "force of the union effected by wedlock."[329] Thus, procreation, faithfulness, and permanence can be grounded in the doctrine of creation.[330]

Review

This chapter has analyzed four distinct contributions by revisionists which address the impasse over how to reconcile the acceptance of same-sex relationships with the church's theology of sex and marriage. I have illuminated the various ways in which these authors engage with Scripture and Christian doctrine to make their claims. In an effort to "test the spirits" (1 John 4:1), these accounts have been placed in conversation with the theological tradition through the lens of Augustine. From this analysis, certain theological trends within the field of Christian sexual ethics have begun to emerge. The next chapter will map these trends and discuss future areas of study.

---

328. Augustine, *City of God* 1.6–7, 26; see also Augustine, *City of God* 14.10, 115.

329. Augustine, *On Genesis* 9.23, 389.

330. It should be noted that Augustine does not ground faithfulness and permanence using covenantal language. He prefers to rely on Paul's statements from 1 Corinthians 7 and the words of Jesus on marriage and divorce (Matt 5, 19; Mark 10; Luke 16).

4

Mapping the Debate

WITH THIS CONCLUDING CHAPTER, our discussion of marriage and same-sex relationships takes an important turn. I will undertake the constructive task for which chapters 1 and 2 on the origins of the church's traditional theology of marriage and chapter 3 on contemporary revisions of that theology have prepared us. It is necessary to address the various questions and conflicts that have been brought to light through engaging Augustine's thought with that of the contemporary revisionists.

This chapter does not represent an effort to harmonize the work of these authors, attempting to force agreement where it does not exist. Nor is it an effort of comparative description, where the differences between these authors are merely articulated. Instead, I endeavor to provide an overview of the state of the discipline of Christian sexual ethics by appealing to the four revisionists described in the previous chapter. As was argued in chapter 3, each of these authors presents a distinct approach to the challenges present in contemporary discussions of sex and marriage. Namely, theological discussion on this topic has reached an impasse. Two reasons have been suggested as to why this deadlock has occurred. First, contemporary traditionalists and revisionists too often display an uneven handling of the theological tradition and the biblical witness. Second, dialogue is further hindered by the grammar employed, with traditionalists relying on theological language and revisionists appealing to secular language to support their arguments. The result is the existence of two divergent, competing grammars that cannot be resolved. Both groups speak past each other rather than engaging in meaningful dialogue. A new framework for the conversation is needed.

The chapter will begin by indicating areas of relative consistency between the revisionists and the theological tradition. I will proceed by examining key traditional doctrines that are being challenged by the revisionists. The chapter will conclude with an analysis of newer theological arguments being employed to revise the church's theology of marriage and create space for same-sex relationships. By exploring areas of broad agreement between these authors, as well as the many competing crosscurrents that exist in their work, my aim is to provide language and theological avenues to reframe the contemporary discussion on marriage and same-sex relationships.

Areas of Broad Agreement

Over the last few decades, the church's theology and practice has been challenged in a variety of ways. Much of what was comfortable, familiar, indeed, considered "normal" for what it means to be a follower of Christ has been called into question. This move away from traditional beliefs and practices is especially evident in the various criticisms levelled at the church's theology of marriage. Perhaps what is most surprising is the speed at which sexual norms are changing. For example, the first judiciary challenges to the illegality of same-sex relationships occurred in the United States in the early 1970s. By 2008, individual states declared the denial of marriage to same-sex couples to be unconstitutional, a decision affirmed by the Supreme Court and extended to the nation in 2015. Compared to other movements, i.e., the abolition of slavery, women's rights, etc., the push to legalize same-sex marriage has moved relatively quickly. When the legalization of same-sex marriage is placed alongside other changing sexual mores, many Christians wonder if the church's entire framework for understanding sex and marriage is up for grabs. It is possible that this book has done little to ease their anxiety. However, it is important to note that there are areas of relative consistency between the revisionists and the theological tradition. Of Augustine's three goods of marriage, two of the goods continue to receive broad support amongst contemporary revisionists who affirm the institution of marriage: fidelity and permanence. In the forthcoming section, I will examine the ways in which each of the revisionists in this study described fidelity and permanence, as well as the doctrinal commitments that are at stake in their descriptions.

Fidelity and Permanence

Thatcher affirmed fidelity and permanence as goods of marriage and grounded the concepts in God's unwavering faithfulness to "the world, the church, and all humanity."[1] Sexual faithfulness to one's marital partner was described as an ongoing action that bears witness to God's faithfulness. However, for Thatcher, fidelity was more than sexual exclusivity or a negative command to refrain from extramarital sex. Fidelity also included the positive commitment

---

1. Thatcher, *Liberating Sex*, 91.

to seek the good for one's partner and ensure that both partners experience the opportunity to flourish. With this definition, Thatcher acknowledged that a commitment to marital faithfulness and permanence is made by sinful individuals. As such, the institution can be a place of psychological, emotional, and physical harm for one or both partners. Therefore, while affirming permanence in principle, Thatcher argued that some actions violate the couple's commitment to joint flourishing. In some instances, the violation of fidelity is so egregious that divorce is required. In such cases, Thatcher argued that remarriage is permitted. Thus, Thatcher presented an affirmation of fidelity and permanence that attempted to integrate both sin and the lived experience of married couples.

Rogers also affirmed fidelity and permanence. Similar to Thatcher, Rogers' commitment to marital fidelity was grounded in covenantal theology. Marital faithfulness depends for its coherence on the God who chose Israel and exercised faithfulness to that people both by bringing the Messiah from Israel and through grafting the Gentiles into the covenant. For Christians, marital fidelity witnesses to Christ's faithfulness to the church, his bride. Rogers' support of permanence rested on two assertions. First, he stated that marriage exists, in part, for the purpose of sanctification: to transform *eros* into *agape*. This process necessarily takes time and requires the confrontation of a marriage partner who will not leave and from whom one cannot escape. Thus, the sanctifying work of marriage requires permanence. Second, Rogers argued that marital love receives its rationale from the Gospel, which represents God's rejection of conditional love in favor of eternal, unqualified love. Through these arguments, Rogers affirmed fidelity and permanence as necessary goods of marriage.

Song also grounded the faithfulness and permanence of marriage in God's fidelity to the covenant with Israel and the church. He argued that marriage reflects and embodies the divine covenantal relationship in a limited way through its commitment to faithfulness and permanence.[2] However, contra Thatcher, Song followed Augustinian logic by arguing that fidelity and permanence are intrinsic goods which require no additional telos. Though these goods may support the raising of children, the deepening of the relational life of the couple, or the wellbeing of society, permanence and faithfulness are not contingent on whether these ends are achieved.

At first glance, Stuart's project appeared to be a departure from the other three revisionists regarding faithfulness and permanence. Initially, Stuart rejected relational fidelity defined as a commitment to remain sexually faithful to one's partner. She provided two arguments to support this

2. Song, *Covenant and Calling*, 36.

claim. First, she challenged the traditional connection between fidelity and covenant. She argued that fidelity depends for its coherence on a biblical model of covenant which is predicated on inequality and is often accompanied by language of servitude. Stuart asserted that a theology of relationship between two ontologically equal human beings should not be grounded in an analogy of inherent inequality. Second, Stuart criticized the doctrine of God which undergirds traditional covenantal theology. Stuart rejected the analogy of the covenantal God who chooses a people and remains steadfast to that people. In place of this model, she proposed the image of a deity characterized as a "promiscuous lover" whose universal love expands beyond monogamy to one people.[3] She asserted that human relationships are grounded in the universal love of God and are, therefore, not intended to be sexually exclusive. Yet, Stuart was unable to maintain the logic supporting her appeal to the universal God. Defining relational sin as the act of "betrayal," a moral judgment grounded in the logic of faithfulness, ran contrary to Stuart's image of "God as the promiscuous lover."[4] Furthermore, Stuart included in her relational theology the category of "radical vulnerability," the pinnacle of friendship which she believes can only be achieved with one person at a time. This ideal friendship necessitates a narrowing of the expression of one's love, an exclusion that is similar to the faithfulness exhibited by monogamy. Granted, in Stuart's theology, it is a situational monogamy which does not require permanence. Despite her attempt to redefine and replace fidelity as a relational good, Stuart not only endorses relational faithfulness but also elevates it as a category to which one should aspire.

Central to this discussion is the doctrine of God. Stuart correctly reminds the church about the complexities of applying the divine/human covenant to marriage. Namely, a straightforward application of the analogy can result in a husband assuming a position of godlike dominance over his female covenant partner. However, Stuart's appeal to the universal God and subsequent attempt to dismiss fidelity as a relational good is less defensible, specifically because of what such a position says about God. By rejecting the covenant God, there is no reason to trust that God will be faithful to God's promises. As in Stuart's description of friendship where commitments are the subject of continual adjustment, God would be free to renegotiate prior commitments, thus bringing the hope of salvation into question. As Thatcher, Rogers, and Song have demonstrated, it is possible to articulate an understanding of relational fidelity and permanence grounded in the God of the covenant that does not include the asymmetrical qualities of the

---

3. Stuart, *Just Good Friends*, 190.
4. Stuart, *Just Good Friends*, 190.

divine/human covenant. Key to the descriptions of covenant by these revisionists is the conviction that marriage reflects the divine/human covenant in a limited way. The two covenants are not mirror images of each other, and therefore they do not share all characteristics in common. Because the marriage covenant is established between equals, it is not necessary or appropriate for the relationship to reflect the asymmetrical qualities of lordship and obedience which characterize the divine/human covenant. Thus, the goods of faithfulness and permanence can be grounded in the faithfulness of the covenant God, so long as the differences between the analogates is sufficiently articulated.

Desire as Positive Theological Category

Now we turn to an area of concordance among the revisionists which is in tension with the overall trajectory of the theological tradition: the attempt to reclaim bodily desire as a positive theological category. Either explicitly or implicitly, there is agreement among the revisionists that theological reflection should begin with the conviction that bodily desire is good because it is created by God. While this statement is not necessarily in conflict with the theological tradition, the tradition has been wary of bodily desire. There has been a tendency to emphasize sin's impact on desire, rather than conceiving the category as a theological resource. It is for this reason, I contend, that the revisionists' use of desire is in tension with the theological tradition.

A version of this position was held by Stuart, who asserted that the Christian tradition, with Augustine as the primary instigator, has had a thoroughly negative understanding of bodily desire.[5] According to Stuart, the church has described bodily desire as a disability which must be overcome, and a powerful, manipulative force of which one must be wary. By contrast, Stuart argued that desire is a positive category. She relied on a christological argument to support her claim. She asserted that Jesus was the one who wept at the death of a friend, angrily overturned tables in the temple, experienced anguish in the garden, and befriended the beloved disciple. All of these actions, Stuart argued, were motivated by desire. The gospels never condemned Jesus' desire or the actions which result from that desire. If Jesus is the model for humans, then theological reflection should begin by affirming the goodness of bodily desire. Based on the affirmation that desire is good, Stuart concludes that desire should be expressed as freely

---

5. She prefers the term "passion" to "desire," but it is clear from her association of passionate friendships with lesbian relationships that bodily desire for the other is one of the meanings she uses for "passion." Stuart, *Just Good Friends*, 89.

as possible so long as the relational context meets the criteria of mutual acceptance, respect, and delight. Expressions of bodily desire that satisfy this threefold criteria are considered good. Stuart correctly recognized the theological tradition's wariness of bodily desire and the need to reconsider whether the church should view the category in a positive light. Yet, she is incorrect in her analysis of Augustine's understanding of human emotions, and, more specifically, bodily desire. Far from the stoicism that Stuart ascribes to him, Augustine claimed that all people experience the gamut of emotions/affections. He further asserted that pleasure, including bodily desire, was a part of creaturely existence. To support these claims, Augustine also appealed to various experiences in Jesus' life: weeping, righteous anger, distress in the garden. Augustine argued affections can be experienced rightly or wrongly based on the orientation of the will and the telos of the affection. Stuart's support for the goodness of desire also requires further qualification. At stake in this discussion is the relationship between bodily desire, sin, and redemption. Stuart's underlying assumption seems to be that human sexual desire is a God-given part of human nature and is therefore unchallengeable. If one's sexual desire is declared good, then it is good through and through; that desire does not need to be redeemed. In Stuart's theology, this view is combined with her conviction that sin is primarily a social phenomenon. Such a position does not leave room for a discussion of the existence of sinful desire or the negative consequences that proceed from acting on sinful desire.

From this standpoint, Thatcher presented a helpful corrective to Stuart's position. The two authors agreed that bodily desire is part of human nature and is good because it was created by God. For Thatcher, desire is both an experience and an expression of human incompleteness that directs one to another. It is a force which encourages humans to move from isolation toward community. However, Thatcher also argued that while desire is good, it is prone to distortion. Prior to the fall, desire directed one toward the other for the mutual good of both parties. As a result of the fall, desire now devolves into a quest for self-fulfillment divorced from seeking the other's good. The inclusion of hamartiology allowed Thatcher to argue that not every desire is good. As such, individual bodily desires are open to criticism. According to Thatcher, the relational context plays a key role in determining whether bodily desire is deemed licit and open to expression. While Thatcher attempted to balance the goodness and fallenness of sexual desire, one feature of his theology problematizes this account. He argued that one of sin's effects on sexual desire is that it becomes a "consuming power" that cannot be tamed.[6] If it is

---

6. Thatcher, *Liberating Sex*, 69. See also Thatcher, *Liberating Sex*, 117.

true that sinful bodily desire cannot be controlled and all desire after the fall is sinful, it is difficult to reconcile how desire can be a positive theological category. Thatcher's theology would benefit from an account of the ways in which redemption impacts sinful sexual desire.

Rogers presented the most detailed account of the goodness of bodily desire. He made three doctrinal arguments to support his position. First, he asserted that the goodness of sexual desire is grounded in God's yearning desire to bring creation to fulfillment. Thus, yearning and longing are characteristic of divine love. While love between the persons of the Trinity may not be erotic, Rogers asserted that God's love for humans, characterized by longing for consummation, is erotic. It is this same desire for consummation with the other that characterizes human love. Second, Rogers argued that in the Incarnation, Christ assumed, redeemed, and transformed human bodily desire into a desire for creation's consummation. The inclusion of the category of redemption is important to Rogers' account of the goodness of bodily desire. More specifically, he never indicates that *eros*, in itself, is good. Sin has distorted bodily desire and turned it into a source of temptation. Yet, Christ's redemptive work on *eros* means that it is not only a source of temptation, but also a means of redemption. Rogers argued that the transformation of human bodily desire from *eros* to *agape* is accomplished through the asceticism of celibacy and marriage. Finally, the interaction between the Father and the Son at pivotal moments in the gospels revealed the Father's approval of the Son's love for humans, a love characterized by *eros*. Thus, God in Christ loves creation and humankind with a love characterized by *eros*. Rogers argued that humans learn of God's love for them through the body and bodily desire. In this framework, the purpose of sexual desire is to teach humans of God's love for them, a task which is accomplished through the vocations of celibate monasticism and marriage. The result of this collection of moves is that human bodily desire is connected to one's knowledge of God. When applied to marriage, Rogers asserts that it is possible to attain knowledge of God's love through loving and being loved by one's spouse.

While agreeing with some of Rogers' position, Song provided two arguments to support a much more qualified understanding of the goodness of bodily desire. First, he argued that while bodily desire is created good by God, it has been distorted by sin. As a result, desire is prone to lust and selfishness. Yet, because desire does not vacate all of the goodness ascribed to it by the Creator, it also serves positive ends. Sexual desire serves as a finite symbol which points humans to the eternal. More specifically, human bodily desire reflects the love of God in the Trinity as well as God's love for creation. Second, Song argued that desire is connected to one's knowledge of God. According to Song, the reciprocal desire experienced and expressed by married couples or covenant partners witnesses in a limited way to the intimacy one will experience with God in the eschaton.

Experiential Difference

Another area in which the revisionists share a measure of agreement is in their affirmation of the uniqueness of same-sex experience. All four authors argue that same-sex relationships differ somehow from those of heterosexuals. However, each revisionist provides a distinct analysis of the similarities and differences between lesbian, gay, and heterosexual couples. They also disagree on how this experiential difference should impact a theology of relationships.

While not a central part of her theology of relationships, Stuart affirmed the uniqueness of same-sex experience.[7] She also acknowledged a further distinction between the experience of lesbian women and gay men, noting that the latter group benefits from societal structures in a way that the former does not. As such, she contended that it is characteristic of gay men to seek a place of equality at the social table by downplaying difference. By contrast, lesbian women seek to overturn the table. This explains why Stuart's project does not seek for marriage to be extended to same-sex couples, but instead works to dismantle the institution.

Thatcher also supported the existence of an experiential difference between same-sex and heterosexual couples. Theologically speaking, the primary difference between the two groups is that one relationship is procreative while the other is not. Based on this distinction, Thatcher argued that same-sex relationships should not be called marriage, because marriage requires an openness to procreation. At the same time, Thatcher also sought to minimize the difference between heterosexual and same-sex couples. He compared being gay to being left-handed. He also argued that all people, regardless of orientation, are susceptible to sin and in need of redemption. Furthermore, all relationships are called to exhibit a form of fruitfulness. Though the fruitfulness of same-sex couples differs from heterosexual relationships, both groups demonstrate a kind of reproduction. Rhetorically, these statements are designed to emphasize what humans have in common, rather than the difference inherent in a discussion set in terms of binary sexual orientation. Thatcher concludes that same-sex relationships should receive the same benefit and be subject

---

7. Stuart relies upon the "experience of lesbian women and gay men," not in opposition but as an alternative to heterosexual experience. See Stuart, *Just Good Friends*, 22.

to the same standards as heterosexual relationships. Through these two moves, Thatcher attempted to balance the similarities and differences between same-sex and heterosexual couples. However, by extending the same benefits to both groups under different relational titles, Thatcher revealed his preference for similarity over difference.

Rogers altered the terms of the discussion but arrived at a similar conclusion as Thatcher. While affirming differential experience for same-sex and heterosexual couples, Rogers sought to minimize difference. Two moves helped Rogers accomplish this goal. First, he rejected procreation as a necessary telos of marriage, instead, arguing that marriage exists to transform bodily desire through asceticism. By removing the primary characteristic which differentiates same-sex from heterosexual couples, i.e., procreation, Rogers reduced the distance between the two groups. Second, Rogers built commonality between heterosexual and same-sex relationships by focusing on the theological characteristics of heterosexual marriage which can be extended to same-sex couples. For example, the call to asceticism applies to all Christians, whether straight or gay. Furthermore, all Christians are called to encourage the church through their relationships. Rogers argued that weddings, both straight and gay, accomplish this by witnessing to Trinitarian love. Thus, Rogers agreed with Thatcher that similarity supersedes difference.

At first glance, one can understand the rationale driving these authors. Humans have the tendency of defining ourselves against the backdrop of an "other" who differs from us. We respond to the foreignness of this individual or group by associating our identity with truth and goodness and that of the other with truth's opposite.[8] This propensity of demonizing the other is especially evident in past and contemporary discussions of the sexual other. In such a setting, there is merit in emphasizing that what unites humankind is greater than that which divides. However, the attempt to deemphasize difference also results in the removal of particularity. The previous chapter noted that gay and lesbian theologians emphasize the particularity of their experience. One immediately wonders if the solution presented by Thatcher and Rogers adequately honors the uniqueness of gay and lesbian experience which queer authors hold in high esteem. While diminishing difference in an effort to reduce or eliminate homophobic violence is commendable, extending heterosexual marriage, or some equivalent in all but name, to same-sex couples results in homogenization. In such a setting, the church is unable to learn from the particular giftedness of lesbian, gay, and heterosexual individuals. It must be acknowledged that, as fallen creatures, we see through a

---

8. See Connolly, *Identity/Difference*.

glass dimly. As institutions comprised of sinful humans, churches and denominational bodies have theological blind spots. Often, these murky points in one's theological system can only be identified by an outsider. As churches and denominations seek to formulate theological positions on marriage and sexuality, the tendency has been to view the sexual other as a problem that must be solved. Perhaps ecclesial bodies would benefit from assuming a different posture toward same-sex-attracted individuals. By emphasizing and honoring the uniqueness of same-sex-attracted individuals and couples, the church has the opportunity to learn from those at the margins, to be both instructed and corrected by those whom the church has traditionally labeled the "sexual other." Assuming such a posture would require a great deal of humility on the part of the church. It would also necessitate repentance for the church's many sins against same-sex-attracted individuals. It remains to be seen if denominations and congregations, particularly in the Evangelical world, are ready for this kind of move.

Thankfully, our final author provides the beginnings of an alternative framework for addressing the difference between heterosexual and same-sex relationships. Similar to the other revisionists, Song affirmed that the experience of lesbian and gay individuals is distinct from that of heterosexual individuals. In agreement with Thatcher, Song asserted that the key theological difference between same-sex couples and heterosexual couples is the ability to procreate. However, contrary to other revisionists, Song argued that this key difference cannot be abandoned in an effort to extend marriage to same-sex couples. Marriage has a distinct theological shape provided by the doctrine of creation. As a creation good, the institution requires an openness to physical procreation and, by extension, sexual difference. Since neither of these criteria are met by same-sex couples, marriage is not an option for them. Song asserted that different theological grounding is needed to make space for same-sex relationships, as well as heterosexual sexually active relationships that are not directed toward procreation.

In an effort to adequately honor the particular experience and giftedness of intentionally non-procreative couples, Song presented covenant partnership as a third relational vocation alongside marriage and celibacy. Covenant partnership shares certain characteristics with marriage. For example, both witness to God's covenant with humankind, and are therefore characterized by the covenant goods of faithfulness and permanence. Marriage and covenant partnership are also both vocations to which one is called and gifted by God. However, as a distinct vocation, covenant partnership also differs from marriage. Whereas marriage is grounded in creation and is directed toward procreation, covenant partnership is grounded in covenant, a doctrinal category which will be fulfilled in the eschaton. In the time between the times in which we now reside, covenant partnership witnesses to the eschaton, a time when there will be no more death and therefore no need for procreation. Thus, it is not open to physical procreation. However, the relationship is open to other forms of fruitfulness in service to the Kingdom of God. Because covenant partnership is a vocation, Song argued that the precise shape of the couple's fruitfulness will be determined, in part, by God's call upon the couple. A key move for Song was his assertion that the parameters of covenant partnership are wide enough to include same-sex couples as well as heterosexual couples who are called to refrain from procreating. In summary, Song honored the distinctiveness of same-sex experience by emphasizing procreation as a theologically significant category which differentiates same-sex couples from heterosexual couples. Rather than assimilate same-sex couples into the heteronormative institution of marriage, Song offered the distinct vocation of covenant partnership, a genitally expressed, relational vocation characterized by faithfulness, permanence, and a commitment to allegorical fruitfulness.

Song's argument is more theologically appealing than that of the other revisionists for several reasons. Thatcher and Rogers attempted to redefine the institution of marriage in such a way that its parameters are wide enough to include same-sex couples. In doing so, both revisionists rejected procreation as a necessary good of marriage. This move resulted in their theologies of marriage relying solely on the goods of fidelity and permanence. In the process, both Thatcher and Rogers obfuscated the connection between marriage and the doctrine of creation. By contrast, Song argued that because marriage is grounded in creation, procreation is essential to the institution. Marriage is required to be open to procreation as the result of the couple's sexual relationship, a possibility that is precluded by same-sex relationships. Covenant partnerships are grounded in covenant and the eschaton, and are therefore not directed toward procreation. Thus, the connection between creation and marriage is preserved, while an option is presented for the inclusion of same-sex couples which relies on different theological logic. Through this move, Song suggests a repositioning of the church's posture toward the challenge presented by same-sex experience. Instead of being a problem that must be solved, same-sex-attracted individuals offer the church an opportunity for communal growth. Thus, Song overcomes the liberal premise that the contemporary church stands in a place of enlightened superiority over and above an archaic theological tradition by affirming that church tradition was correct to articulate and support a theology of marriage characterized by procreation and sexual difference. He also breaks with the biblicism of traditionalists by reading Scripture through a christological lens, thereby encouraging the expansion of what it means to be the church community in light of same-sex relationships.

Areas of Contention

This chapter has examined theological claims by the revisionists which are in concordance with the theological tradition, as well as areas of agreement between the revisionists which places them in relative tension with the overall trajectory of the tradition. There are also two topics where the stances of the authors place them at odds with the historical claims of the theological tradition: sexual difference and procreation.

Sexual Difference

As has been discussed above, all four revisionists affirm the distinctiveness of lesbian and gay experience. However, it is necessary to examine the grounding for the claim that the experience of lesbian and gay couples differs from that of heterosexual couples. This claim can be parsed a variety of ways. Consider an argument posed by Stuart, who traced the difference in experience between same-sex and heterosexual individuals to a divergence in their experience of societal norms. Stuart lamented the forces which form and construct human sociality through norms, sex, gender, class, etc., calling the phenomenon the "original sin" of socialization. A second way to describe the difference in same-sex and heterosexual individuals is to appeal to the difference in the direction of their bodily desires. The latter group's desire is directed toward the opposite sex, while the desire of the former group is directed toward members of the same sex. However, this argument depends for its coherence on sexual difference, a third way of describing why the experience of heterosexual and same-sex-attracted individuals differs from each other. While this analysis has been brief, these descriptions reveal that the question of experiential difference involves a confluence of societal norms, bodily desire, and sexual difference. I now turn my attention to the issue of sexual difference as it relates to a theology of relationships.

This project has argued that the church's traditional theology of marriage requires sexual differentiation. Augustine provided two arguments to support this position. First, he affirmed the goodness of the body and its created form. He argued that God created humans as sexually differentiated beings before the fall, and as such the anatomical features that distinguish male and female bodies are good. Second, he asserted that marriage and marital intercourse exists for the purpose of procreation. Procreation is a direct result of the sexual relationship between a sexually differentiated couple. Therefore, the telos of marriage requires sexually differentiated partners. The previous chapter demonstrated a trend by revisionists in the field of theological ethics regarding their approach to sexual difference. Three of the four revisionists denied the necessity of sexual differentiation to a theology of marriage. I will briefly review the various arguments used to support this claim, followed by an examination of Song's approach to the issue of sexual difference.

Stuart argued that theology's attempt to require relationships to be sexually differentiated is a patriarchal construction. To refute the necessity of sexual difference, Stuart criticized marriage, the institution which undergirds the requirement. She argued that marriage is a social construct developed by men to distribute their property and power to their male heir. According to this narrative, marriage is an institution established to afford men the opportunity to achieve and maintain social dominance over women. This aim is accomplished through sexually differentiated, procreative, monogamous marriage where a patriarch is assured the sexual loyalty of woman and the purity of his bloodline. Stuart's argument is that sexual difference is a necessary relational component only because marriage, a patriarchal institution, makes it so. Stuart's project and mine agree in emphasizing the connection between sex, procreation, and sexual differentiation in marriage. Where we differ is that Stuart described this connection in social terms, while I account for this connection in theological terms. If the importance of sexual difference is to be negated or altered, this task must be accomplished using the doctrinal resources available to the church.

Thatcher chose a different means of negating the importance of sexual difference. To make his case, Thatcher combined a limited doctrine of creation with social Trinitarianism. He argued that while a theology of marriage is often grounded in creation, it is necessary to take the discussion "back" one step further. According to Thatcher, the inner relationship of the Triune God, rather than creation, is the appropriate grounding for a theology of human relationships and marriage. Thatcher argued that the Godhead is a community of persons-in-relationship characterized by love. He described the act of creation as an overflow or a sharing of divine love. Humans are created in the image of God, and therefore reflect the characteristics seen in the Trinity in a limited way. Thus, humans are relational beings created to share love with the other. Thatcher asserted that humans share love through their sexuality, which he defined as the way one relates to the world and others as male and female.

This description reveals Thatcher's method for addressing the question of sexual difference as it relates to the church's theology of marriage. On the one hand, Thatcher asserted that humans are created male and female, a reference to the doctrine of creation. On the other hand, Thatcher made clear that the doctrine of the Trinity is the driving force behind his relational theology. Because marriage is grounded in the Trinity, the Trinity supplants creation in Thatcher's account. Two additional moves by Thatcher make this clear. First, Thatcher asserted that sexual difference is not necessary in human relationships. He supported this claim by arguing that in the Trinity, "each of the Persons transcends gender difference."[9] Divine love is not defined by sexual differentiation. Because human love is based on divine love, its expression need not be limited to sexually differentiated relationships. Second, Thatcher argued that sexuality is part of created human nature and is therefore good. However, he made no direct statement concerning his conviction that sexual differentiation is good. A generous reading would be that because sexuality is intimately connected to being male and female in Thatcher's definition, he would consider sexual difference to be good as well. However, it may be that Thatcher intentionally refrains from making such a statement. Affirming that sexual differentiation is good would necessitate some level of articulation regarding the content of that statement. It would also require Thatcher's theology to rely more heavily on the doctrine of creation, a move which would complicate Thatcher's claim that the necessity of sexual difference is overcome by an appeal to the Trinity.

In his effort to define the parameters of marriage widely enough that the institution can include same-sex relationships, Rogers presented, perhaps, the most sophisticated challenge to the importance of sexual difference. He brought together two arguments to support this move. First, Rogers affirmed the significance of the human body as it relates to sharing love. Like Thatcher, Rogers argued that Trinitarian love is the basis for human love. Whereas Triune love has no spatial or temporal limits, human love requires both time and space. Bodies are the special medium through which humans express and share love. They are the creaturely limit that allows for the possibility of touch and embrace. Defining human love as a bodily expression which takes place in time and space enabled Rogers to introduce his second argument. Not only did he support the goodness of bodies, he also affirmed the goodness of sexuality and sexual orientation. According to Rogers, sexuality serves two purposes. It enables humans to express love in time and space, and it also serves as the seat of desire. Sexual orientation, which Rogers described as "a special appreciation for the particular delights of special finitudes, or bodily forms," is the medium through

---

9. Thatcher, *Liberating Sex*, 146.

which bodily desire is expressed.[10] Because humans were created to image God by sharing love, Rogers argued that sexuality and sexual orientation are fundamental characteristics of human nature.

Rogers brought bodies and sexuality together through his use of the doctrine of election. He asserted that God's election of the Hebrews, signified by circumcision, and God's engrafting of the Gentiles without requiring circumcision are both concerned with the body. Because the penis is the body part in question, Rogers deduced that election involves the way in which one lives one's sexual differentiation. Therefore, election is connected to both bodies and sexuality. This afforded Rogers the space to refer to lesbian, gay, and heterosexual bodies.

From the designations of lesbian, gay, and heterosexual bodies, it initially appears that Rogers affirmed the importance of sexual difference. However, these descriptions conflate sexual difference with sexual orientation. The pairing of "gay," "lesbian," and "heterosexual" with "bodies" indicates that those bodies are understood and unified through the category of sexual orientation. Two problems arise from this description. First, the claim that bodies are understood through sexual orientation relies on the assumption that the latter category is stable enough to bring intelligibility to the former. However, the requirement that one's orientation must be continually performed to prove its stability presents a challenge to the presumed fixed character of the category. Thus, the unity of the self which is achieved through the performance of one's sexuality will only ever be partial and unstable. Second, Rogers' description of gay, lesbian, and heterosexual bodies was not a reference to real male or female bodies, but to sexualized bodies. Throughout his work, Rogers affirmed the goodness of bodies, bodily desire, and sexuality, apart from reference to humans created male and female. Rogers' solution to the problem that sexual difference poses for the inclusion of same-sex-attracted individuals within the church's traditional theology was to ignore bodily difference and speak only of the sexualized body.

Affirming sexual difference as a good, God-given part of human nature would problematize Rogers' account. By way of example, consider Rogers' argument against requiring lesbian and gay individuals to be celibate. He asserted that all humans have a specific bodily vocation. To put it another way, vocations are a God-given calling that are specific to each individual. As such, the concept of vocation affirms particularity while rejecting genetic determinism. Because of the particularity of calling, one's vocation cannot be predetermined based on membership to a specific people group. According

---

10. Rogers, *Sexuality and the Christian Body*, 201.

to Rogers, forcing lesbian and gay individuals to a life of celibacy violates the particularity of vocation, i.e., the specific bodily vocation to which one is called by God. Pressing further, Rogers rightly recognizes that Paul describes both marriage and celibacy as gifts (1 Cor 7:7). Thus, forced celibacy does not recognize the specific gift that God bestows on the individual. Unfortunately, based on the construction of his argument, Rogers denies that created givenness, i.e., genetics, plays any role in God's calling on an individual's life. The issue that Rogers' account is unable to resolve is whether God's creation of humans as male and female has any bearing on the specific bodily vocation to which individuals are called. Referring to the goodness of bodies apart from their specific shape, i.e., their creation as male or female, enabled Rogers to deny the importance of sexual difference. However, this move is made at the cost of the doctrine of creation.

Song provided a unique solution to the problem that sexual difference poses to the church's inclusion of same-sex-attracted individuals. Whereas Thatcher denied the importance of sexual differentiation by appealing to Trinitarian love as the basis for human love, and Rogers appealed to sexualized bodies rather than male and female bodies, Song affirmed the goodness of sexed bodies. He asserted that rejecting the importance of sexual difference borders on the gnostic tendency to deny the goodness of the material creation and its created form. He stated that this move also results in the obfuscation of the link between sexual difference and procreation in marriage. According to the first creation account, humans are commanded to have dominion over the earth. Dominion is accomplished through procreation, which is the result of the one-flesh relationship of the sexually differentiated couple. Based on this logic, the doctrine of creation ties marriage to procreation; procreation can only be accomplished through sexual differentiation. Thus, marriage requires sexual differentiation.

Key for Song's account was his assertion that sexual difference is only necessary because of its link to procreation. As will be discussed in greater detail below, Song argued that Christ fulfilled dominion, thereby rendering procreation redundant. If procreation is no longer necessary, Song argued, then there is no theological reason to insist that relationships be sexually differentiated. Stated succinctly by Song, "Baptism and the new identity in Christ take us beyond the creation categories of male and female in a way that renders them no longer of defining significance."[11]

This quotation raises an important question: how deeply are bodies gendered in Song's account? One of the contemporary issues at stake in this question is the challenge that transgendered individuals pose to a traditional

11. Song, *Covenant and Calling*, 49.

understanding of the body and gender. It is no longer clear that anatomical sex readily corresponds to gender for all people. Some individuals who identify as transgender have elected to undergo hormone therapy and/or sex-reassignment surgery in effort to repair the dissonance they experience between body and gender. While a more in-depth discussion of this topic cannot be undertaken here, it allows the initial question of this paragraph to be posed another way: does Song believe it is possible for a male body to become a female body, whether through surgery, hormone therapy, or through some other means? If so, then Song's response would challenge his affirmation of the goodness of human bodies created male and female. If he denies that such a transformation is possible, presumably he would support the claim by relying on the doctrine of creation.

Song attempted to strike a delicate balance by honoring the importance of sexual difference in the creation accounts, while taking seriously Paul's claim that in Christ there is "no longer male and female" (Gal 3:28). This enabled him to refer to "the sexed nature of bodies that is *in some sense* given with creation."[12] The italicized phrase reveals an important aspect of Song's account of sexual difference. Song refrained from articulating how humans are to live in the world as beings created male and female. To put it another way, he did not clearly describe the relationship between bodies and gender. Such descriptions often attempt to negate the dissonance that humans experience between sexed bodies and gender. Rogers presented one such account. He portrayed the ideal self as a unified entity. Such unity is achieved through the performance of a fixed, intelligible sexuality within the vocation of marriage. Gay and lesbian individuals, like heterosexuals, experience division within the self. However, unlike heterosexuals, lesbian and gay individuals are denied the means by which unity is restored: marriage. Thus, marriage is the solution to gender/body dissonance in Rogers' account. Song's hesitation to eliminate the dissonance between sexed bodies and gender is what differentiates his account from that of Rogers. While this posture leaves the reader feeling a bit unsatisfied, perhaps Song's willingness to live within this tension points to a deep theological truth.

From Augustine, we learned that sin has destroyed the unity of the self. In a fallen world, it is not possible to achieve self-unity, here, parsed as gender/body unity, through marriage, sex, or any other means. According to this perspective, humans will continually be required to navigate how they respond to their creatureliness; discerning what it means to be created male and female in the image of God is part of what it means to be human.

---

12. Song, *Covenant and Calling*, xvi.

Procreation

Not only did the revisionists seek to alter the church's traditional understanding of sexual difference, they also challenged the necessity of procreation to marriage. This project argued that the church has held procreation to be an essential telos of marriage, more or less consistently, since Augustine's articulation of his theology of marriage. Concurrently, it has been acknowledged that procreation is one of the two crucial theological barriers to the church's affirmation of same-sex relationships. In attempting to create space for same-sex couples within the church, the revisionists bear the burden of demonstrating how a same-sex relationship that is genitally expressed but not procreative is compatible with the church's theology, which has consistently linked sexual expression with *proles*.

In seeking to navigate this tension, three of the revisionists examined in this project denied procreation as a necessary telos of marriage. For example, Stuart argued that the church has tended to support *proles* as the only good to which the couple's sexual relationship is directed. She identified three outcomes of this position. First, because of the singular focus on procreation, the church has had difficulty recognizing other goods of sexual intimacy. To combat this deficiency, Stuart argued that all actions receive meaning in a specific context. More specifically, it is the couple who provides meaning to its sexual relationship. It follows that the significance of sexual intimacy will vary widely between couples, rather than sex being limited to one meaning. While affirming that sexual intimacy serves a variety of ends, Stuart also argued that sex is a good in itself. She asserted that sexual intimacy is one way in which humans are invited to enjoy bodily existence and celebrate the goodness of the body. Second, by focusing on the procreative good of a sexual relationship, the church has been slow to identify and denounce forms of violence which exist in procreative marriage. Physical, verbal, and emotional abuse are tolerated or overlooked so long as the relationship fulfills its procreative end. Finally, identifying procreation as the primary telos of marriage results in one's partner becoming merely a means to an end. In this schema, one's marital partner is not a person to whom sacrificial love is directed. Instead, he becomes an instrument by which the proper telos of marriage is accomplished. Based on these arguments, Stuart rejected procreation as a necessary good of marriage.

Stuart's project correctly identifies several dangers associated with the church's historical tendency to identify procreation as the primary or only good of a couple's sexual relationship. However, it is unclear that her criticism provides the theological grounding necessary to sever the link between sex and procreation. Furthermore, even if the reader decides that she has succeeded, Stuart stops short of the constructive task of describing what purpose a couple's sexual relationship serves once the procreative telos is negated. Chapter 2 demonstrated Augustine's commitment to the link between sex and its procreative telos. His motive for supporting this connection was not a prudish attempt to remove joy or pleasure from the sexual experience, as Stuart hints in her work. The reason for this connection stems from Augustine's conviction that sexual intimacy requires an external telos, without which the couple's sexual life will become little more than an embodiment of self-centered hedonism. Sex serves the purpose of procreation, but even procreation is not an ultimate end. For Augustine, procreation and the raising of children exists for the good of the church. The point is, if procreation is no longer the external good to which a couple's sexual relationship is directed, Augustine asks that a new theological telos be provided.

Thatcher provided a more constructive argument about the relationship between sex and procreation. On the one hand, he asserted that procreation is a good of marriage, and a way for married couples to image the divine. This description highlights two aspects of Thatcher's thought on the subject. First, procreation belongs to marriage. While Thatcher allowed for various levels of sexual activity to occur outside of marriage, he argued that procreation is reserved only for marriage. The reason for this is because children expect lifelong commitments, and only marriage provides the commitment to permanent fidelity that fulfills those expectations. So emphatic was his commitment to keeping procreation in the context of marriage, that Thatcher described extra-marital *proles* as running contrary to the best interests of the child. Second, Thatcher asserted that procreation is a way that married couples image God. Thatcher argued that humans are called to reflect the characteristics of the Triune God in whose image they are created. Through procreation, the married couple mirrors God's creative power.

On the other hand, Thatcher also sought to limit the theological connection between sexual intimacy and procreation. He made three arguments to support this move. First, Thatcher asserted that the necessary link between sex and procreation is a patriarchal construct. The assumption supporting the necessity of procreation is that the separation of pleasure from its function is sinful. Therefore, the pleasure of sex must be connected to its procreative function. However, Thatcher argued that this statement assumes male bodies and male sexual experience to be normative. While there is an anatomical link between pleasure and reproduction in male bodies, it is possible to separate pleasure from reproductive function in female bodies. Based on this argument, Thatcher concluded that creating a necessary link between sex and procreation does not account for the experience of women and should therefore be rejected. Second, Thatcher argued that though procreation is a good of marriage, it is not a necessary good. While he affirmed the divine command for humans to "be fruitful and multiply," Thatcher also asserted that physical procreation is but one way in which married couples demonstrate obedience to that command. Based on his preference for an allegorical reading of the procreative command, Thatcher contends that fruitfulness is not exhausted by *proles*. Obedience to the command to be fruitful, whether by physical procreation, adoption, or some other form of fruitfulness, satisfies the external telos needed to keep marriage from collapsing into coupledom. Finally, Thatcher argued that the sexual intimacy of the married couple has meaning beyond procreation. Sex also exists for the good of the couple. In marital lovemaking, each partner shares his or her body that it might be received by the other. Thatcher calls this act a sacrament that mirrors Christ's eucharistic act. Because of its sacramental character, lovemaking allows married couples to participate in divine love. For Thatcher, the argument that sex serves goods beyond procreation supports his claim that *proles* is not necessary to marriage.

In summary, Thatcher's solution to the tension in the relationship between procreation and sexual intimacy is twofold. First, he argued that obedience to the command to be fruitful and multiply is part of imaging God in the context of marriage. Thus, he affirmed the procreative command to be normative for his account Christian sexual ethics. Second, he demonstrated his preference for an allegorical reading of this command. The result is that the link between physical procreation and marriage is rejected in favor of allegorical fruitfulness.

Rogers relied on a different set of arguments but arrived at a similar conclusion. He challenged the necessity of procreation in four ways. First, Rogers asserted that requiring marriage be linked to procreation results in a distorted understanding of God's act of creation. A traditional interpretation of creation asserts that humans image God's creative act through procreation. Here, rejecting procreation in marriage amounts to a refusal to image God. Thus, where *proles* is necessary to marriage, Rogers argued, creation becomes a necessity by extension. Because theology understands creation to be a gift rather than a necessity, Rogers asserted that procreation must be considered a non-necessity in order to properly reflect God's creative act. Second, Rogers argued that procreation is primarily concerned with the good of the species rather than with individual couples. According to Rogers, this move is necessary to account for the celibacy of Jesus and to explain how the church considers the marriages of infertile couples to be licit. Since procreation applies to the species, then it is not necessary for every marriage to bring forth children. Third, Rogers argued that Jesus' virgin birth and his decision to remain celibate, despite the command to be fruitful, problematize the necessity of physical procreation. Finally, he argued that marriage and sex serve sanctifying, rather than procreative, ends. According to Rogers, both sex and marriage exist to sanctify *eros,* thereby contributing to the transformation of marriage partners into children of God. While children may contribute to sanctification, they are not necessary to the task. Based on these arguments, Rogers asserted that procreation is not a suitable metaphor to describe how humans image God.

In place of the procreative metaphor, Rogers argued that Trinitarian love expressed in creation through election should be the primary analogate for marriage. In this paradigm, humans image God not through procreation, but through adoption. According to Rogers, adoption serves as a reminder that a child, like creation, is a gift rather than a necessity or an achievement. Adoption also better represents God's choosing of Israel as a covenantal partner and the extension of that covenant to the Gentiles.

The rejection of procreation as a primary telos of marriage, coupled with the affirmation of election as primary grounding for marriage has two implications that are important for our current discussion of the relationship between procreation and marriage. First, the doctrine of election supersedes the doctrine of creation in Rogers' account. Second, like Thatcher, Rogers elevates an allegorical reading of the procreative command to the exclusion of physical procreation. In essence, adoption is privileged over procreation.

Throughout his career, Augustine wrestled with this tension between an allegorical and a more historical, concrete interpretation of the creation accounts. In his early work, Augustine privileged an allegorical reading, while toward the middle of his career he preferred a historical interpretation. In his more mature work, Augustine concluded that both interpretations are needed to make sense of the creation accounts and the command to be fruitful and multiply. For Augustine, creation is a real event in history, and that event also points to a spiritual truth. He argued that the various elements of the creation story "stood for something other than what they were, but all the same they were themselves bodily realities."[13] The last phrase of that quotation encapsulates what is at stake in the attempt by Rogers and Thatcher to jettison a concrete reading of creation in favor of a purely allegorical interpretation: the ability for the doctrine of creation to say anything normative about actual human bodies.

In contrast with the previous three authors, Song affirmed procreation as a necessary good of marriage. According to Song, marriage is a creation

---

13. Augustine, *Literal Meaning of Genesis* 8.8. See also Augustine, *Literal Meaning of Genesis* 8.9–11, 13; 9.12, 20–22; 11.38–39, 50–55.

good, and as such the institution must receive its shape from the doctrine of creation. From the creation accounts, Song deduced that marriage has a definitive structure. As Genesis 1:28 indicates, humans are created male and female for the purpose of completing the task of having dominion over the earth. This task is accomplished through obedience to the command to be fruitful and multiply. Therefore, the logic of Scripture indicates that procreation is a necessary good of marriage. Procreation is essential, in part, because it provides an external telos for marital sex in the form of children. This external telos prevents a couple's sexual relationship from merely satisfying selfish desire. Pressing further, Song argued that procreation is the key feature that distinguishes heterosexual relationships from same-sex relationships. He described the ability to procreate as a "morally relevant difference," and called into question attempts by Stuart, Thatcher, and Rogers to indicate that same-sex and heterosexual relationships are analogous. Thus, Song affirmed a concrete interpretation of the command to be fruitful, indicating that marriage is necessarily directed toward procreation.

At the same time, Song also endorsed an allegorical reading of marital fruitfulness. To support this claim, he pointed to the example of infertile marriages. In instances where a couple discovers that procreation is not an option, the church still affirms that the relationship is a marriage. Song argued that while procreation is not a possibility for these couples, their marriages are open to other kinds of allegorical fruitfulness. While Song, Rogers, and Thatcher all appeal to the existence of infertile couples to support their allegorical reading of the creation stories, Song's reference differs from the other two authors. Thatcher and Rogers equated infertile heterosexual couples with both fertile heterosexual couples who are deliberately childless and same-sex couples who are biologically unable to procreate. This argument is used to sever the connection between procreation and marriage, thereby overcoming the claim that same-sex relationships are illegitimate because they are unable to procreate. By contrast, Song argued that learning that one cannot have children differs from rejecting procreation or entering a relationship with prior knowledge that procreation is not an option. The moral difference between these groups is significant enough that they cannot be equated, nor can the existence of infertile couples be used directly as an argument to reject the necessity of procreation to marriage. According to Song, both an allegorical and a concrete interpretation of the command to be fruitful are needed to ensure that a theology of marriage is grounded in a robust doctrine of creation.

Song's arguments on procreation and sexual difference fundamentally alters the conversation within Christian sexual ethics regarding same-sex relationships.[14] Prior to Song, the primary arguments determining whether a relationship is licit centered on sexual differentiation or the orientation/direction of one's desires. However, Song has argued that sexual difference is necessary only in its relationship to procreation. If procreation has been fulfilled by Christ and is no longer necessary, then the theological logic requiring relationships to be sexually differentiated no longer holds. According to Song, sexual difference is no longer a theologically all-determining category. Rather, the ability to procreate is the primary theological category used to differentiate between couples. Thus, the central issue of debate has been altered.

New Claims in Christian Sexual Ethics

My examination of the various ways in which revisionists are appropriating and adapting Augustine's theology of marriage has revealed two relatively new avenues being pursued in an effort to create space for same-sex couples. The first is an appeal to the inner life of the Trinity as an analogy for sex, and the second is the claim that covenant serves as the basis for a new relational vocation alongside marriage and celibacy.

Social Trinitarian Theology and Sex

Whereas Augustine's psychological analogy for the Trinity dominated the West since the fifth century, the revitalization of the social model of the Trinity is one of the prominent shifts in twentieth-century theology.[15] It is beyond the scope of this project to examine the validity of the social trinitarian model to describe the Godhead. My aim, here, is to examine the ways in which the revisionists employ the social Trinity in a discussion of marriage and sex.

Social trinitarian theology is not prevalent in Stuart's theology of friendship, so I will proceed to Thatcher's use of the doctrine. According to Thatcher, knowledge of the Triune life is derived from the gospels' accounts of life, teachings, death, and resurrection of Christ. However, this is not the only source of knowledge about the inner life of the Trinity. Thatcher also asserted that the Incarnation shows that revelation is experienced in the body. Therefore, human relationships disclose something about the nature of the Triune God. Based on his analysis of information gleaned from Scripture and experience, Thatcher argued that the three equal, distinct, yet

---

14. To my knowledge, Song is the first scholar to make this argument.
15. Gresham, "Social Model of the Trinity," 325–43.

unified persons of the Trinity exist in a relationship of love characterized by "interdependence, interrelation, and communion."[16] Because humans are created in the image of the Triune God, Thatcher deduced, these same characteristics are reflected in human relationships in a limited way. To flesh out this move, Thatcher combined the social trinitarian model with the doctrines of creation and incarnation. He asserted that while divine love is completely self-sufficient, God chose to share Triune love more widely through the act of creation and by sharing God's self in the person of Jesus. From these arguments, Thatcher reasoned that divine love, and by extension, human love are meant to be shared. Creaturely love is shared through sexuality, a part of human nature that God uses to invite humans into relationship with others. Thus, the Triune God is the grounding for a theology of human relationship, sex, and marriage.

Rogers' account of the social trinitarian model differed from Thatcher's in the way the analogy functioned. Whereas knowledge of the Triune life can be gleaned from creaturely relationships in Thatcher's theology, Rogers insisted that human experience is unreliable because of sin. Therefore, knowledge of the Triune life must begin with what is revealed in Scripture and described by the theological tradition. Thus, Rogers' account represented an improvement over Thatcher's, precisely because Rogers combined his trinitarian theology with hamartiology. Rogers then made three moves to establish a connection between the Trinity and marriage. First, Rogers asserted that the Trinity is made up of three distinct, unified persons who share love and celebrate the sharing of love. In the Godhead, the reciprocal sharing and celebrating of love occurs free from temporal and special constraints. Second, Rogers argued that creation is an overflow of divine love, where the reciprocal love of the Trinity is embodied in time and space. Bodily boundaries enable the possibility for touch and embrace, while time allows for relationships to develop through sequential mutual self-giving. Third, the creaturely constraints of time and space make possible the vocations of monasticism and marriage. It is in faithfulness to a specific location and a commitment to permanence that marriage and monasticism mirror Trinitarian love.

As was noted above, Rogers' decision to ground marriage in the Trinity enabled him to bypass the creation categories of procreation and sexual difference. While this move benefited Rogers' goal of extending marriage to same-sex couples, it did not afford a way for him to provide a theological account of why humans are created male and female or why children are the result of a sexually differentiated couple's sexual intercourse. Grounding

---

16. Thatcher, *Liberating Sex*, 54.

marriage in the Trinity resulted in procreation and sexual difference being insufficiently integrated into Rogers' theology. Based on this criticism, it is unclear whether a doctrine of the Trinity can do sufficient work to sustain a theology of marriage.

Song presented a more qualified use of trinitarian theology to undergird his theology of relationships. He asserted that the analogy between Trinitarian relationality and human relationality must function in a top-down manner, with the Triune God as the primary analogue. The characteristics that God exhibits in the inner life of the Trinity are disclosed in God's relation to creation. God's relational characteristics are demonstrated to humans through election and covenant. The constant commitment that God shows toward God's covenant people reveals the relational characteristics of faithfulness and permanence. As humans reflect these relational characteristics, they image God. Thus, in a limited and finite way, the faithfulness and permanence of marriage reflects God's covenant with human beings, which reflects the relationship between the Trinitarian Persons. Song's application of the Trinity to his theology of marriage differed from that of the other two revisionists in one important aspect. Thatcher and Rogers argued that the Trinity provides the primary grounding for a theology of marriage. By contrast, Song asserted that the doctrine of the Trinity offers logic for the marital goods of faithfulness and permanence, but creation is needed to account for procreation. According to Song, both doctrines are needed to articulate a robust theology of marriage.

Covenant and Same-Sex Relationships

While the use of the covenantal metaphor for marriage is not new, the mode in which the concept is being employed by contemporary revisionists differs greatly from that of theologians of previous eras. For example, Augustine did not rely on covenant as a primary analogy to support his theology of marriage. Of his works on marriage, the only reference to Ephesians 5:22–33, the primary passage cited in support of the analogy, is found in his late work, *Continence*. Augustine used the reference to support the logic of dualistic, hierarchical submission of the wife to the husband, not to undergird the goodness of marriage.[17] For Augustine, the concept of covenant was primarily associated with a divine command which requires human obedience.[18] In chapter 3, Stuart argued that this kind of application of the covenantal metaphor, employed here by Augustine, is characteristic

---

17. Augustine, *Continence*, 207.
18. Augustine, *City of God* 16.27.

of the way covenant has been used throughout the Christian tradition. As a result, marriage has been a relationship of dominance and submission, characteristics integral to the covenantal metaphor in Scripture. Based on this analysis, Stuart rejected covenant as an appropriate metaphor for a relationship between two ontologically equal persons.

Stuart correctly asserted that the relationship between covenant and marriage is not without its problems. The examples of covenants found in Scripture illustrate the issue. Covenants between humans in the Hebrew Scriptures occur between unequal parties. Further complicating matters is the New Testament's association of marriage with the divine/human covenant. The latter is an agreement between beings of ontologically disproportionate power, while the former is made between equals. Therefore, the application of the divine/human covenant to human relationships is not a straightforward exercise. However, rejecting the covenantal metaphor entirely has wide-ranging consequences. For example, Song demonstrated that covenant provides a link between creation, Christology, and eschatology in salvation history. Removing that link disconnects marriage from a wealth of doctrinal resources available to support the institution. Consider another example. Covenant is one of the doctrines in which faithfulness and permanence are grounded for Thatcher, Rogers, and Song. Commitment to these goods of marriage reflects God's eternal faithfulness to God's covenant. If faithfulness and permanence do not rely on the God of the covenant for their coherence, other grounding must be provided. It is probable that such alternatives will not possess the theological weight necessary to ensure stability of these marital goods. Therefore, despite the difficulties associated with the covenantal metaphor, I am suggesting that the analogy is essential to an articulation of a theology of marriage. Application of the concept to human relationships should emphasize the everlasting faithfulness of the covenant God, but reject the domination and submission which characterize unequal relationships. This methodological choice hinges on the difference in the particular kind of relationship being referenced. The divine/human relationship is, by definition, unequal. As a result, human faithfulness to God includes obedience, submission, worship, etc. By contrast, marriage relationships are symmetrical. As such, it would be inappropriate for marital faithfulness to be defined in asymmetrical terms. Therefore, faithfulness in marriage is characterized by mutual submission. This application preserves the connection between marriage and covenant, while also highlighting the key difference between God's covenant with humans and human covenants.

Thatcher and Rogers appealed to covenant to support their efforts to make space for same-sex relationships. Thatcher asserted that the permanence and faithfulness of marriage are grounded in the faithfulness of the covenant God. As such, they are necessary goods of marriage. As previously discussed, Thatcher also rejected procreation as necessary to marriage by privileging an allegorical reading of the procreative command. Because marriages are only required to fulfill the covenantal goods of faithfulness and permanence, Thatcher argued, the logic of marriage is wide enough to include same-sex couples. Both heterosexual and same-sex couples can reflect the steadfast faithfulness of the covenant God. This project has argued that procreation is a necessary good of marriage. As such, *proles* cannot be bypassed by appealing to an allegorical reading of the procreative command paired with covenantal theology. From Thatcher's account, it is not entirely clear that he has demonstrated sufficient theological arguments to reject procreation while affirming faithfulness and permanence. Thatcher's approach could have been furthered by a more thorough appeal to covenantal theology. The covenant is the grand narrative of God's interaction with humankind in salvation history. It serves as the link between creation, Christology, and eschatology. In support of his allegorical reading of the procreative command, Thatcher could have appealed to the impact of Christ on the place of procreation in salvation history, or to the claim that in the eschaton marriage will be no more.

Rogers presented a more elegant use of the covenantal metaphor. Like Thatcher, Rogers grounded marital permanence and faithfulness in covenant. God's continued commitment to Israel, and the engrafting of the Gentiles demonstrate God's unending faithfulness to the covenant. Rogers extended this argument by appealing to Christology. He asserted that the God who initiates the covenant with Israel is made manifest in Christ, the bridegroom of the church. Thus, the covenantal God, embodied in Christ, becomes grounds for the covenant of marriage. Rogers' account of the engrafting of the Gentiles was critical to his project. Rogers asserted that the Gentiles were brought into the covenant as Gentiles, i.e., without being circumcised. Gentile nature, which Rogers identified with sexuality, was not a barrier to salvation. Based on this assertion, Rogers argued that the sexuality of same-sex-attracted individuals should not be a barrier to their inclusion within the church. Like Thatcher, Rogers also argued that procreation is not necessary to marriage. Therefore, a commitment to faithfulness and permanence is sufficient to constitute a marriage for heterosexual and same-sex couples.

The gain of this approach is its detailed engagement with covenant as it relates to salvation history. However, Rogers' use of the covenant metaphor does present a problem. By making salvation of the Gentiles analogous to the inclusion of same-sex marriage, Rogers gives similar weight to salvation and sexuality. The argument is constructed so that sexuality is given salvific importance. Therefore, refusing to affirm the sexuality of same-sex-attracted individuals by denying them the opportunity to marry represents a denial of God's salvific work. I am not intending to deny that there is a category called "sexuality," which serves as one of the ways through which humans understand themselves; I am intending to question the central place it has been given by Rogers. His claim about the salvific importance of sexuality, combined with his preference for the homogenization of same-sex and heterosexual experience, has two outcomes.

First, it reinforces a romantic view of marriage, placing weight on marriage that the institution was never meant to bear. It is a popular misconception that one can be made whole or complete through relationship with one's marriage partner. This romantic view remains intact in spite of the experiential evidence to the contrary, i.e., high divorce rates. Theologically speaking, it is impossible for fallen humans to regain the unity of self that sin destroyed by means of relationship with another fallen human. Acknowledging that the wholeness or salvation that we seek can only come from God in Christ allows marriage to be enjoyed properly. It can be a source of mutual love, encouragement, and growth. Based on this more qualified description of the institution, it may be that marriage serves as a location of sanctification, but, contrary to Rogers, it is not *the location* where sanctification takes place.

Second, Rogers' methodological choice hides the distinctiveness of same-sex relationships, essentially forcing lesbian and gay individuals back into the closet. By taking this route, the church misses a great opportunity. Difference is a much better teacher than similarity. What might the unique experience of same-sex individuals and their relationships have to teach us? Perhaps same-sex couples will remind the church that, eschatologically speaking, Christians have no ultimate stake in the preservation of the human race through physical procreation. Or maybe same-sex couples will challenge traditional gender roles. Here, seemingly silly questions posed to same-sex couples by heterosexuals about who takes out the trash and who does the dishes reveal important ethical implications regarding how couples relate to each other. Or perhaps same-sex individuals will call into question the image of masculinity, characterized by an obliteration of femininity, that is so often intertwined with our descriptions of God. There are certainly many other possibilities that have yet to be discovered. If the church is to profit from these occasions for instruction, she will need to emphasize the uniqueness and variety of same-sex experience.

Song presented a theologically rich analysis of the ways in which the concept of covenant might be applied to theologies of marriage and sexuality as they relate to same-sex couples. As previously mentioned, Song demonstrated that marriage is grounded in creation. The doctrine of creation provides marriage with its theological shape, namely, that the institution requires sexual differentiation and openness to physical procreation. Because of this trajectory, marriage is not open to same-sex couples because they do not meet these criteria. If the church is to find a way to include and bless the relationships of same-sex couples, she must rely on logic other than that which is supplied by the doctrine of creation.

Song argued that the doctrine of the covenant, understood through a christological lens, provides a possible way to navigate this challenge. Song asserted that the marital good of procreation is grounded in creation. Humans image God by having dominion over the earth, a task accomplished through procreation by the sexually differentiated couple. Song also contended that while creation provides the basis for procreation, the goods of fidelity and permanence are rooted in covenant. This move relies on a description of God as steadfastly faithful and then applies these characteristics to human relationships. Through the couple's commitment to faithfulness and permanence, marriage reflects and embodies God's covenant with God's people.

Following Augustinian logic, Song argued that the advent of Christ altered marriage and its place within salvation history. First, Song asserted that procreative marriage is no longer inevitable for Christians. Where Adam failed to have dominion over the earth, Christ succeeded through means other than procreation. Through Christ's triumph on the Cross and in the Resurrection, the necessity of procreation, and by extension, the necessity of marriage itself, were nullified. Therefore, it is no longer compulsory for the people of God to marry; instead, marriage remains a licit option, but Christians can also be called to bear witness to an eschatological future when marriage will be no more. Second, not only did the coming of Christ alter the inevitability of marriage, Song also argued that Christ revealed the divergent logics of the three goods of marriage. The creation good of procreation has been fulfilled by Christ, and therefore, procreation has a different theological value. *Proles* is no longer essential to the way humans image God. Instead, children are a sign of the goodness that God continues to display toward creation. By contrast, the goods of faithfulness and permanence are rooted in covenant, a theological category which points to the eschaton. Third, the divergent logics of the three goods reveals the possibility of a third relational vocation alongside marriage and celibacy: covenant partnership. Since this vocation is grounded in covenant, it is committed to the covenantal goods of faithfulness and permanence. Also because of its covenantal ties, covenant partnership points to the eschaton, a time where there will be no need for procreation or marriage. Therefore, the vocation is defined by expressions of allegorical fruitfulness, but not an openness to physical procreation. This claim has a direct impact on the place of sexual difference in a theology of relationship. According to Song, procreation provides the only theological logic for requiring marriage to be sexually differentiated. However, Christ has resituated these categories in such a way that "baptism and the new identity in Christ takes us beyond the creation categories of male and female in a way that renders them no longer of defining significance."[19] By denying covenant partnerships the possibility of procreation, the vocation is open to both heterosexual and same-sex couples. Thus, Song argued that the theological category of covenant provides the church with an avenue to include and bless same-sex couples, honoring their distinct calling and giftedness, while still affirming heterosexual marriage as a good of creation.

Of the revisionist efforts to create space for same-sex couples within the church's theology of marriage and sexuality, Song's account of covenant partnership shows the most theological promise. Clarification is needed regarding the ways in which sexual differentiation fits within the tension of creation and eschatology. Specifically, an account of the relationship between sex and gender in light of the advent of Christ would enrich Song's theology. Further work is also needed to demonstrate that covenant partnership is a relational vocation that is able to make sense of the whole of the biblical witness. Song's significant contribution to the church's ongoing discussion makes these undertakings all the more necessary and worthwhile.

Dialogue and Discernment

The contemporary discourse on the inclusion of same-sex individuals and their relationships within the church's theology of marriage and sexuality has devolved into diametrically opposed positions. These positions are summarized by two distinct ways of approaching the conversation. At times, the debate is framed as being between those who comply with the authority of Scripture and those who would rather appeal to the authority of love. On other occasions, the argument is purportedly between those who cling to a tired, obsolete past and those who are leaving the dark ages of tradition, institution, or anything else that slows the wheels of "progress," to march into the light of a more just and equitable future. The premise of my proposal is that the current debate is overly simplistic and cannot be resolved while couched in terms of us versus them. If the impasse is to be overcome, work must be done to unpack these two positions, moving

---

19. Song, *Covenant and Calling*, 49.

beyond superficial surface polarities to uncover the actual theological issues at stake in the church's theology of sexuality and marriage.

I have sought to reconceive the terms of the debate by mapping the contested zones within various revisionist accounts, searching for areas of agreement and disagreement between those authors and the Western theological tradition articulated by Augustine. Such an approach breaks the liberal premise that the past should be rejected based on a judgment about the moral superiority of one's vantage point in the present. Assumed moral superiority ends the possibility for discussion. Instead, I have encouraged contemporary authors to learn from history and to reason from within the bounds of the theological tradition. In this work, I have also revealed the ways in which arguments found in some public church documents on sex and marriage cannot be resolved in the terms set by the current debate. For example, I have suggested that this discussion is not primarily concerned with the authority of Scripture: those who believe the Bible versus those who do not. The disagreement is taking place between Christians, both revisionists and traditionalists who affirm the authority of Scripture. The more pressing question concerns the ways in which Scripture is deployed to discuss theological issues pivotal to sexuality and marriage, i.e., sexual difference, procreation, covenant, etc. Placing the revisionists in conversation with the theological tradition has allowed for greater clarity about the key issues at stake, the new doctrinal connections available to address the discussion, and theological work that still needs to be done.

In response to the stalled conversation on same-sex relationships, Oliver O'Donovan invited the church to a time of discernment. He argued that discernment involves delineating the contours of the discussion, demonstrating an "awareness of the peculiar temptations of the situation," while also "identifying the possibilities of service in a specific vocation."[20] This project has responded to O'Donovan's call to break the conversational impasse by linking it with the theological tradition, thereby contributing to ecclesial discernment. There is no guarantee that this approach will succeed in bringing meaningful resolution to a disagreeing church. However, it is my sincere hope that it will initiate and elucidate the conversation that is waiting to begin.

---

20. O'Donovan, *Conversation Waiting to Begin*, 108.

Bibliography

Augustine. *Adulterous Marriages*. In *Marriage and Virginity*, edited by John E. Rotelle, 142–85. Translated by Ray Kearney. Works of Saint Augustine 1.9. Hyde Park, NY: New City, 1999.

———. *Against Julian*. Translated by Matthew A. Schumacher. Fathers of the Church 35. Washington, DC: Catholic University of America Press, 1957.

———. *Against Pelagius*. In *Anti-Pelagian Writings*, translated by Peter Holmes, 374–435. New York: Christian Literature, 1887.

———. *City of God*. Edited by Boniface Ramsey. Translated by William Babcock. Works of Saint Augustine 1.6-7. Hyde Park, NY: New City, 2012.

———. *Commentary on the Lord's Sermon on the Mount: With Seventeen Related Sermons*. Translated by Denis J. Kavanagh. Fathers of the Church 11. Washington, DC: Catholic University Press, 1951.

———. *Confessions*. Translated by Maria Boulding. Works of Saint Augustine 1.1. Hyde Park, NY: New City, 1997.

———. *Continence*. In *Marriage and Virginity*, edited by John E. Rotelle, 192–216. Translated by Ray Kearney. Works of Saint Augustine 1.9. Hyde Park, NY: New City, 1999.

———. *The Excellence of Widowhood, Marriage, and Virginity*. In *Marriage and Virginity*, edited by John E. Rotelle, 111–36. Translated by Ray Kearney. Works of Saint Augustine 1.9. Hyde Park, NY: New City, 1999.

———. *The Good of Marriage*. In *Treatises on Marriage and Other Subjects*, edited by Roy J. Deferrari, 9–51. Translated by Charles T. Wilcox et al. Fathers of the Church 27. New York: Catholic University Press of America, 1955.

———. *Holy Virginity*. In *Marriage and Virginity*, edited by John E. Rotelle, 69–107. Translated by Ray Kearney. Works of Saint Augustine 1.9. Hyde Park, NY: New City, 1999.

———. *The Literal Meaning of Genesis*. In *On Genesis*, edited by John E. Rotelle, 168–506. Translated by Edmund Hill. Works of Saint Augustine 1.13. Hyde Park, NY: New City, 2002.

———. *On Genesis: A Refutation of the Manichees*. In *On Genesis*, edited by John E. Rotelle, 39–102. Translated by Edmund Hill. Works of Saint Augustine 1.13. Hyde Park, NY: New City, 2002.

———. *On Marriage and Concupiscence*. In *Anti-Pelagian Writings*, translated by Peter Holmes, 258–309. New York: Christian Literature, 1887.

———. *On Original Sin*. In *Anti-Pelagian Writings*, translated by Peter Holmes, 214–57. New York: Christian Literature, 1887.

———. *The Trinity*. Translated by Stephen McKenna. Fathers of the Church 45. Washington, DC: Catholic University of America Press, 1963.

Barth, Karl. *Church Dogmatics* 3/1. *The Doctrine of Creation*. Translated by J. W. Edwards et al. Edinburgh: T. & T. Clark, 1958.

———. *Church Dogmatics* 3/4. *The Doctrine of Creation*. Translated by G. W. Bromiley and T. F. Torrance. London: T. & T. Clark, 2010.

BeDuhn, Jason. *Augustine's Manichaean Dilemma 1: Conversion and Apostasy, 373–388 CE*. Philadelphia: University of Pennsylvania Press, 2010.

Bennett, Jana. *Water Is Thicker than Blood: An Augustinian Theology of Marriage and Singleness*. Oxford: Oxford University Press, 2008.

Brock, Brian, and Bernd Wannenwetsch. *The Malady of the Christian Body: A Theological Exposition of Paul's First Letter to the Corinthians*. Vol. 1. Eugene, OR: Cascade, 2016.

Brown, Peter. *The Body and Society: Men, Women, and Sexual Renunciation in Early Christianity*. New York: Columbia University Press, 2008.

Brownson, James V. *Bible, Gender, Sexuality: Reframing the Church's Debate on Same-Sex Relationships*. Grand Rapids: Eerdmans, 2013.

Brubaker, Eric. "A Christian View of Marriage." *Bretheren Life and Thought* 55.1–2 (2010) 28–37.

Burrus, Virginia, et al. *Seducing Augustine: Bodies, Desires, Confessions*. New York: Fordham University Press, 2010.

Butler, Judith. *Gender Trouble: Feminism and the Subversion of Identity*. New York: Routledge, 1990.

Butting, Klara. "Pauline Variations on Genesis 2:24: Speaking of the Body of Christ in the Context of the Discussion of Lifestyles." *Journal for the Study of the New Testament* 23 (2000) 79–90.

Cameron, Andrew. "The Logic of Love: A Theological Approach to the Relationship between Ethics and Emotion." PhD diss., King's College London, 2001.

Coakley, Sarah. *God, Sexuality, and the Self: An Essay "On the Trinity"*. Cambridge: Cambridge University Press, 2013.

———. *Powers and Submissions: Spirituality, Philosophy, and Gender*. Oxford: Blackwell, 2002.

Coleman, Peter. *Christian Attitudes to Marriage: From Ancient Times to the Third Millennium*. London, SCM, 1992.

Connolly, William E. *Identity/Difference: Democratic Negotiations of Political Paradox*. Ithaca: Cornell University Press, 1991.

Countryman, L. William. *Dirt, Greed, & Sex: Sexual Ethics in the New Testament and Their Implications for Today*. London: SCM, 1988.

Davies, Jon, and Gerard Loughlin, eds. *Sex These Days: Essays on Theology, Sexuality, and Society*. Sheffield: Sheffield Academic Press, 1997.

Engels, Friedrich. "The Origin of History and the Family, Private Property, and the State." In *Selected Works*, 191–334. Vol. 3. Moscow: Progress, 1970.

Ernst, Waltraud, ed. *Histories of the Normal and Abnormal: Social and Cultural Histories of Norms and Normativity*. New York: Routledge, 2006.

Evdokimov, Paul. *The Sacrament of Love: The Nuptial Mystery in the Light of the Orthodox Tradition*. Translated by Anthony P. Gythiel and Victoria Steadman. Crestwood, NY: St. Vladimir's Seminary Press, 1985.

Finer, Lawerence. "Trends in Premarital Sex in the United States 1954–2003." *Public Health Reports* 122 (2007) 73–78.

Flannery, Austin, ed. *Vatican Council II: The Conciliar and Post-Conciliar Documents*. Leominster: Fowler Wright, 1980.

Foucault, Michael. *The History of Sexuality*. Translated by Robert Hurley. 3 vols. London: Penguin, 1990–92.

Gagnon, Robert A. J. *The Bible and Homosexual Practice: Texts and Hermeneutics*. Nashville: Abingdon, 2001.

Garland, David E. *1 Corinthians*. Grand Rapids: Baker Academic, 2003.

González, Justo L. *The Story of Christianity*. Vol. 1, *The Early Church to the Dawn of the Reformation*. San Francisco: Harper & Row, 1984.

Gregory of Nyssa. *On Virginity*. In *Ascetical Works*, edited by Joseph Deferrari, 3–78. Translated by Virginia Woods Callahan. Fathers of the Church 58. Washington, DC: Catholic University of America Press, 2014.

Gresham, John, Jr. "The Social Model of the Trinity and Its Critics." *Scottish Journal of Theology* 46 (1993) 325–43.

Haflidson, Ron. "Outward, Inward, Upward: Why Three Goods of Marriage for Augustine?" *Studies in Christian Ethics* 29 (2016) 51–68.

Hauerwas, Stanley. "The Family: Theological and Ethical Reflections." In *A Community of Character: Toward a Constructive Christian Social Ethic*, 167–74. Notre Dame: University of Notre Dame Press, 1981.

———. "The Moral Value of the Family." In *A Community of Character: Toward a Constructive Christian Social Ethic*, 155–66. Notre Dame: University of Notre Dame Press, 1981.

———. "The Politics of Sex: How Marriage Is a Subversive Act." In *After Christendom? How the Church Is to Behave if Freedom, Justice, and a Christian Nation Are Bad Ideas*, 113–31. Nashville: Abingdon, 1999.

———. "Resisting Capitalism: On Marriage and Homosexuality." In *A Better Hope: Resources for a Church Confronting Capitalism, Democracy, and Postmodernity*, 49–55. Grand Rapids: Brazos, 2000.

———. "Sex in Public: Toward a Christian Ethic of Sex." In *A Community of Character: Toward a Constructive Christian Social Ethic*, 175–95. Notre Dame: University of Notre Dame Press, 1981.

Hodgson, Leonard. *The Doctrine of the Trinity: The Croall Lectures, 1942–1943*. New York: Scribner's, 1944.

Hunt, Mary. *Fierce Tenderness: A Feminist Theology of Friendship*. New York: Crossroad, 1991.

Hunter, David G. "Augustine and the Making of Marriage in Roman North Africa." *Journal of Early Christian Studies* 11 (2003) 63–85.

———. "Reconstructing Jovinian." In *Marriage, Celibacy, and Heresy in Ancient Christianity: The Jovinianist Controversy*, 3–25. Oxford: Oxford University Press, 2007.

———. "The Virgin, the Bride, and the Church: Reading Psalm 45 in Ambrose, Jerome, and Augustine." *Church History* 69 (2000) 281–303.

Isherwood, Lisa, and Dorothea McEwan. *Introducing Feminist Theology*. 2nd ed. Sheffield: Sheffield Academic Press, 2001.

Jerome. *Against Jovinianus.* In vol. 6 of *Nicene and Post-Nicene Fathers*, Series 2, edited by Philip Schaff and Henry Wace, 346–416. Translated by W. H. Fremantle. Grand Rapids: Christian Classics Ethereal Library, 1892.

———. *Commentary on Matthew.* Edited by Thomas Halton. Translated by Thomas P. Scheck. Fathers of the Church 117. Washington, DC: Catholic University of America Press, 2008.

———. *Letter 22/5.* In vol. 6 of *Nicene and Post-Nicene Fathers*, Series 2, edited by Philip Schaff and Henry Wace, 22–40. Translated by W. H. Fremantle. New York: Christian Literature, 1893.

———. *On the Perpetual Virginity of the Blessed Mary against Helvidius.* In *Dogmatic and Polemical Works*, translated by John N. Hritzu, 3–43. Fathers of the Church 53. Washington, DC: Catholic University of America Press, 1965.

John, Jeffrey. *Permanent, Faithful, Stable: Christian Same-Sex Marriage.* London: Darton, Longman & Todd, 2012.

Jungling, Laurie A. "Passionate Order: Order and Sexuality in Augustine's Theology." *Word & World* 27 (2007) 315–24.

Kelly, David. "Sexuality and Concupiscence in Augustine." *The Annual of the Society of Christian Ethics* (1983) 81–116.

Küng, Hans. "A Dignified Death." In *On Moral Medicine: Theological Perspectives in Medical Ethics*, edited by M. Therese Lysaught et al., 1090–96. 3rd ed. Grand Rapids: Eerdmans, 2012.

Mathewes, Charles T. "Original Sin and the Hermeneutics of Charity: A Response to Gilbert Meilander." *Journal of Religious Ethics* 29 (2001) 35–42.

McPake, John L. "Theological Commission on Same-Sex Relationships and the Ministry." Church of Scotland General Assembly, May 2013. http://www.churchofscotland.org.uk/__data/assets/pdf_file/0004/39253/2013_Theological_Forum.pdf.

Meilaender, Gilbert. "Sweet Necessities: Food, Sex, and Saint Augustine." *Journal of Religious Ethics* 29 (2001) 3–18.

Moltmann, Jürgen. *The Trinity and the Kingdom: The Doctrine of God.* Translated by Margaret Kohl. San Francisco: Harper & Row, 1981.

Moore, Stephen D. *God's Beauty Parlor: And Other Queer Spaces in and around the Bible.* Stanford: Stanford University Press, 2001.

Nietzsche, Friedrich. *Beyond Good and Evil: A Prelude to a Philosophy of the Future.* Translated by Helen Zimmern. New York: Dover, 1997.

Nikkel, David H. "St. Augustine on the Goodness of Creaturely Existence." *Duke Divinity School Review* 43 (1978) 181–87.

O'Donovan, Oliver. *A Conversation Waiting to Begin: The Churches and the Gay Controversy.* London: SCM, 2009.

Oliphant, David. "Modern Marriage—a Union of Equals?" The 1991 Mary Body Memorial Lecture. *St Mark's Review* 149 (1992) 15–21.

Olson, Roger. *The Story of Christian Theology: Twenty Centuries of Tradition & Reform.* Downers Grove, IL: InterVarsity, 1999.

Ornella, Alexander. "Posthuman Pleasures: Transcending the Human-Machine Boundary." *Theology & Sexuality* 15 (2009) 311–28.

Otten, Willemien. "Augustine on Marriage, Monasticism, and the Community of the Church." *Theological Studies* 59 (1998) 385–405.

Paris, Jenell Williams. *The End of Sexual Identity: Why Sex Is Too Important to Define Who We Are*. Downers Grove, IL: InterVarsity, 2011.

Paul VI, Pope. *Humanae Vitae*. Encyclical Letter, July 25, 1968. http://w2.vatican.va/content/paul-vi/en/encyclicals/documents/hf_p-vi_enc_25071968_humanae-vitae.html.

Primavesi, Anne. *From Apocalypse to Genesis: Ecology, Feminism and Christianity*. Tunbridge Wells: Burns & Oates, 1991.

Raymond, Janice G. *The Transsexual Empire: The Making of the She-Male*. London: Women's Press, 1992.

Rees, Geoffrey. *The Romance of Innocent Sexuality*. Eugene, OR: Cascade, 2011.

Roberts, Christopher C. "Book Review: Robert Song, *Covenant and Calling: Towards a Theology of Same-Sex Relationships*." *Studies in Christian Ethics* 29 (2016) 115–19.

———. *Creation & Covenant: The Significance of Sexual Difference in the Moral Theology of Marriage*. New York: T. & T. Clark, 2007.

Rogers, Eugene F., Jr. "The Celebration and Blessing of a Marriage from the Book of Common Prayer." In *Theology and Sexuality: Classic and Contemporary Readings*, edited by Eugene F. Rogers Jr., 45–52. Oxford: Blackwell, 2002

———. *Sexuality and the Christian Body: Their Way into the Triune Body*. Oxford: Blackwell, 1999.

Rogers, Jack. *Jesus, the Bible, and Homosexuality: Explode the Myths, Heal the Church*. Rev. and expanded ed. Louisville: Westminster John Knox, 2009.

Ruether, Rosemary Radford. *Sexism and God-Talk: Toward a Feminist Theology*. Philadelphia: Fortress, 1984.

Song, Robert. *Covenant and Calling: Towards a Theology of Same-Sex Relationships*. London: SCM, 2014.

Spong, John Shelby. *Living in Sin? A Bishop Rethinks Human Sexuality*. San Francisco: Harper & Row, 1988.

Stuart, Elizabeth. *Just Good Friends: Towards a Lesbian and Gay Theology of Relationships*. New York: Mowbray, 1995.

Talbert, Charles. *Reading Corinthians: A Literary and Theological Commentary on 1 and 2 Corinthians*. New York: Crossroad, 1987.

Tertullian. *An Exhortation to Chastity*. In *Treatises on Marriage and Remarriage*, edited by Johannes Quasten and Joseph C. Plumpe, 42–64. Translated by William P. Le Saint. London: Longmans, Green, 1951.

———. *Monogamy*. In *Treatises on Marriage and Remarriage*, edited by Johannes Quasten and Joseph C. Plumpe, 70–108. Translated by William P. Le Saint. London: Longmans, Green, 1951.

———. *To His Wife*. In *Treatises on Marriage and Remarriage*, edited by Johannes Quasten and Joseph C. Plumpe, 10–36. Translated by William P. Le Saint. London: Longmans, Green, 1951.

Thatcher, Adrian. *Liberating Sex: A Christian Sexual Theology*. London: SPCK, 1993.

———. *Marriage after Modernity: Christian Marriage in Postmodern Times*. Sheffield: Sheffield Academic Press, 1999.

———. "Postmodernity and Chastity." In *Sex These Days: Essays on Theology, Sexuality and Society*, edited by Jon Davies and Gerard Loughlin, 122–40. Sheffield: Sheffield Academic Press, 1997.

Thistlethwaite, Susan Brooks. *Sex, Race, and God: Christian Feminism in Black and White*. New York: Crossroad, 1989.

Torrance, Iain. "Theological Forum." Church of Scotland General Assembly, May 2017. http://www.churchofscotland.org.uk/__data/assets/pdf_file/0009/39573/Theological_Forum.pdf.

Trible, Phyllis. *God and the Rhetoric of Sexuality*. Philadelphia: Fortress, 1978.

———. *Texts of Terror: Literary-Feminist Readings of Biblical Narratives*. Philadelphia: Fortress, 1984.

Vasey, Michael. *Strangers and Friends: A New Exploration of Homosexuality and the Bible*. London: Hodder & Stoughton, 1995.

Via, Dan O., and Robert A. J. Gagnon. *Homosexuality and the Bible: Two Views*. Minneapolis: Fortress, 2003.

Ware, Kallistos. *The Orthodox Way*. Crestwood, NY: St. Vladimir's Seminary Press, 1979.

Webb, William J. *Slaves, Women & Homosexuals: Exploring the Hermeneutics of Cultural Analysis*. Downers Grove, IL: InterVarsity, 2001.

Wilcox, W. Bradford, ed. *When Marriage Disappears: The New Middle America*. Charlottesville, VA: National Marriage Project, 2010. http://nationalmarriageproject.org/wp-content/uploads/2012/06/Union_11_12_10.pdf.

Williams, Robert. "Toward a Theology for Lesbian and Gay Marriage." *Anglican Theological Review* 72 (1990) 130–43.

Williams, Rowan. "The Body's Grace." In *Theology and Sexuality: Classic and Contemporary Readings*, edited by Eugene F. Rogers Jr., 309–21. Oxford: Blackwell, 2002.

———. "Forbidden Fruit." In *Intimate Affairs: Sexuality & Spirituality in Perspective*, edited by Percy Martin, 21–31. London: Darton, Longman & Todd, 1997.

Wink, Walter. *Homosexuality and the Christian Faith: Questions of Conscience for the Churches*. Minneapolis: Fortress, 1999.

Witherington, Ben. *Conflict & Community in Corinth: A Socio-Rhetorical Commentary on 1 and 2 Corinthians*. Grand Rapids: Eerdmans, 1995.

———. *Women in the Earliest Churches*. Cambridge: Cambridge University Press, 1988.

Zizioulas, John. *Being as Communion: Studies in Personhood and the Church*. Crestwood, NY: St. Vladimir's Seminary Press, 1985.

www.ingramcontent.com/pod-product-compliance
Lightning Source LLC
Chambersburg PA
CBHW051739230426
43670CB00012B/2086